CIVIC EDUCATION IN POLARIZED TIMES

NOMOS

LXVI

NOMOS

Harvard University Press
I *Authority* 1958, reissued in 1982 by Greenwood Press

The Liberal Arts Press
II *Community* 1959
III *Responsibility* 1960

Atherton Press
IV *Liberty* 1962
V *The Public Interest* 1962
VI *Justice* 1963, reissued in 1974
VII *Rational Decision* 1964
VIII *Revolution* 1966
IX *Equality* 1967
X *Representation* 1968
XI *Voluntary Associations* 1969
XII *Political and Legal Obligation* 1970
XIII *Privacy* 1971

Aldine-Atherton Press
XIV *Coercion* 1972

Lieber-Atherton Press
XV *The Limits of Law* 1974
XVI *Participation in Politics* 1975

New York University Press
XVII *Human Nature in Politics* 1977
XVIII *Due Process* 1977
XIX *Anarchism* 1978
XX *Constitutionalism* 1979
XXI *Compromise in Ethics, Law, and Politics* 1979
XXII *Property* 1980
XXIII *Human Rights* 1981
XXIV *Ethics, Economics, and the Law* 1982
XXV *Liberal Democracy* 1983
XXVI *Marxism* 1983
XXVII *Criminal Justice* 1985

NOMOS LXVI
Yearbook of the American Society for Political and Legal Philosophy

CIVIC EDUCATION IN POLARIZED TIMES

Edited by

Elizabeth Beaumont and Eric Beerbohm

NEW YORK UNIVERSITY PRESS • *New York*

NEW YORK UNIVERSITY PRESS
New York
www.nyupress.org

Please contact the Library of Congress for Cataloging-in-Publication data.

ISBN: 9781479829064 (hardback)
ISBN: 9781479829088 (library ebook)
ISBN: 9781479829071 (consumer ebook)

This book is printed on acid-free paper, and its binding materials are chosen for strength and durability. We strive to use environmentally responsible suppliers and materials to the greatest extent possible in publishing our books.

Manufactured in the United States of America

10 9 8 7 6 5 4 3 2 1

Also available as an ebook

CONTENTS

CONTRIBUTORS

Rima Basu
Assistant Professor of Philosophy, Claremont McKenna College

Elizabeth Beaumont
Associate Professor of Politics, University of California, Santa Cruz

Lisa García Bedolla
Political Science and Graduate School of Education, University of California, Berkeley

Eric Beerbohm
Professor of Government and Director of the Edmund and Lily Safra Center for Ethics, Harvard University

Sigal Ben-Porath
Professor, Graduate School of Education, Philosophy, and Political Science, University of Pennsylvania

Kristine L. Bowman
Professor of Law and Professor of Education Policy, Michigan State University

Justin Driver
Robert R. Slaughter Professor of Law, Yale University

Amy Gutmann
Christopher H. Browne Distinguished Professor of Political Science, School of Arts and Sciences, and Professor of Communications, Annenberg School for Communication, University of Pennsylvania

Wurud Jayusi
Head of the Arab Academic Institute, Beit Berl College

Jennifer Morton
*Presidential Penn Compact Associate Professor of Philosophy and
Education, University of Pennsylvania*

Ilana Paul-Binyamin
Dean of Faculty of Education, Beit Berl College

Seana Valentine Shiffrin
*Professor of Philosophy and Pete Kameron Professor of Law and Social
Justice, University of California, Los Angeles*

Yael (Yuli) Tamir
*President, Beit Berl College, and Adjunct Professor, Blavatnik School of
Government, Oxford University*

Brandon M. Terry
*John L. Loeb Associate Professor of the Social Sciences, and Co-Director
of the Institute on Policing, Incarceration, and Public Safety at the
Hutchins Center for African and African American Research, Harvard
University*

Dennis Thompson
*Alfred North Whitehead Professor of Political Philosophy Emeritus,
Harvard University*

Robert L. Tsai
Professor of Law and Law Alumni Scholar, Boston University

PREFACE

ERIC BEERBOHM AND ELIZABETH BEAUMONT

This sixty-sixth volume of NOMOS emerges from the scholarly papers and conversations at the annual meeting of the interdisciplinary American Society for Political and Legal Philosophy in 2021. The conference was organized by Eric Beerbohm and Elizabeth Beaumont, and hosted by the Edmund and Lily Safra Ethics Center at Harvard University, October 29–30, 2021. Due to the COVID-19 pandemic, the conference was held in a hybrid webinar format, with remote participation enabled through videoconferencing. Our topic, "Civic Education in Polarized Times," was selected by the Society's members. It is telling that this volume follows several recent NOMOS volumes that have focused on other aspects of contemporary democratic decay and conflict, and responses to these: *Democratic Failure, Truth and Evidence, Protest and Dissent,* and *Repair and Reconciliation.*

The ASPLP conference on Civic Education in Polarized Times included three panels: (1) "Democratic Civic Education and Democratic Law"; (2) "Advancing Civic Awareness through Cross-Communal Teaching"; and (3) "Civic Education, Students' Rights, and the Supreme Court." This volume includes revised versions of the principal papers delivered at the conference by Seana Shiffrin; Ilana Paul-Binyamin, Wurud Jayusi, and Yael (Yuli) Tamir; and Justin Driver. It also includes essays that developed from initial original commentaries on those papers by Robert Tsai, Brandon Terry, Kristine Bowman, Rima Basu, Jennifer Morton, and Lisa García Bedolla. The volume also features a solicited paper from Sigal Ben-Porath, Amy Gutmann, and Dennis Thompson, which served as the keynote address for the conference. We are very grateful to this set of authors for their excellent contributions. We also greatly appreciated the audience and members of the ASPLP for their interest and engagement, and for sharing insightful questions and comments—despite the limitations of the hybrid conference format.

Many thanks are also due to the Edmund and Lily Safra Ethics Center at Harvard University for hosting the conference, and to the very helpful team that made it a successful endeavor, especially Emily Bromley and Alex Ostrowski Schilling. We also thank our conference co-sponsors: Princeton University's Center for Human Values and Department of Politics; Boston University School of Law; University of California, Santa Cruz's Institute for Social Transformation and the Politics and Legal Studies Programs; and the University of Pennsylvania's Andrea Mitchell Center for the Study of Democracy.

We extend further thanks to Amanda Safi for help with indexing, to the editors and production team at New York University Press, especially Sonia Tsuruoka, Associate Editor for Social Sciences, Alexia Traganas, Senior Production Editor, and to our copyeditors, Karen Verde, and Nicholas Taylor from Grit City Creative. On behalf of the Society, we convey gratitude for the Press's continued support for the NOMOS series and its tradition of interdisciplinary scholarship. We also express appreciation to Boston University School of Law, Brown University's Political Theory Project, Duke University School of Law, New York University's College of Arts & Science–Social Sciences, Princeton University's Center for Human Values, and Stanford University's School of Humanities and Sciences, as well as for a bequest by Professor John Ladd of Brown University, a former secretary-treasurer and president of the Society, for subventions to support this and other NOMOS volumes.

Finally, we also we wish to thank the members of the ASPLP Council: President David Estlund, Vice Presidents Anna Stilz and Anita Allen, and Secretary-Treasurer James Fleming, as well as past president Stephen Macedo, Vice Presidents Derrick Darby and Yasmin Dawood, and past editor Melissa Schwartzberg, who helped support and guide our work to organize the conference and develop this volume.

INTRODUCTION

CIVIC EDUCATION IN, AND FOR, A DEEPLY POLARIZED ERA

ELIZABETH BEAUMONT

What is the role of civic education in polarized times? In recent years, scholars have chronicled the rise of pernicious polarization that not only deepens partisan and ideological divides, but fuels movement into hostile camps with a dangerous "us vs. them" mentality.[1] While extreme polarization is especially acute in the United States, it presents significant threats to democracy in many countries, from Turkey to Brazil to Poland to India.[2] Fears that polarization contributes to democratic corrosion and crisis are prompting many people to turn attention to civic education as a possible remedy, exemplified by headlines such as "Can Teaching Civics Save Democracy?"[3] The hope is that civic education could help young citizens strengthen democratic culture and institutions, and perhaps counteract or remedy the harmful aspects of political antipathy. Yet the dynamics and circumstances of polarization do not stop at the schoolhouse gates—they bring both added pressures and new constraints to all civic education projects. Thus, as political polarization has intensified across the world, civic education seems more urgent, but it has also become more challenging.

This volume invites us to think deeply about some of these complex issues by bringing a range of philosophical, political, legal, and educational perspectives to bear. The authors share an overarching belief in the need for civic education that informs and empowers young people to confront political problems and improve democracy. But they part ways, sometimes dramatically, on the specific questions of what type of civic education is needed, and what is possible, in this discordant era. In grappling with these questions, they help illuminate the difficult problems and choices many contemporary democracies are facing as they consider how to educate the next generation for democratic citizenship.

Thinking about the place of civic education in polarized times requires looking at some of the ways that civic learning and political divisiveness may mutually interact, and how each may influence the other. One line of consideration involves questions about educating citizens *in* a polarized era: asking how polarization affects democracy, and how polarized circumstances shape and constrain the conditions and possibilities for civic education. How are efforts for civic teaching affected when schools, administrators, teachers, parents, and students are also operating in a divided world?

Another line of consideration involves questions about how to educate citizens *for* a polarized era: In a time of intensifying political schisms and dysfunctions, what should the goals of civic education be, and how should they be implemented? What types of civic learning hold promise for preparing students for navigating their way through a political landscape of escalating hostile factions, distrust, truth decay, and disagreement about basic facts? Could or should civic education attempt to reduce or counteract polarization, or should it focus on other aims?

This volume is a timely and much needed contribution to these questions. Despite widespread concerns about polarization, and calls for revitalizing or reforming civic education, there has been relatively little discussion of how we should try to educate democratic citizens in this context. Indeed, a review of the research found little work that considered how to undertake or implement civic education for decreasing political polarization or for supporting students' development of democratic knowledge, skills, and engagement in the face of polarization.[4] This collection brings valuable attention to these topics, demonstrating how concerns for civic education weave across academic fields, and across political, legal, and social spheres. In the following chapters, we will see how the contributors wrestle with some of the important normative and practical questions about civic education in a polarized and polarizing era, and the considerations and proposals they offer.

There are a number of thorny debates at stake. These involve not only central questions regarding civic education and polarization, but broader issues of modern democratic conditions, democratic conflicts, and efforts for democratic invigoration.

In a polarized era characterized by growing distrust in institutions,[5] do modern democracies need to adopt models of civic education that can better prepare emerging citizens to be "co-authors of the law" and possessors of legal-civic literacy? Given the centrality of law to so many elements of modern life and politics,[6] could promoting substantive legal knowledge help student-citizens contribute to a more robust democracy, and help them feel less disaffected and distrusting of institutions? Or, do approaches focused on the historical paths and rationales for existing laws risk undermining students' capacities to advocate for change?

In an era of heated divisions over the content of civic education—epitomized in the United States by clashes between the *New York Times' 1619 Project,* former president Trump's *1776 Commission Report,* and a slate of legislation restricting teaching, lessons, and books about racism and gender identity[7]—could there be consensus on a "student-centered" approach focused on studying the development of students' constitutional rights? Or might this approach fall short by sidestepping the controversies, or by failing to prepare and motivate students from all walks of life to be democratically engaged in the present?

When political conditions are highly contentious and many people are less supportive of compromise,[8] should civic education programs try harder to teach students how to engage in negotiation and cooperation and to seek common goals? Or does it become more important to learn how to participate effectively in competition and become skilled and prepared for the rivalrous and increasingly adversarial and conflictual aspects of democratic politics?

If polarization reflects and intersects with long-standing socioeconomic, racial, ethnic, and political inequalities,[9] should civic education include more focus on understanding the causes and manifestations of those problems, and considering efforts to address them? Do we need increased emphasis on research-backed teaching approaches and active pedagogies that can reach students from groups that have been historically disenfranchised or disempowered, and help them gain political agency?

To help students understand and respond to political problems that are shaped not only by current polarization, but also by historic injustices and formative rifts involving unresolved debates over citizenship and national identity,[10] do we need models of civic teaching with more critical and transformative goals? Do emerging citizens need knowledge and skills for "political diagnosis" to understand the causes of current problems and possible solutions, and capacities to "reason from injustice" and work for political change, as many groups and movements from the past have done?

If current polarization is fueled partly by democratic disfigurements, and reflects persistent problems of racism and racial subordination,[11] should civic education do more to help students understand these patterns and consider ideas and approaches for correcting them? Do we need to look for models, agents, and sites of civic teaching that can draw from historic models of dissent to injustice and work for democratic justice, such as those of Black freedom struggles?

With polarization further exacerbating ethnic and religious prejudices and intolerance in societies,[12] can teachers from minority groups help students learn how to respect diversity and shared humanity, thereby ameliorating polarization? Or might such projects risk tokenizing or placing undue burdens on teachers from underrepresented backgrounds?

As polarization makes conditions for political speech and discourse more challenging and stressful,[13] including on college campuses, should campus leaders and community members consider a new "democratic model" for free speech? Could this approach enable a wider array of students and members of school communities to engage in more robust civic discourse and communication?

These are just some of the questions that the authors invite us to grapple with. While most of the chapters consider US contexts, where polarization is especially potent, and increasingly studied and discussed, the issues they raise are relevant for the many countries confronting these challenges.[14]

To ground these debates, we need to consider the significant concerns raised by extreme political polarization. We also need to consider how rising polarization increases desire and demand for civic education while simultaneously making the work of civic education more difficult and more fraught. Delving into these issues and some of the important literature will help set the stage for the important lines of inquiry and argument that follow.

THE PROBLEMS EXTREME POLARIZATION PRESENTS FOR DEMOCRACY

What is meant by "political polarization," why is it increasingly identified as a serious threat to democracies, and how does it present challenges for civic education? The general concept of political polarization can refer to several things, including basic partisan and ideological divides and "self-sorting" into different political groups.[15] And although most recent discussions emphasize negative impacts, not all types of political polarization are problematic for democracy. Indeed, some degree and some effects of polarization can be politically beneficial—such as by unifying a group or consolidating a party; motivating individual political engagement or energizing social movements; helping to disrupt an unjust status quo; and creating real alternatives or new ideas and directions for laws and policies.[16]

Indeed, some scholars believe increased polarization in the United States could be a positive sign that the country is traveling a rough road necessary for progress, because it reflects passionate disagreements that might ultimately lead to reforms on racial inequality and other issues.[17] In this volume, Brandon Terry reminds us that the capacity to mobilize a group and create moral outrage and energy for change has been necessary for groups such as African Americans struggling against slavery, segregation, and other injustices. Thus, he warns against assumptions that political polarization is always harmful for democracy, or that a primary aim of civic education should be to dissolve polarization.

Yet there is also important evidence that dangerous forms of extreme political polarization—also referred to as pernicious, severe, toxic, or hyperpolarization—have risen over the past two decades, and that these are linked to harmful effects on the functions and ethics of democratic citizenship, and on the operation of democratic institutions and norms.[18] Pernicious polarization goes far beyond disagreement over political views and policies: It is defined by division into two hostile camps with fierce animosities and distrust akin to political sectarianism or tribalism, by its entrenchment in political dynamics, and by its array of harmful effects on democracy.[19] Operating at the level of individual democratic citizenship, hyperpolarization corrodes citizens' capacities for political learning, dialog and debate, trust and cooperation, and informed decision-making. This is because it involves a combination of psychological antipathies and cognitive biases, such as "motivated reasoning," "othering," and intense "aversion" that undermine our abilities to consider relevant information, discuss views, evaluate policies, find commonalities with others, uphold democratic ethics and principles, and hold leaders and parties accountable.[20]

And, looking at the broader scale of institutions and societal relations, comparative research shows that hyperpolarization contributes to overarching patterns of democratic corrosion. These patterns of democratic dysfunctions and dangers include political violence and extremism; weakening or corruption of democratic institutions; the rise of autocracy, inflated executive powers, and leaders who exploit supporters' fears; abuses of power, gridlocked institutions, incentives for politicians to use anti-democratic tactics to achieve electoral and political victories; widespread and general distrust of major institutions; and willingness to set aside or violate democratic principles and norms to support one's own political camp.[21]

A further challenge with the mounting political polarization of the twenty-first century is that it is not a static or self-contained problem. Rather, polarization is dynamic and diffuse, overlapping and intersecting with many other serious conflicts and strains: rising economic inequality and financial crises; misinformation and media siloing; surges in xenophobia, racism, hate crimes, and violence targeting ethnic or religious minorities; reckonings with legacies of colonialism and slavery; new waves of migration and refugees; and dangerous climate and health crises. Polarization fuels and can be fueled by such challenges and the disagreements over them. And, as it intensifies, polarization makes it even more difficult to address the serious issues societies face. So while democracy is always a "work in progress," and fully inclusive and egalitarian democracy exists only as an ideal, hyperpolarization seems to undermine existing levels of democracy and the democratic advances a country has made—such as work toward free and fair elections, robust civil liberties—as well as creating impediments for improving democracy.[22]

Moreover, the negative consequences of pernicious polarization are not limited to overtly political activities or arenas. They can affect individual interactions and health and stress levels, and they can create hostilities and breakdowns in cooperation in families, neighborhoods, religious organizations, workplaces—and schools.[23] Thus, hyperpolarization poses risks not only for democratic institutions, but for the ethics of democratic citizenship, the terrain of democratic culture, civil society and "everyday democracy," and the entire core "civic infrastructure" for democracy, including education.[24]

This is why some liken extreme polarization to a monster problem: a problem that makes us see others as monsters and a problem that "eats" and exacerbates other problems.[25] Navigating the conditions of pernicious polarization is difficult for democratic citizens. And trying to reverse extreme polarization is daunting: Not only is it a complex problem shaped by institutional features, historic cleavages, and patterns of inequality, but its dynamics can become entrenched and self-reinforcing.[26] In the United States, there have been many suggestions for trying to "depolarize" through a number of institutional reforms, or through civil society projects.[27] And there have also been many calls for civic education to help strengthen democracy.[28]

The Demands for, and Challenges of, Civic Education in a Divided Era

What role might civic education play in this deeply polarized era? The health of democracies depends on informed, thoughtful, and participatory citizens.[29] And there is now an expanding body of research showing that high-quality civics courses, programs, and experiences can promote political knowledge and engagement for students from many backgrounds.[30] Thus, many people across the political divide consider civic education especially urgent at this time.[31] As Linda McClain and James Fleming have urged, "civic education is a necessary but not sufficient step" to reduce the polarization contributing to "rot" in constitutional democracy.[32] Organizations that study democracies around the world, such as

The Freedom House, identify investment in civic education as a method for addressing growing disregard for the "foundations of democracy—including respect for the rights of minorities and migrants, space for critical dissent, and commitment to the rule of law."[33] And studies of youth voting and civic knowledge urge that "Teaching a new generation to be civil, responsible, and constructive citizens may be part of the solution to our polarized and dysfunctional politics."[34] For instance, one recent report on civic education suggested that, in addition to long-standing goals of promoting civic knowledge, the goals of civic learning should include "reducing political polarization," including learning and skills to support discourse and argument and media literacy.[35]

Yet, at the same time that civic education seems especially urgent, and is encouraged as a method for countering democratic threats and reversals, political polarization is creating a more fraught terrain for civic education. Civic education has long been limited and uneven in the United States, with declining investments since the 1960s, and many teachers who have lacked sufficient preparation, time, and support for civic teaching.[36] But the circumstances of hyperpolarization mean that civic education is now being asked to tackle more problems, even as schools are in the crosswinds of these problems and educators are being forced to operate on precarious terrain.

Civic education has become part of the political tug-of-war— one magazine article referred to civic education as "the most bitterly contested subject in America today."[37] These bitter contests are most dramatically exemplified by controversies over teaching issues pertaining to race and racism, sexuality, and gender, and state legislation prohibiting teaching such topics. As of June 2023, thirty gag order laws have passed in sixteen US states, some with harsh punishments for schools and teachers, such as fines or loss of state funding, and threats of termination or criminal charges for teachers.[38] According to the American Library Association, there has also been a massive increase in book bannings: 1,651 books were challenged or removed from US schools, universities, and libraries in 2022.[39] Moreover, in a number of communities, school board meetings and elections have become especially contentious, and sometimes violent, and a number of teachers and school staff have faced verbal abuse or confrontations with students or parents.[40] These are just some of the dramatic indicators of how extreme polarization is affecting public schools, teachers, and the landscape of possibility for civic education. As Paula McAvoy's and Diana Hess's work emphasizes, and further studies confirm, polarization has fueled intense disagreements over school curricula and what should or shouldn't be taught in public schools, and it has made some people more distrustful of schools and civic education efforts.[41]

The heightened divisions and animosities resulting from polarization are creating tensions and problems for educational institutions, teachers, and students, and making civic education work far more difficult. We can consider a few elements of this. First, the aspects of hyperpolarization connected to political bias, motivated reasoning, distrust, aversion, and othering all interfere with or cut against fundamental goals of civic learning—such as developing abilities to engage in thoughtful, fair-minded consideration and discussion of diverse perspectives.[42] Moreover, conditions of pernicious polarization affect students' perceptions of politics and their interest in civic learning, as well as their motivation for their own democratic engagement. As the Commission on Youth Voting and Civic Knowledge has noted, "Civic education is especially difficult when young people have good reasons to view politics as polarized and dysfunctional."[43]

In addition, civic education also confronts problems of misinformation and "truth decay" that crisscross between society at large and classroom contexts. To take just one recent example, a survey of US teachers across all grade levels identified commonly reported challenges in which students made "unfounded claims in class based on unreliable media sources," as well as problems with students "sharing hateful posts on social media." These were especially problematic concerns at the secondary level (more than 80% and more than 60%, respectively). And among secondary teachers, nearly 80 percent described "limited ability to evaluate the credibility of online information" as a moderate or major problem.[44]

In addition, the current conditions of polarization make it even more difficult for many teachers to engage in evidence-based "best practices" of civic education, such as those related to open classroom climates, democratic deliberation, and discussion of current events and controversies.[45] For instance, there is extensive evidence from studies in the United States and internationally that more open or democratic classroom climates—climates in which students are encouraged to express opinions, where different opinions are respected—and classrooms with discussions of current events and politics, have significant positive effects on students' development of civic knowledge, attitudes, dispositions, and behaviors.[46] In contrast, students who perceive their classroom climates as less open tend to experience fewer civic gains. Research also suggests that engaging in classroom deliberations about meaningful political controversies is needed to develop capacities to understand complex political disagreements, to consider a range of viewpoints and perspectives, and to encourage political engagement.[47]

But hyperpolarization makes it more difficult to carry out the type of high-quality civic education that has been shown to contribute the most to civic knowledge, skills, and interest. In a strongly polarized political context, when teachers fear hostile reactions to political discussions, or when schools and teachers face proposed or enacted legislation barring discussion of topics of current controversy, this has a chilling effect on civic education. It leads many school administrators and teachers to want to avoid or remove anything "political" or potentially controversial from the classroom.[48]

As a result, in the United States and other countries where there are heated debates over curricula and national history, it has become even more challenging to teach civic education, topics related to politics, national history, and a wide range of social issues, including race, sexuality, and gender, and some topics related to science and health, such as those involving COVID-19, vaccines, and climate change.[49] One study of public school teachers found that although teachers believed there was a need to help students develop their civic skills and dispositions, they were facing many challenges integrating civics in the classrooms, and did not feel systematically supported to provide such opportunities.[50] Moreover, a major study of civic learning in US public high schools found that the hyperpolarized political climate, and legislation banning topics related to race, sexuality, gender, and others, were making it much more difficult for teachers to prepare their students for participation in a diverse democracy. The political context created broad chilling effects that resulted in "limiting the opportunities for students to practice respectful dialogue on controversial topics." This made it more difficult for them to "build capacities for respectful, evidence-based dialogue," and harder to address rampant misinformation, and permitted fewer opportunities to "develop commitments to robust civil liberties and recognition of the dignity of fellow citizens."[51]

Thus, while civic education is always a challenging endeavor, it must now operate on a far more stressful terrain. Hyperpolarization creates a tremendous need for democratic education, while simultaneously making it more difficult to undertake this work.

CONTRIBUTIONS TO THE VOLUME

Given the problems of polarization for democracy, and the demands for and challenges of civic education in this polarized time, what type of civic education should we promote? What civic learning might help students navigate divides, avoid being swept up by forces of polarization, or perhaps even try to mitigate it? Could civic education help reduce animosity and distrust between groups, or provide more opportunities for open political conversation and deliberation about social problems? Should existing, traditional approaches to civic education be continued? Or is there a need for reforms and new approaches, even though some educational researchers have warned that "Attempts to reemphasize or reform citizenship education in our high schools may trigger traditional fault lines in American politics"?[52] The authors in this volume have valuable and distinct takes on these questions and others. They offer a range of arguments touching on the following important issues.

One question the contributors help us consider is what types of civic learning are needed in a period of polarization that includes growing distrust in political institutions tasked with making, interpreting, and executing law. In the United States, polls show declining trust in institutions—including legislatures and courts—and they show significantly higher levels of distrust among younger generations and among racial and ethnic minorities than in other groups.[53] In "Democratic Civic Education and Democratic Law," Seana Shiffrin calls for a type of legal-civic learning. Her aim is to encourage more informed and participatory citizenship, and to help people serve as "co-authors of law," thus supporting core ideals of democracy and justice. She sees this as an important model of civic learning for polarized times because fostering legal literacy and a "sense of shared agency and responsibility for the content and success of democratic law" could prevent young people from being overwhelmed by the types of "generalized, unsubstantiated distrust" associated with political polarization.

Young citizens need to be equipped, Shiffrin believes, to "deliberate about the law's aims and values and how, in good faith, to bring them about." This is in part because important legal principles and standards, such as "equal treatment," prohibitions on "harassment," requirements to provide "reasonable accommodation," are neither self-defining nor self-implementing, and the "lived existence" of such principles depends importantly on individual actions. For instance, Shiffrin believes that when individuals have opportunities to learn about free speech principles, they may be inspired to adopt values and practices of "tolerance, open-mindedness, and engagement" that are important for democratic culture. Similarly, if individuals are inspired to adopt social norms of equal treatment, they can complement civil rights and help to implement them. Social critics often criticize the gaps between the principles of democracy and law, on the one hand, and actual practices on the other. Shiffrin's vision is that legal-civic education would create participatory citizens who could help close these gaps and co-create more democratic law through their informed judgment and actions.

While Shiffrin believes infusing civic learning with legal learning could improve participation and democracy, Brandon Terry and Robert Tsai raise cautions. They propose quite different goals for civic learning, and approaches that would include a strong focus on diagnosing and addressing sources of political and social division in the United States, especially racial and ethnic injustices. In "Civic Education and Polarized Politics: Transition, Critique, and Dissent," Brandon Terry calls for deeper questioning of the aims and content of civic education, and the causes and functions of polarization. He brings a critical and historically contextualized lens to the questions of what type of civic education is valuable and necessary—and where and how it can occur—when political animus limits the capacity to teach about race. In these polarized times, he argues, it is not helpful to use philosophical "ideal theory" to advocate for consensus or for reconciling citizens to existing political and legal institutions through civic education. Instead, it is important to begin by considering the reasons and conditions contributing to intense political antagonisms. Terry highlights historical and social scientific studies examining how racism and racial dynamics have shaped the patterns of partisanship, distrust, and violence tied to polarization.

For Terry, the racial underpinnings of political fault lines demonstrate the need for a "justice-oriented civic education" that is informed by the lessons and from African American critique and dissent, and that may occur outside the formal classroom. He calls for recognizing different ideals, sites, agents, and practices of civic education. These include the "praxis of resistance to oppression and injustice," and the "fugitive pedagogies" taught by Black activists and educators such as Martin Luther King Jr., Carter G. Woodson, and Huey Newton, and the ideals of "genuinely emancipatory and democratic civic learning" that have come from movements for dissent and reconstruction.

For Robert Tsai, too, a program of civic education focused on legal-civic knowledge appears too limited. He suggests such a model remains too abstract and "too incomplete to equip the citizen to tackle the problems facing an aging political order." In "Civic Education and Democracy's Flaws," Tsai argues that not only is a civic education that prioritizes legal literacy unlikely to bridge the deepening divides of the era, but, if undertaken in the narrow and conventional ways used in many law schools, teaching about law and encouraging legal proficiency could be demoralizing, fail to empower democratic action, and even reinforce existing problems and inequalities. Tsai's prescription for a civic education that can "make a meaningful impact at this historical moment" calls for a different approach.

He believes that democratic citizens not only need capacities for "listening, truth-telling, and toleration," but they also need capacities for "righteous outrage" when they see abuses and injustices; they need ways to learn how to understand "the multiplicity of relationships and identities in modern life"; and they need to learn about how some despised political and legal decisions have influenced the structures and institutions of political life.

Building from some of the content and pedagogy he has developed in his own courses, Tsai suggests that civic education should help students learn "the ability to diagnose democracy's shortcomings and the capacity to reason from injustice."

As Terry's and Tsai's contributions indicate, some people believe that there is a particular need for civic education work to recognize and confront the pressing problems of this era and legacies of the past, even though taking more critical or radical approaches may make civic education a more challenging or controversial endeavor. Others, however, such as Justin Driver, believe it is important for K-12 civic education efforts to offer bipartisan appeal if they want to operate in the political fray of the current era and be considered for adoption by schools across the country.

Justin Driver's "Civic Education, Students' Rights, and the Supreme Court" argues that the lack of robust civic education in schools has helped to exacerbate political tensions and conflict. He urges what he calls a "student-centered approach" as a superior alternative to conventional approaches. Driver believes this approach promises multiple benefits, including a greater ability to engage students as well as the capacity to find widespread, bipartisan support even amidst polarized times. Driver suggests a central focus on historic struggles for students' rights. This is an approach he believes—partly from his own experience teaching high school students—will inspire students' interest in learning about the operation and development of constitutional democracy and make them more aware and critically evaluative of the rights they have.

For Driver, learning about the landmark US Supreme Court decisions that have shaped students' rights and experiences in schools can serve as an entry for discussions of broader issues and arguments. This student-centered approach can be used to illuminate students as active participants in creating rights, and to encourage students to "become engaged, able stewards of our constitutional democracy." Thus, Driver views this model of civic education not simply as a retrospective lens on the arc of national history and past constitutional development, but as a tool for encouraging students' sense of civic agency and a sense of possibility for further advancing democracy and justice in the present.

While many will see the pragmatic benefits of improving upon and augmenting civic education's traditional focus on political and legal institutions, others, such as Jennifer Morton and Lisa García Bedolla, hope for approaches to civic education that might better inspire critical and creative democratic citizenship. Jennifer Morton views Driver's model as a potentially fruitful avenue for civic education reform, but her contribution, "Can Driver's Civic Education Model Circumvent Partisanship?," also identifies concerns. Although she agrees that Driver's student-centered learning approach could gain broad support and help provide "a common ground of core institutional knowledge," Morton worries that an overwhelming focus on Supreme Court opinions limits civic education too much to learning about institutions as they are, rather than providing students tools for thinking about alternatives for how institutions ought to be.

Thus, she sees this type of model as being in tension with another critical aim of civic education: "to enable students to reimagine the terms on which our society is built, including the Constitution and the legal process it enshrines." Morton draws on Derrick Bell's critique of *Brown v. Board of Education*, which pointed out the continued inequalities that persisted in *Brown's* wake, to suggest how studying students' rights and Supreme Court decisions could include more progressive potential. However, she recognizes that a more radical approach to civic education would not generate the broad-based political common ground that Driver seeks to cultivate. Thus, Morton raises the difficult question of whether "we cannot do better at this historical moment in the United States than aiming for some common civic ground, even if it falls short of our more progressive ideals."

Lisa García Bedolla's "Race, Equity, and Civic Education" agrees with Driver that a call to action is needed to improve civic education. However, she is concerned that his recommended approach would fall short of providing a powerful civic learning experience that could make students from all backgrounds feel engaged and efficacious in the US political system. García Bedolla suggests that scholars developing civic education approaches, such as Driver, should clarify their anticipated goals for civic education. She also emphasizes that civic education efforts should be informed by the robust literature on effective pedagogical practices for fostering youth civic engagement, such as problem-based learning and structured political conversations. In addition, she points to the need to recognize different school contexts, and the challenges of racial, gender, and socioeconomic inequalities that exist in US schools and society.

Ultimately, for García Bedolla, there is need for deeper consideration and conversation about the civic education approaches required to promote a multiracial democracy. She argues that "there has never been a national conversation about what civic education needs to look like in order to support a truly inclusive multiracial democracy," and that it is "only by facing all our truths—the good and the bad" that we can teach young people that "this democracy truly is theirs and that they have both the power and the obligation to nurture and sustain it."

In addition to considering the content or pedagogy of civic education for polarized times, it is also important to consider the crucial roles of teachers as role models and transmitters of civic learning. Ilana Paul-Binyamin, Wurud Jayusi, and Yael (Yuli) Tamir highlight the potential for cross-community teaching—when teachers and students come from different ethnic or religious groups—to help reduce distrust and hostility in divided societies. In "Moving Beyond the 'Poitier Effect': Examining the Potential to Advance Civic Respect through Cross-Community Teaching," Binyamin, Jayusi, and Tamir consider the opportunities for and difficulties of promoting intergroup empathy and connection in the midst of polarization and "thick diversity."

They revisit the so-called Poitier effect, named for Sidney Poitier's famous movie role as an inspirational teacher who helps break down racial divides, and they consider whether there are ways that teachers from different backgrounds can help reduce prejudice and humanize others. Because teachers are influential authority figures for students, the authors believe students from majority groups can be deeply affected when they are learning from an "other" who is a figure of expertise, a mentor, and perhaps a friend. Drawing on intergroup contact theory, research on cross-cultural interactions in educational contexts, and their own study of a cross-community teaching program in Israel, they argue that these approaches may have deep and lasting effects, including a positive impact on students and communities of schoolteachers. While they identify significant cautions and challenges, Binyamin, Jayusi, and Tamir argue that cross-community teaching by teachers from minority backgrounds could make important contributions to developing more inclusive societies, nurturing the connections and civic virtues needed to reduce prejudices and create more empathetic and just societies.

Rima Basu's "The Challenges of Thick Diversity, Polarization, Debiasing, and Tokenization for Cross-Group Teaching," considers Paul-Binyamin, Jayusi, and Tamir's argument that teachers who don't share the same background as their students can help counter increasing polarization. Basu suggests several challenges to their proposal for encouraging this approach. These include concerns that research on intergroup contact interventions reveals that such efforts can have backlash effects and unintended consequences, and sometimes increase rather than reduce prejudice.

In addition, Basu raises concerns that the type of cross-community teaching program suggested by Paul-Binyamin and colleagues can entail serious risks, such as harmful tokenization of minority teachers, or placing the burdens of combating prejudice and injustices of racial and ethnic oppression on them. Basu invites the authors, and us, to consider that civic education in divided and polarized societies could benefit from Olúfémi O Táíwò's idea of the need to "be accountable and responsive to people who aren't yet in the room, and [let us] build the kinds of rooms in which we can sit together, rather than merely seek to navigate more gracefully the rooms history has built for us."[54]

We can also consider the importance of broader campus climates for civic education beyond the classroom. There are important types of civic learning that students may experience through the voices, ideas, civic discourse, and diversity of perspectives they may encounter in their campus spaces and communities. Increased political polarization has contributed to heated controversies over free speech on university campuses. Many schools have struggled with finding ways to support the ability for all voices to be heard, while trying to avoid climates of hostility that can undermine students' learning and membership.[55] In "Exploring an Epistemic Conflict over Free Speech on American College Campuses, and the Promise of the New Democratic Model," Kristine Bowman focuses on concerns regarding the ideas and conditions of free speech on college campuses.

She explores two different views of higher education and free speech and how they may relate to diversity and to polarization. The traditional model prioritizes the university's knowledge production function and adopts a generally absolutist understanding of free speech as a negative right. This model of higher education and its view of free speech, argues Bowman, involves ideas and approaches that can tend to maintain or increase polarization. But an emerging "new democratic model" understands universities as institutions of learning and knowledge creation where inclusion is central to the mission, and where free speech is more akin to a "compound right" in which individual liberty balances with considerations of speech harms. Bowman argues that this new democratic model and compound rights approach has greater potential to combat polarization on campuses and in society, and is likely to continue developing outside of courts—even though more absolutist approaches to free speech remain strongly entrenched in Supreme Court jurisprudence.

Last but not least, Sigal Ben-Porath, Amy Gutmann, and Dennis Thompson raise the question of whether students living in a polarized world need a civic education that helps them learn skills for cooperation that would seem to suit a more idealized democracy, or skills for competition that would seem to suit politics as it is. In "Teaching Competition and Cooperation in Civic Education," they argue that students need to learn both sets of skills. Although approaches that focus on competition might seem most useful for hyperpolarized politics, Ben-Porath, Gutmann, and Thompson believe it would be a mistake to teach students only "how to be more effective in fighting for their own causes," to use strategies emphasizing opposition and techniques for mobilizing partisans.

They also believe it would be a mistake to teach students only skills of cooperation: "strategies for finding common ground, dialog that bridges differences, rhetoric that is mutually respectful, techniques that bring opponents together." Instead, students need opportunities to learn and practice "alternating the experiences of competition with the practices of cooperation in the classroom," in order to learn their respective strengths and weaknesses, and how they can be combined for democratic citizenship. To develop their case, the authors consider examples and evidence of how to combine cooperation and competitive approaches to civic learning from a Legislative Semester program, as well as other curricular and extracurricular programs, such as Ethics Bowl, Model UN, and Action Civics.

The Need for Critical and Creative Civic Education for a Divided Era

Civic education is always shaped by the political concerns and disagreements of its era. When an earlier group of scholars of philosophy, law, and politics came together twenty years ago to tackle the topic of "Moral and Political Education," they expressed a core concern that "deep disagreement about moral and religious values" created significant challenges for educational projects and policies related to modern democratic life.[56] Much has happened in the intervening years. But the concerns of civic education in the present polarized era are not entirely new or separate from those raised earlier. Indeed, some of the present concerns relate to the ways that older fissures in politics, society, and education have deepened or expanded as they have intersected with new fractures.

Extreme polarization interferes with norms and processes that are considered fundamental for democratic citizenship and the health of democratic institutions and culture: citizens' capacities for political learning, interaction, debate, and informed decision-making; citizens' abilities to hold leaders and parties accountable for their actions and policies; individual and group commitments to democratic norms, including tolerance for difference, acceptance of political opposition, and avoidance of political violence; leaders' incentives for pursuing cooperation and broad-based coalitions, and for rejecting inflammatory rhetoric, corruption, and abuses of power.

So, as worries of democratic decay and threats mount, civic education should be part of the solution to these crises. Civic education cannot be the only response to pernicious polarization—it must be part of more comprehensive efforts to change the social conditions and confront the institutional and societal factors and problems that have fueled it. But more attention to, and support for, civic learning in school is especially crucial, since the future of democracy will lie in the hands of today's students and emerging citizens. "The Hill We Climb," the poem written and recited by Amanda Gorman for the US presidential inauguration, is one poignant expression of an attempt to navigate the circumstances of extreme political division in the United States that led to the assault on the Capitol:

> When day comes, we ask ourselves, where can we find light in
>   this never-ending shade?
> The loss we carry. A sea we must wade. . . .
> And, yes, we are far from polished, far from pristine, but that
>   doesn't mean we are striving to form a union that is perfect.
> We are striving to forge our union with purpose.
> To compose a country committed to all cultures, colors,
>   characters and conditions of man.
> And so we lift our gaze, not to what stands between us, but what
>   stands before us.

Gorman's verse expresses some of the pains and aspirations some young people feel and face as they try to place themselves in the uneven and unfolding story of democracy—they want to feel hopeful, but they also want honest confrontations with problems, and they want to be prepared for helping to address these problems and to build a more vibrant and just democracy. As Gorman's words help convey, the pernicious effects of polarization require us to think more critically, but also more creatively, about the difficult work of democracy—and of educating for a healthier democracy.

NOTES

1 See Jennifer McCoy, Tahmina Rahman, and Murat Somer, "Polarization and the Global Crisis of Democracy: Common Patterns, Dynamics, and Pernicious Consequences for Democratic Polities," *American Behavioral Scientist* (Beverly Hills) 62, no. 1 (2018): 16–42.

2 McCoy et al., "Polarization and the Global Crisis."

3 Ariana Figueroa, "Can Teaching Civics Save Democracy?" NPR, September 22, 2017. www.npr.org. Accessed January 7, 2022. See also George Packer, "Can Civics Save America," *The Atlantic*, May 15, 2021.

4 Jason C. Fitzgerald, Alison K. Cohen, Elena Maker Castro, and Alexander Pope, "A Systematic Review of the Last Decade of Civic Educa-

tion Research in the United States," *Peabody Journal of Education* 96, no. 3 (2021): 235–246. Some important existing discussions of civic education in relation to polarizing include Paula McAvoy and Diana Hess, "Classroom Deliberation in an Era of Political Polarization," *Curriculum Inquiry* 43, no. 1 (2013): 14–47; Maren Tribukait, "Students' Prejudice as a Teaching Challenge: How European History Educators Deal with Controversial and Sensitive Issues in a Climate of Political Polarization," *Theory & Research in Social Education* 49 no. 4 (2021): 540–569; and Daniela Kruel DiGiacomo, Erica Hodgin, Joseph Kahne, and Sara Trapp, "Civic Education in a Politically Polarized Era," *Peabody Journal of Education* 96, no. 3 (2021): 261–274.

5 Henry E. Brady and Thomas B. Kent, "Fifty Years of Declining Confidence & Increasing Polarization in Trust in American Institutions," *Daedalus* (Cambridge, MA) 151, no. 4 (2022): 43–66. https://doi.org/10.1162/daed_a_01943; Kevin Vallier, *Trust in a Polarized Age* (New York: Oxford University Press, 2021).

6 On the proliferation of law in modern societies and its influence on many realms of human experience, see Robert A. Kagan, "What Socio-Legal Scholars Should Do When There Is Too Much Law to Study," *Journal of Law and Society* 22, no. 1 (1995): 140–148.

7 For the initial Pulitzer Prize–winning publication of *The 1619 Project* from the *New York Times*, see www.nytimes.com. Accessed July 12, 2022. This became the basis for the Pulitzer Center's 1619 Project for Educators, which "challenges us to reframe U.S. history by marking the year when the first enslaved Africans arrived on Virginia soil as our nation's foundational date" and offers "reading guides, activities, and other resources to bring *The 1619 Project* into your classroom." https://pulitzercenter.org. Accessed July 12, 2022. For the Trump Administration's President's Advisory 1776 Commission's 1776 Report, see https://trumpwhitehouse.archives.gov. Accessed July 12, 2022. This has become the basis for a 1776 action pledged to "advance the values that made America great" and to oppose teaching related to race and other characteristics, and Action Civics. 1776 Action. https://1776action.org. Accessed July 12, 2022. For proposed and adopted anti–Critical Race Theory legislation, see PEN America's Index of Educational Gag Orders, https://docs.google.com. Accessed April 12, 2023.

8 Pew Research Center, Section 4: Political Compromise and Divisive Policy Debates, Political Polarization in the American Public. June 12, 2014. www.pewresearch.org. See especially the data on "Political Compromise in Principle," www.pewresearch.org.

9 On these issues, see Kay Lehman Schlozman, Henry E. Brady, and Sidney Verba, *Unequal and Unrepresented: Political Inequality and the People's*

Voice in the New Gilded Age (Princeton, NJ: Princeton University Press, 2018); Alan I. Abramowitz and Jennifer McCoy, "United States: Racial Resentment, Negative Partisanship and Polarization in Trump's America," *Annals of the American Academy of Political and Social Science* 681 (2019): 137–156; Yanna Krupnikov and John Barry Ryan, *The Other Divide: Polarization and Disengagement in American Politics* (Cambridge: Cambridge University Press, 2022).

10 Murat Somer and Jennifer McCoy, "Transformations through Polarizations and Global Threats to Democracy," *Annals of the American Academy of Political and Social Science* 681, no. 1 (2019): 8–22.

11 Rachel Kleinfeld and Joel Olsen, among others, identify racism as a significant contributor to inequality, polarization, and violence in the United States. Kleinfeld, "The Rise of Political Violence in the United States," *Journal of Democracy* 32, no. 4 (October 2021): 160–176. Joel Olson, "Whiteness and the Polarization of American Politics," *Political Research Quarterly* 61, no. 4 (2008): 704–718.

12 Thomas Carothers and Andrew O'Donahue, *Democracies Divided: The Global Challenge of Political Polarization* (Washington, DC: Brookings Institution Press, 2019).

13 Knight Foundation, "Free Expression in America Post-2020," January 6, 2022. https://knightfoundation.org. Accessed July 17, 2022. See also Sigal R. Ben-Porath, *Free Speech on Campus* (Philadelphia: University of Pennsylvania Press, 2017).

14 In one US national poll, 28 percent of respondents said "political extremism or polarization" was one of the most important issues facing the country—a higher share than those that named racism, immigration, economic inequality, climate change, taxes, the government budget, and other types of concerns. Well over a majority (62%) said they want the US to work to reduce political polarization. Geoffrey Skelley and Holly Fuong, "3 in 10 Americans Named Political Polarization as a Top Issue Facing the Country," FiveThirtyEight, June 14, 2022. https://fivethirtyeight.com.

15 Nolan McCarty, *Polarization: What Everyone Needs to Know* (New York: Oxford University Press, 2019). While earlier political research focused on polarization among political elites and parties, more recent work emphasizes that there is also extreme polarization in the public or masses. See, for instance, Steven W. Webster and Alan I. Abramowitz, "The Ideological Foundations of Affective Polarization in the U.S. Electorate," *American Politics Research* 45, no. 4 (2017): 621–647, and Lilliana Mason, "Ideologues without Issues: The Polarizing Consequences of Ideological Identities," *Public Opinion Quarterly* 82, no. S1 (2018): 280–301.

16 Several different perspectives are presented in A. LeBas, "Can Polarization Be Positive? Conflict and Institutional Development in Africa,"

American Behavioral Scientist 62, no. 1 (2018): 59–74; Y. Stavrakakis, "Paradoxes of Polarization: Democracy's Inherent Division and the (Anti-) Populist Challenge," *American Behavioral Scientist* 62 (2018): 43–58; Gordon Heltzel and Kristin Laurin, "Polarization in America: Two Possible Futures," *Current Opinion in Behavioral Sciences* 34 (2020): 179–184. https://doi.org/10.1016/j.cobeha.2020.03.008.

17 See, e.g., Peter T. Coleman, "The U.S. Is Suffering from Toxic Polarization. That's Arguably a Good Thing," *Scientific American*, April 2, 2021. www.scientificamerican.com; Lilliana Mason, *Uncivil Agreement: How Politics Became Our Identity* (Chicago: University of Chicago Press, 2018).

18 See, e.g., Carothers and O'Donahue, *Democracies Divided.*

19 Political scientists and others differentiate between benign types and degrees of political polarization, and the type of extreme polarization that is dangerous for democracy. Benign ideological polarization involves "sorting" into opposing political groups or parties based on shared political values, interests, and policy views, while pernicious polarization involves "affective dimensions," particularly hostility, aversion, and othering. Eli Finkel and his colleagues identify three core elements of hyperpartisanship that make it as "political sectarianism," "othering," or the tendency to view opponents as fundamentally different or alien from oneself; "aversion," or intense dislike and distrust of this other; and "moralization," or perceiving the other as evil. See Eli J. Finkel et al., "Political Sectarianism in America," *Science* 370 (2020): 533–536. Jennifer McCoy and her colleagues describe pernicious polarization as being distinguished from lesser forms by "the strength of animosity and distrust between the camps, its entrenchment in political dynamics, and its [more severe] negative consequences for democracy." Jennifer McCoy, Benjamin Press, Murat Somer, and Ozlem Tuncel, "Reducing Pernicious Polarization: A Comparative Historical Analysis of Depolarization," Carnegie Endowment for World Peace, May 2022. https://carnegieendowment.org. Accessed March 7, 2023.

For a specific focus on the United States, see Shanto Iyengar et al., "The Origins and Consequences of Affective Polarization in the United States," *Annual Review of Political Science* 22, no. 1 (2019, May 11): 129–146.

20 Finkel et al., "Political Sectarianism in America." See also Dan M. Kahan, "The Politically Motivated Reasoning Paradigm, Part 1: What Politically Motivated Reasoning Is and How to Measure It," in *Emerging Trends in the Social and Behavioral Sciences*, edited by Robert A. Scott, Marlis Buchmann, and Stephen Kosslyn, for Wiley Online Library (2016), 1–16. Although there is mixed evidence on the operation of motivated reasoning, a number of studies find it has problematic effects.

21 Carothers and O'Donahue, *Democracies Divided*; Finkel et al., "Political Sectarianism in America"; Milan Svolik, "Polarization Versus Democ-

racy," *Journal of Democracy* 30, no. 3 (July 2019): 20–32; Levi Boxell, Matthew Gentzkow, and Jesse M. Shapiro, "Cross-Country Trends in Affective Polarization," *Review of Economics and Statistics* (2022): 1–60.

22 One of the most influential twentieth-century political theorists, Robert Dahl, argued that complete democracy remains an ideal because of the challenges of providing full political equality and inclusion. But Dahl also argued that there are important democratic achievements, as well as shortcomings, that can be measured. See Robert A. Dahl, *Democracy and Its Critics* (New Haven, CT: Yale University Press, 1989), especially chapters 8–9, and pp. 109–115, 129–131. For a more contemporary discussion of democracy as an ideal in the popular press, see Astra Taylor, *Democracy May Not Exist But We'll Miss It When It's Gone* (New York: Verso, 2019).

23 Zaid Jilani and Jeremy Adam Smith, "What Is the True Cost of Polarization in America?," *Greater Good Magazine*, March 4, 2019. https://greatergood.berkeley.edu. Accessed May 18, 2022.

24 On everyday democracy, see Nancy Rosenblum, *Good Neighbors: The Democracy of Everyday Life in America* (Princeton, NJ: Princeton University Press, 2016). On the ethics of democratic citizenship, see Ronald D. Glass, "Education and the Ethics of Democratic Citizenship," in *Education, Democracy, and the Moral Life*, ed. M. S. Katz, S. Verducci, and G. Biesta (Dordrecht: Springer, 2009); and Eric Beerbohm, *In Our Name: The Ethics of Democracy* (Princeton, NJ: Princeton University Press, 2012). The concept of a "civic infrastructure," including civic education, as a foundation for democratic problem-solving began to be emphasized and studied by the National Conference on Civic Renewal in the late 1980s. See Christopher T. Gates, "The National Civic Index: A New Approach to Community Problem Solving," *National Civic Review* 76 (1987): 472–479. A more recent set of measures is provided in Julia H. Kaufman, Melissa Kay Diliberti, Douglas Yeung, and Jennifer Kavanagh, *Defining and Measuring Civic Infrastructure* (Santa Monica, CA: RAND Corporation, 2022), pp. 56–58. www.rand.org.

25 Monica Guzman, *I Never Thought of It That Way: How to Have Fearlessly Curious Conversations in Dangerously Divided Times* (Dallas, TX: BenBella Books, 2022).

26 Ezra Klein's analysis of the causes of polarization in the United States identifies multiple factors, including unequal distributions of power and representation through institutional and constitutional characteristics (such as single-member, winner-take-all legislative districts and the design and functions of the US Senate and Electoral College) as well as the country's political legacies of slavery and racial and ethnic exclusion. Klein also points to the ways that polarization can be self-reinforcing. See Ezra Klein, *Why We're Polarized* (New York: Avid Reader, 2020). Klein's anal-

ysis reflects long-standing critiques of the undemocratic features of the US system, such as in Robert A. Dahl, *How Democratic Is the American Constitution?* New Haven, CT: Yale University Press, 2001).

27 There are an array of important suggestions for how to "depolarize" politics ranging from institutional reforms, such as ranked choice voting; to new policy initiatives, such as voter education or mandatory national service; to suggestions for civic interventions such as projects for cross-partisan civic discussions or Citizens' Assemblies. See, for instance, Jennifer McCoy and Murat Somer, "Overcoming Polarization," *Journal of Democracy* 32, no. 1 (2021): 6–12. For one set of ideas offered for the United States by scholars, politicians, and others, see the twenty contributions to the *Politico* magazine symposium, "How to Fix Politics in America," 2019. www.politico.com. Accessed February 28, 2022.

28 See, for instance, Rebecca Winthrop, "The Need for Civic Education in 21st-Century Schools," Brookings Institution, June 2020; and Rick Hess, "Tackling Polarization Via a 'Cross-Partisan' Approach to Civics Education," *Education Week*, December 16, 2021. www.edweek.org. Accessed February 28, 2022.

29 Influential arguments include Benjamin Barber, *An Aristocracy of Everyone: the Politics of Education and the Future of America* (New York: Ballantine Books, 1992); Amy Gutmann, *Democratic Education* (Princeton, NJ: Princeton University Press, 1987); Eamonn Callan, *Creating Citizens: Political Education and Liberal Democracy* (Oxford: Clarendon Press, 1997); and Stephen Macedo, *Diversity and Distrust: Civic Education in a Multicultural Society* (Cambridge, MA: Harvard University Press, 2000).

30 For research on the positive effects of civic education, see, for instance, David E. Campbell, "What Social Scientists Have Learned About Civic Education: A Review of the Literature," *Peabody Journal of Education* 94, no. 1 (2019): 32–47; Judith Torney Purta and JoAnn Amadeo, "Civic and Political Knowledge and Skills," in *SAGE Encyclopedia of Political Behavior* (2017), 87–90; Jonathan Gould, ed., *Guardian of Democracy: The Civic Mission of Schools* (Philadelphia: Leonore Annenberg Institute for Civics of the Annenberg Public Policy Center at the University of Pennsylvania, 2011); Diane Hess and Paula McAvoy, *The Political Classroom: Evidence and Ethics in Democratic Education* (New York: Routledge, 2015); and Meira Levinson, "The Civic Empowerment Gap: Defining the Problem and Locating Solutions," in *Handbook of Research on Civic Engagement*, ed. Lonnie Sherrod, Judith Torney-Purta, and Constance A. Flanagan, 331–361. (Hoboken, NJ: John Wiley & Sons, 2010). My co-authors and I studied and wrote about some of these issues at the college level in Anne Colby, Elizabeth Beaumont, Thomas Ehrlich, and Jason Stephens, *Educating for Democracy: Preparing Undergraduates for Responsible Political En-*

gagement (San Francisco, New York: Jossey-Bass, 2008). One of the most ambitious new K-12 civic programs, developed to incorporate research and proven practices, is the "Educating for American Democracy" program, www.educatingforamericandemocracy.org. Accessed December 1, 2022.

31 CivXNow, "Civic Education Has Massive Cross-Partisan Appeal as a Solution to What Ails Our Democracy" (Cambridge, MA: CivXNow, 2020). https://civxnow.org. Accessed August 7, 2022. However, bipartisan agreement on the importance of civic education does not mean agreement on the content of civic education. See Frederick M. Hess and Matthew Rice, "Where Left and Right Agree on Civics Education, and Where They Don't," *EducationNext.* March 25, 2020. www.educationnext.org. Accessed August 7, 2022.

32 Linda C. McClain and James Fleming, "Civic Education in Circumstances of Constitutional Rot and Strong Polarization," *Boston University Law Review* 101 (2021): 1771–1792. See also Peter Levine and Kei Kawashima-Ginsberg, "The Republic Is (Still) at Risk—and Civics Is Part of the Solution: A Briefing Paper for the Democracy at a Crossroads National Summit" (Medford, MA: Jonathan M. Tisch College of Civic Life, Tufts University, 2017).

33 Sarah Repucci and Amy Slipowitz, "Democracy under Siege," *Freedom House* (2021), p. 29; and Sarah Repucci and Amy Slipowitz, "The Global Expansion of Authoritarian Rule," *Freedom House* (2022), p. 11.

34 Commission on Youth Voting and Civic Knowledge, *All Together Now: Collaboration and Innovation for Youth Engagement* (Medford, MA: Center for Information & Research on Civic Learning and Engagement, 2013).

35 Rajiv Vinnakota and Red & Blue Works. "From a Civic Education to a Civic Learning Ecosystem: A Landscape Analysis and the Case for Collaboration," Institute for Citizens and Scholars, 2019.

36 See, for instance, Judith Torney-Purta et al., *Citizenship and Education in Twenty-Eight Countries: Civic Knowledge and Engagement at Age Fourteen* (Amsterdam: IEA Secretariat, 2001); Carol Hahn, "Challenges to Civic Education in the United States," in *Civic Education across Countries: Twenty-four National Case Studies from the IEA Civic Education Project,* ed. Judith Torney-Purta, J. Schwille, and JoAnne A. Amadeo, pp. 583–607 (Amsterdam: IEA Secretariat).

37 George Packer, "Can Civics Save America?," *The Atlantic,* May 15, 2021. Kathleen Hall Jamieson argues, somewhat similarly, that one of the main challenges facing civic education is that efforts to improve and reform civic education "are complicated by the fact that civics education has become a pawn in a polarized debate among partisans." Jamieson, "The Challenges Facing Civic Education," *Daedalus,* Spring 2013.

38 See PEN America, Index of Educational Gag Orders, above. In 2021 and 2022, PEN America tracked more than 191 proposed educational gag orders from thirty-six different US states. See also Stephen Sawchuck, "What Is Critical Race Theory, and Why Is It Under Attack?," *Education Week*, May 18, 2021.

39 "American Library Association Releases Preliminary Data on 2022 Book Bans," American Library Association, September 16, 2022. www.ala.org. Accessed February 3, 2023.

40 Katie Reilly, "As Teachers and School Boards Face a Spike in Violent Threats, the Justice Department Is Stepping In," *Time*. https://time.com. Katie Reilly, "Culture Wars Could Be Coming to a School Board Near You," *Time*, March 23, 2022. https://time.com. Accessed March 5, 2023. See also S. D. McMahon, E. M. Anderman, R. A. Astor, D. L. Espelage, A. Martinez, L. A. Reddy, and F. C. Worrell, "Violence Against Educators and School Personnel: Crisis During COVID." Policy Brief. American Psychological Association, 2022.

41 Hess and McAvoy, *The Political Classroom*.

42 Gould et al., *Guardian of Democracy*.

43 Commission on Youth Voting and Civic Knowledge, "All Together Now: Collaboration and Innovation for Youth Engagement" (Medford, MA: Center for Information & Research on Civic Learning and Engagement, 2013).

44 See Laura S. Hamilton, Julia H. Kaufman, and Lynn Hu, "Media Use and Literacy in Schools: Civic Development in the Era of Truth Decay" (Santa Monica, CA: RAND Corporation, 2020). www.rand.org.

45 Paula McAvoy and Diana Hess, "Classroom Deliberation in an Era of Political Polarization," *Curriculum Inquiry* 43, no. 1 (2013). Hess and McAvoy believe that teaching students how to deliberate about political controversies not only helps students become more informed citizens and learn discussion skills needed for democracy, but that "the aims of deliberative democracy" might be "the solution to a highly polarized and nasty political climate."

46 Judith Torney-Purta and Britt S. Wilkenfeld, "Paths to 21st Century Competencies through Civic Education Classrooms: An Analysis of Survey Results from Ninth-Graders" (American Bar Association, Division for Public Education, 2009), www.americanbar.org; E. Quintelier and Mark Hooghe "The relationship between political participation intentions of adolescents and a participatory democratic climate at school in 35 countries." *Oxford Review of Education*, 39, 567–589. For research demonstrating positive effects of open discussion of current events at the college level, see David E. Campbell, "Voice in the Classroom: How an Open Classroom Climate Fosters Political Engagement Among Adolescents," *Political Be-*

havior 30 (2008): 437–454, and Elizabeth Beaumont, "Promoting Political Agency, Addressing Political Inequality: A Multilevel Model of Internal Political Efficacy," *Journal of Politics* 73 no. 1 (2011): 216–231.

47 Hess and McAvoy, *The Political Classroom.* Torney-Purta et al., "Paths to 21st Century Competencies. For a further examination of political discussion and deliberation in higher education contexts, see Anne Colby, Elizabeth Beaumont, Thomas Ehrlich, Josh Corngold, "Learning through Discussion and Deliberation," in *Educating for Democracy: Preparing Undergraduates for Responsible Political Engagement* (San Francisco: Jossey-Bass, 2008), 156–174. More broadly, Diana Mutz's work has found that people exposed to cross-cutting views learned more legitimate reasons for political disagreement, and they became more tolerant of political groups with opposing views. See Diana Mutz, *Hearing the Other Side: Deliberative Versus Participatory Democracy* (Cambridge: Cambridge University Press, 2006).

48 Hess and McAvoy, *The Political Classroom.*

49 See, for instance, McAvoy and Hess, "Classroom Deliberation," and Maren Tribukait, "Students' Prejudice as a Teaching Challenge: How European History Educators Deal with Controversial and Sensitive Issues in a Climate of Political Polarization," *Theory & Research in Social Education* 49, no. 4 (2021): 540–569.

50 DiGiacomo et al., "Civic Education in a Politically Polarized Era," https://doi.org/10.1080/0161956X.2021.1942705.

51 J. Rogers and J. Kahne, with M. Ishimoto et al., *Educating for a Diverse Democracy: The Chilling Role of Political Conflict in Blue, Purple, and Red Communities* (Los Angeles, CA: UCLA's Institute for Democracy, Education, and Access, 2022).

52 Lautzenheiser et al., p. 6, in Hess and McAvoy, *The Political Classroom*; see also the cautions from Jamieson, "The Challenges Facing Civic Education."

53 Jeffrey M. Jones, "Trust in Federal Government Branches Continues to Falter," October 11, 2022. Gallup. https://news.gallup.com. Accessed January 15, 2023. See also Pew Research Center, July 2019, "Trust and Distrust in America," www.pewresearch.org.

54 Olúfẹ́mi O. Táíwò, *Elite Capture: How the Powerful Took Over Identity Politics (And Everything Else)* (Chicago: Haymarket Books, 2022), cited in Basu, chapter 8 of this text.

55 See Ben-Porath, *Free Speech on Campus.*

56 Stephen Macedo and Yael Tamir, eds., *Moral and Political Education: NOMOS XLIII* (New York: New York University Press, 2002).

1

DEMOCRATIC CIVIC EDUCATION AND DEMOCRATIC LAW

SEANA VALENTINE SHIFFRIN

The substantive law is a neglected topic in civic education. To be sure, the US Constitution is often an object of fixation in civic education and it will feature in my discussion too. Yet, though it is important, it's a small part of the law. Primarily, it directly regulates state actors, and that fact, along with the rather text-bound way it is often presented, can encourage a shallow and distant model of citizenship. This emphasis does not nurture the attitude that the law is ours, and that it is our joint responsibility, together, to make it work. A more robust model of democratic citizens and their duties would require providing a deeper exposure to a broader band of the substantive law, its purposes, and the associated moral education that citizens need to execute those purposes well.

I will start by discussing some shortcomings, from a democratic point of view, in the implicit picture of citizenship and the relation between citizens and government that is embedded in much civic education, whether in schools or the culture. I will then proceed to defend the importance of a more participatory form of citizenship that requires greater citizen initiative and engagement with substantive law and its purposes, directly and in the supportive social culture. Finally, I will offer some examples and some cautions concerning how civic education could incorporate the sort of moral and legal education necessary to empower a more participatory democratic citizenry.

THE MODEL OF SEPARATION

Civic education, in school and in public discourse, sends conflicting messages about the role of citizens in government. Alongside the self-congratulatory (and historically revisionary) references to "We the people" wafts a model of civic participation that implicitly emphasizes distance, opposition, and a dilute, haphazard integration of the citizen with the democratic state.

For example, although there is a discourse about citizens having a duty to vote, the invocation of the idea of duty is truncated. The deontic language often does not continue through to framing *how* one should vote or to any idea that one's representatives are delegates of our mutual duties to one another.

The dominant models of representation often portray the choice confronting the representative as one of whether to vote as their constituents wish, to vote in their constituents' actual interests, or to vote in the general interest of constituents, as a community. The first two options understand representatives as agents of the principal voters, but the conception of the principal is as either a (mere) rights holder or as a beneficiary, defined in welfarist terms. Notice that if, instead, you conceived of citizens as duty-holders, who were delegating their power to discharge their duties, and of representatives as fellow duty-holders, this would affect what we expected of *citizens*—whether or not representatives are empowered to implement their own judgment, must reflect citizens' judgment, or should strive for a position that emerges from their joint engagement about their shared collective duties. In selecting a representative, the citizen's primary question would not be who would best implement their interests, but rather who is qualified to execute their duty. Answering that question requires a civic education and some level of informed civic engagement. For, in delegating a duty responsibly, one must have sufficient judgment about what the duty requires and who is qualified to discharge it. Further, the responsibility of anyone delegating a duty lingers with the primary duty-holder. She must not only keep an eye on matters to ensure her delegate actually discharges the duty faithfully, but must also stay in the picture to complement the delegate's work where needed and to engage in consultation and joint deliberation about how to execute their shared duties. These activities require both oversight and a developed sense of judgment about what the duty requires. Moreover, the relevant duties would be the duties to realize justice and fulfill our other collective responsibilities. Ensuring one's delegates discharged these duties faithfully would require forming judgments not just about one's own interests, but having a conception of the conditions, rights, and needs of others. Assuming our collective responsibilities range outside ourselves, this understanding would demand that citizens develop an understanding of our joint global, as well as our domestic, responsibilities.[1]

Not only does the framing of the representative's charge in terms of citizens' interests encourage a flaccid conception of citizenship, so does the common, if implicit, hand-off model on which citizens vote and hand over power to their representatives. In the interim periods, their everyday participation is conceived of at best in terms of thin compliance, oversight, and accountability. The good citizen observes the speed limit, pays their taxes, reads the newspaper, dashes off the occasional note to their representative, and when things get dire, as they have, attends a protest or donates to a cause or campaign. So long as they color within the lines, compliance-wise, there is no sense that citizens in fact play a crucial role in the everyday implementation of the law that may be performed in better or worse ways. It's a model that suits a capitalist, individualist, consumer culture, but that's more a diagnosis and indictment than praise for the synergy.

The way we talk about law, in formal civic education and in the culture, reinforces this separation of government from citizens. Much civic education concerns the structure of government—the three branches, separation of powers, bills on Capitol Hill, etc. In formal civic education, very little law is presented, apart from the Constitution, perhaps the fact—but little substance—of some super-statutes, and some discussion of certain statutes as historical landmarks of pitched political battles.[2] The Constitution is prominently discussed, but it is usually presented as a document about limitations on government. This is understandable in some sense because the Constitution only explicitly regulates individuals directly in the Thirteenth Amendment, but as I will go on to argue, many constitutional protections create a culture that must be accepted and supported by citizens for those protections to succeed and achieve the values that justify them.

Yet, in the common model, citizens appear mainly as rights-holders against potential, illegitimate forms of governmental power. They are situated to complain, but not to assume regular responsibility as co-authors of law. In this picture, lay citizens have little role to play in government but as legally compliant beneficiaries, potential victims with government-issued shields, observers, and occasional contributors, in elections, suits against government, and protests. Common law, for instance, is a stranger to the civics classroom. Its exclusion perpetuates the myth that the judiciary's role is simply to interpret statutes and constitutions. It also thereby submerges any recognition of citizens' roles in the development and articulation of law through their instigation of and participation in common law cases as well as their daily habits and interactions with each other that establish the law on the street but also the customary practice that the law then draws from when identifying and codifying its norms.[3]

This model of separation also implicitly dominates the cultural conversation about interpretation of law. Consider the debates over what methodology should guide legal interpretation, such as the disputes about whether originalist, textualist, purposivist, or moral reading approaches to the Constitution should govern. Although it is understandable during confirmation hearings that these debates are framed in terms of what a judge or a justice should do, it is less understandable that the cultural discourse about methodology almost always contorts itself to fit the limits of this frame. Many arguments about methodology center around what judges are qualified to do and how they should wield their power. But, if one thought of citizens as the co-authors of law, co-authoring with their contemporaries and with their forbearers, and as the co-implementers of law, this nearly univocal focus on the judiciary should seem strange. To proceed with the project of joint authorship and to engage in joint implementation, citizens need to be able to understand the content of the law. One might have thought that a desideratum for an interpretative theory is that *citizens* and judges alike could use it to understand the law and that the theory appropriately reflected the status of citizens as co-authors of the law. Putting aside for the moment what theory or theories satisfy that desideratum, the dominance of the judicial perspective in cultural and academic conversations about legal interpretation reveals rather low expectations and constrained opportunities for citizen engagement.

Put bluntly, this model of separation is not a sensible fit for a democratic polity, in which we citizens constitute the government and are responsible to each other to ensure that we create and maintain conditions of justice and that we fulfill our other collective responsibilities. A more integrated model of the relation between a democratic government and a participatory citizenry is essential to democracy, and its system of civic education should be designed to prepare and empower citizens to play that role. As I will now argue, part of the education of a participatory citizenry must include a greater focus on law.

ENGAGEMENT WITH LAW: FULL COMPLIANCE vs. COMPLYING TO CODE

Our current practices of under-education about substantive law and the architecture of its implementation represent a missed opportunity in at least four respects. The first two are familiar, if neglected, and are compatible with the standard model of citizen as both subject and principal/consumer. First, knowing more about law's content would aid citizens in knowing what resources they may call upon and what treatment they may demand, when implementation has gone awry, and when provisions are inadequate and demand reform. Second, understanding how the legal infrastructure facilitates daily living may also inspire greater appreciation for law and generate more substantive and affective grounds for the general motives of compliance with law and democratic participation. The virtues not only serve the interests of citizens qua consumer/beneficiary but also serve the general mission of justice. Still, they both have an easy fit with the separation model in which government provides a service to consumer/beneficiary citizens whose knowledge and pattern of compliance grease the wheels of production and delivery.

I want to focus on some, to my mind, underappreciated points about the advantages of deeper knowledge of the substantive law by citizens. These are points that emerge from taking the more participatory perspective on citizenship seriously, a perspective that expects citizens to do more than act as critics and the occasional auditors of the process by which articulate law is generated. To flesh out this more participatory perspective, I will begin by identifying what more with respect to law would be expected from citizens and why.

Note that I discuss "adherence" or "compliance" rather than "obedience." I regard the latter as an entirely odious term that has no proper place in a democratic model of government but is at home in and primes one toward the behaviors, attitudes, and expectations appropriate to a hierarchical model of law and government. Adherence and compliance, by contrast, I take to be more neutral. They do not have the connotations of submission that obedience has and are compatible with a range of behaviors from mere compliance to more cooperative, participatory forms of engagement with a system of rules. The points I will make all build on this observation that not all conceptions of legal adherence are alike. A flourishing democratic legal system requires citizens to relate to the law in ways that are a far cry from what obedience often conjures.

To start, for social conditions to remain largely free, citizens must, as a general rule, take their own initiative to follow the law without regard to the likelihood of punishment for noncompliance. What I mean by "social conditions remaining largely free" may be obscure since some may think that compliance under any threat of penalty renders that compliance coerced. I do not believe that the existence of some background, no greater than proportionate, penalties for noncompliance renders all compliance *ipso facto* involuntary for all compliers.[4] Consider those who agree with the law's validity and comply because of the law's validity and not because of the penalty. Consider also those who comply because of the law's validity, conditional upon assurance of reciprocal behavior by other citizens. The penalty may reassure them that reciprocity will be forthcoming, thereby paving the way for their voluntary compliance.

So, put that dispute aside. In saying that citizens must take their own initiative to follow the law for social conditions to remain free, what I have in mind is the degree of intrusiveness of the enforcement measures on social life. If a society had to depend upon external enforcement measures alone to achieve the ends of law, it would have to rely on an extraordinary and intrusive level of surveillance,[5] deceptive tactics,[6] disproportionate or even draconian levels of threat, or some combination thereof. For social conditions to offer a modicum of privacy and the freedom that accompanies it, citizens must both generally accept the law and its aims as legitimate and accept that compliance is a matter of personal commitment and initiative; it is not enough to take the view that some have about parking meters, namely that it would be fair if one were ticketed but one will take one's chances at being a free rider. An attitude of *that* sort practiced regularly by many people, about all kinds of legal requirements, starts to make the case for the surveillance state. So, a democratic legal regime depends on voluntary adherence to law to achieve the democratic end of fostering an environment of (felt) freedom. That dependence also conveys a sense of trust in citizens, which may produce a virtuous feedback loop as citizens aspire to vindicate that trust.

Yet, merely voluntary compliance to the explicit letter of the law will not be enough, as I will try to demonstrate by taking an illustrative detour to another site of social interaction, the workplace, in which some participants can often use a reminder that it is a cooperative venture that thrives when its participants treat it that way and that stalls when participants exhibit various forms of alienation and disrespect. One way that reminder is delivered is through "work to rule" actions in labor disputes, in which workers do not strike but tailor and confine their participation to what is explicitly delineated in their contracts and employee manuals. It can be an effective strategy in a labor dispute, but that is because it reveals the deep inadequacies of a textualist, top-down approach to cooperation that treats workers as mere subjects rather than as active cooperators. So, too, if at least some corners of the law represent our community's commitments to express and achieve our shared values, our aspirations for the citizen's role cannot be the sort of compliance that resembles "working to rule" in labor contexts.

In the workplace, working to rule is a rational, ethical response when one is reasonably alienated from the workplace and its authority figures, when one is being exploited and attempting to demonstrate how much the system relies upon one's good will, and when it is part of a coordinated effort to renegotiate the balance of power to achieve greater equity and fairer terms. The reasons it is such an effective technique during moments of crisis in labor management relations, however, demonstrate why it cannot be a way of life or standard operating procedure in the workplace. Explicit instructions, when read literally, cannot cover every situation a worker encounters, cannot address the variable abilities and struggles of each worker, and cannot substitute for the judgment the skilled worker brings to bear on assessing the needs of a situation to make adjustments, invent ad hoc solutions, and respond to the efforts and needs of colleagues. The frustration that management experiences when its labor force works to rule is not ameliorated by writing a more elaborate performance code, but rather by making environmental adjustments that demonstrate trust and appreciation and that elicit the workers' expertise and judgment, as well as the generous application of their efforts to advance the cooperative mission.[7]

We might glean at least two lessons about a successful democratic legal culture from reflecting on work to rule. One is that minimal conditions of justice are a precondition of truly cooperative activity. Minimal conditions of justice are a precondition to fostering the willingness and sustained morale of participants to participate, whereas exploitation and under-appreciation are toxic to those motives. Minimal conditions of justice also play a supportive role in enabling the success of those participants' efforts. As we know, decent pay, flexible schedules, child care, and guaranteed health care provide the supportive conditions that allow workers to devote their best, focused efforts to their work, rather than their strained and distracted efforts, disrupted by external anxieties. Because our political and legal system is our largest domestic cooperative activity, we have reason to think the successful achievement of democratic law's aims may depend upon its being situated within a conducive social environment that undergirds morale and that is structured to complement and support its particular aims. In this case, as I will go on to argue, the production of the conducive, complementary social environment requires a deeper understanding of law and its purposes.

The second lesson we might glean is that, as a general matter, work to rule does not represent a minimally acceptable approach to one's labor duties as an individual. Work to rule is a protest strategy, used by *organized* groups as an expressive mechanism, when minimal conditions of justice and fair negotiation tactics have broken down. The strategic power of its expressive message hinges on the fact that work to rule is an untenable approach to cooperative activity. The cooperative activity of the workplace depends upon workers often going beyond the letter of the rule and taking various forms of initiative and care that are not required or explicitly spelled out in detail. This may sometimes, I agree, involve the use of discretion to "*deviate* from [the rules] when common sense demands it."[8] But, the discretion that we rely upon from workers is not mainly that they ignore or file down the sharp corners of overbearing rules. Reflecting on work to rule also brings out the converse idea: that the explicit rules, themselves, are often insufficient to address the wide range of circumstances that workers confront. Cooperative rule-following involves an understanding of the aim of the enterprise as well as the willingness and ability to take initiative to *fill in* the gaps where the explicit rules do not reach.[9] That is, the flourishing of the cooperative activity of the workplace depends on workers regularly applying their discretionary judgment and acting in good faith to advance the ends of their position and the workplace more generally.[10]

So too with law. Were we to think of society as a cooperative activity, structured by a set of laws, then the idea that the citizen's sufficient everyday role is to "comply to code," even without explicit threats or the probability of penalties for failure, would analogously fall flat. A literal approach to compliance may be a coping mechanism or a protest mechanism enacted under conditions of injustice and alienation, but it is not an aspiration, nor is it even a baseline standard for a flourishing polity that makes progress toward achieving its cooperative aims. Full compliance is not and cannot always be thoughtless, reflexive, and simplistically textualist. New laws, new social circumstances, and new recognitions about insufficiently addressed social circumstances may require fresh interpretation to discern what should be done and even imagination and effort to execute. That is, the path is not always laid out with a red carpet. It might be more like a trail-under-construction, one that is built by individual hikers forging the way and subsequent others deciding to reinforce their tracks. Such interpretation may require a broader understanding of a particular law's aims and purposes, its scope, and how it is situated in the broader legal landscape.

FULLER COMPLIANCE INSIDE LEGAL CULTURE
AND SUPPORTING LEGAL CULTURE

Although we are not exactly flourishing at present, the civic behavior I am discussing is not entirely foreign to us—even if I wish it were more familiar. Here are a few examples to consider.

First, we often comply without certainty of enforcement. With respect to our taxes, for instance, the law expects and receives our regular, if perhaps sometimes rough, compliance, despite the net expected financial utility of evasion for many given low penalties and the high likelihood that evasions may be missed.[11] As mentioned earlier, voluntary compliance does not simply further the aim of the law complied with, but serves other collective legal aims, including the protection of privacy and the use of resources to advance purposes other than enforcement and surveillance.

Second, our implementation often elicits deliberation and understanding beyond reflexive and reactive fulfillment of pre-specified demands. Whenever the law deploys standards rather than rules (such as when it requires "equity" or "equal treatment," forbids "harassment," appeals to the "reasonable person," permits "fair use" of copyrighted materials, requires "reasonable accommodation" that does not present an "undue hardship," or requires "good faith"), citizens cannot robotically "comply to code" except in those cases in which an agency has issued highly specific rule-like guidance or a court has ruled on a factually similar case. Standards induce citizens to deliberate about the law's aims and values and how, in good faith, to bring them about.[12] Creative deliberation will also be necessary when laws are new and their gaps have not yet been identified and filled, or when background understandings that once filled in gaps dissipate under scrutiny, but nothing has taken their place.[13]

Third, on important occasions, we act on the law's values in our social and personal lives in ways that support legal culture, even when it is ambiguous or clear that such action exceeds the law's expectation. This behavior is by no means uniform or universal but it is at least familiar. For example, many citizens in their everyday, social lives take inspiration from the First Amendment and the values that underlie it. They affirm some version of free speech principles for their personal interactions, although they are not state agents. The content of the principles (and/ or their application, depending on the height of one's perch of abstraction) may vary, of course. By contrast with state distributive schemes, private individuals and associations may respect freedom of speech without acting evenhandedly toward all viewpoints in their own distribution of benefits, for instance. Nonetheless, it seems difficult to deny that private dispositions and practices of tolerance, open-mindedness, and engagement play a significant role in the success of a legal culture of freedom of speech in myriad ways.

For one thing, these habits of listening and engaged, responsive toleration and open-mindedness to divergent views acculturate citizens to enduring, rather than suppressing, uncomfortable ideas. This may prepare and support officials to respect freedom of speech. It may also reduce some of the flashpoints that inspire government abuse as a response to public outcry. That is, the acculturation of endurance may reduce pressure on the state to engage in suppression and also may blunt the shock of state toleration of uncomfortable ideas. The private practice, by partly mirroring the state practice, helps to support the legal climate by lowering the political temperature and costs of state compliance.

But the success of the legal culture is not judged solely by the costs of enforcement and legal compliance. The success of the legal culture is also judged by the degree to which the values underlying the law are achieved. The First Amendment's values are not limited to the control of state abuse and excess. The First Amendment's justifications also include its role in promoting the sort of robust debate necessary for democracy's flourishing as well as its role in promoting the advancement and appreciation of knowledge, intellectual development, moral agency, and authentic social relationships.[14] The achievement of these ends is valuable in itself but also important to the success of the democratic state. Yet, while state action can stymie or facilitate their attainment, state action cannot achieve them alone. A complementary social free speech culture allowing and encouraging citizens to cultivate their minds, entertain and evaluate new (and old) ideas, and exchange them with others without debilitating repercussions for voicing divergent views or making mistakes, is essential for the realization of these ends, even to a modest degree.

THE ROLE OF CITIZEN DISCRETION AND JUDGMENT—
THE EXAMPLE OF FREEDOM OF SPEECH

A final ingredient worth mentioning in the interplay of the social and legal culture of free speech is that of individual judgment and discretion in how to exercise freedom of speech and in what venues. The citizen's role in a free speech culture is not exhausted by participation, respectful engagement with others, and toleration of difference in the form of abstention from private suppression and recriminations that exceed substantial criticism. The generous application of good faith judgment about what to say and when and where to say it serves both the legal and the social culture by reducing pressure on the systems and avoiding unnecessary flashpoints.

What sort of "good faith" judgment do I have in mind? I'll take some examples from the US context in which lying without proof of audience harm is protected by the First Amendment,[15] as is much offensive speech that causes emotional distress,[16] as is some hate speech that does not threaten or harass specific persons and that occurs outside work and educational contexts.[17] The "pure lie" (by which I mean a lie whose false content is not relied upon by the recipients to their detriment) may be protected under First Amendment doctrine, but its production is not a good faith exercise by any citizen. Insincere factual claims advanced as testimony as well as covert insincere advocacy do not reveal or express the speaker's thoughts and do not advance the listener's knowledge; insincere opinions do not contribute to the process of democratic negotiation because they do not represent real perspectives to which citizens should attend out of mutual respect. But, their production does corrode mutual trust and exhausts the attention. Their prevalence may deplete citizens of an interest in responsive, respectful participation.

Protected lies represent just one example of the claim that citizens acting in good faith should not exercise their speech rights up to the legal limit. Offensive speech that causes emotional distress and hate speech offer further examples, although the details here differ. Offensive speech and hate speech (overlapping categories) may indeed express the speaker's thoughts. Further, their expression may educate listeners at least as to the speaker's mindset, if not directly through the content. Even where the content is simply abhorrent, the content's expression may alert listeners to ignorance or dangerous instability on the part of the speaker that requires refutation or another sort of attention. These categories of speech engage with free speech values in a way that pure lies do not. At the same time, a free speech culture will not thrive if these objectionable utterances are regularly voiced and, in particular, if they are regularly voiced in fora of mass dissemination. It isn't primarily because their content is factually or normatively mistaken, although that is true of hate speech and is often true of other forms of offensive speech that cause emotional distress. To be sure, the ignorance embedded within them can exacerbate the damage they inflict, but, at the same time, part of the point of the free speech protection is to give citizens space to entertain mistakes and to come to exorcise them through conversation, realizations, and intellectual evolution.

In these cases, the primary culprits are the animus and insensitivity contained and conveyed in the speech, which, when widely or carelessly deployed, may inflict substantial emotional distress, reinforce systemic inequality, and undermine the foundations of mutual trust and respect that sustain the willingness of citizens to engage in genuine, reciprocal communicative exchanges. For these reasons, even those who believe such speech cannot be comprehensively banned should agree that cooperative citizens should not regard or encourage this speech as ordinary, as unexceptional, as entertainment, as a perfectly respectable form of self-expression, or as simply blowing off steam. Mass media sites have good reason to discourage or prohibit its expression on their channels and to shunt it into smaller fora where its free speech values could be realized but that would insulate others, especially captive audiences, from some of its destructive impact and that may be more likely to elicit the close engagement, whether therapeutic, resistant, or substantively responsive, that is appropriate. That is, citizens may need space to entertain and exorcise mistakes but that space need not be the size of a football arena. Of course, the sensibility of these prescriptions depends mightily on one's conceptions of hate speech, where the line falls between productively provocative speech and truly offensive speech, and the relevant causes of emotional distress. Alighting on the correct conceptions and on a sense of what fora are appropriate calls for careful judgment. This is not the occasion to defend any specific conceptions of these categories. The more limited point I want to make is that while it may be foolhardy, dangerous, or inappropriate for the state to make precise judgments about where the boundaries of acceptable and unacceptable public speech in these areas lie, that does not mean it is foolhardy, dangerous, or inappropriate for every citizen to make such judgments. The arguably necessary abdication of judgment by the state renders it incumbent that citizens and other private parties exercise their own judgment.

Free speech may be the most familiar and perhaps the most developed example of a parallel social culture that provides a critical complement and support to a legal culture, but it isn't an outlying case. Parallel (though not always isomorphic) social cultures complement legal cultures by developing extralegal norms of equality and equal treatment, of procedural fairness in nongovernmental institutional and other group settings, and of dispute resolution (both with respect to norms of impartiality as well as discretion about what disputes to pursue to resolution and what disputes to let go). In these domains as well, parallel social norms reduce tensions over demanding legal norms, and prepare citizens with the knowledge, character, abilities, and habits necessary for legal compliance and implementation without draconian enforcement. They also establish the sort of social relations, including forms of abstention from standing on one's rights on every possible occasion, that are necessary for the full achievement of our collective legal ends.[18]

At the same time, these parallel cultures are insufficiently developed and ensconced across all corners of our legal lives. For instance, the woefully inadequate absorption of norms of equality and the appreciation of the causes and manifestations of inequality reverberate across nearly every aspect of our collective lives. Although we have some budding practices of equality of recognition and anti-discrimination in informal social life, the absorption of the importance of equality of status and its wider ranging implications represents one of many places where citizens and the officials they become could do substantially better; their doing so might bolster and strengthen the legal culture here as well. My diffident suggestions are that civic education has a role to play in achieving progress and that these examples of our partial successes offer reasons for optimism.

Some Implications for Civic Education

What are the implications of these arguments for civic education? Preparing and empowering a democratic citizenry to address a wide range of imperatives, problems, and temptations, quotidian and structural, requires a multifaceted approach, drawing on the humanities, the social sciences, and the sciences.[19] My basic contention is that this multifaceted approach should include greater attention to legal literacy to encourage and inform democratic participation. To sustain the participatory culture of citizenship we have and to achieve a more thoroughgoing and substantive sort of participatory compliance, the substantive content and normative underpinnings of law should be a greater part of civic education, alongside some philosophical training about how to interpret and apply rules and values. What I have in mind would represent a corrective to the dominant focus on the highlight reels from the US Bill of Rights plus a smattering of procedure (elections, the three branches, and how a bill becomes law), supplemented by the social history of upheavals (wars and social protests) when these procedures fail or are stymied.

Understanding the justifications for more of the law that structures our lives would serve at least five purposes. First, where the law is just, it offers an internal reason for compliance for the sake of the law itself, deepening the motivations for voluntary compliance beyond a thin commitment to the rule of law. Second, as I have argued, legal interpretation often requires understanding the justifications and aims of law, and to the extent that citizens serve as first-line interpreters of law, understanding the values and purposes is necessary for this role. Third, successful realization of the law's aims often depends upon a hospitable social environment that supplements state action and legal purposes and enacting such an environment requires an understanding of the purposes of law. Fourth, understanding the best justifications for law also informs voters' understanding of how legal institutions must function and coordinate and what sorts of officials are best placed to serve and reform those institutions. Fifth, understanding the best justifications for the law may also expose the weaknesses, failures, and inequities of the law itself or our track record at implementing it fairly and effectively. This understanding may help to inform reform efforts and inspire more effective and meaningful resistance.

Some might object that the recommendation to teach the purposes and justifications of law presupposes a particular interpretative methodology that by no means commands a consensus of the public or of jurists. To be candid, as I signaled earlier, I do think that a democratic, citizen-oriented approach to interpretation has implications for interpretative theory.[20] In the constitutional context, classic forms of originalism and textualism involve an exaggerated posture of deference to the particular judgments of prior citizens, many of which were forged under discriminatory conditions of exclusion. This posture and the conditions of origin seem difficult to square with a democratic commitment to the self-governance of contemporary citizens. Further, originalism and textualist variants that advert to originalist understandings place high epistemic demands on interpreters that would be difficult for ordinary citizens to meet. Even outside the constitutional context, approaches to statutory interpretation that afford extraordinary or exclusive emphasis on legislative intent or the explicit wording of the text are susceptible to similar criticisms and are more vulnerable to others, given that statutes and regulations often govern nonstate actors. As the prior discussion of work-to-rule was meant to reveal, full and effective compliance requires a more active and collaborative form of interpretation. Interpretative theories that stress how contemporary citizens would achieve the purposes and commitments of the law are more appropriate for democratic law.

Rather than defending this position further, it seems more important to note that the objection can be answered more directly. Although resolving interpretative disputes is important in many legal contexts, their resolution is not central to my argument about civic education. Whether a grasp of the purposes of law is essential to understanding the law or whether it is essential to understanding how to contribute to a social culture that supports the purposes of law, or both, the democratic citizen will need some practice at identifying those purposes and their implications.

To nurture this understanding requires developing a certain form of moral intelligence that is philosophical, although it may not be best learned by everyone through the exclusive study of philosophical essays. History and literature, for example, may also convey philosophical lessons. Sometimes and for some students, more narrative depictions, whether fictional or nonfictional, may convey certain lessons more powerfully than abstract argument. On the other hand, abstract argumentation may activate the critical perspective and stimulate cross-contextual, imaginative applications of principles. I won't evaluate the comparative merits of teaching philosophy directly versus through another discipline, but I will posit that there is some role for more direct philosophical education to impart some of the skills of interpretation, analogous reasoning, critical evaluation, and extension of principles to new situations. In any case, I'll focus on moral and political philosophy here given my expertise and just offer a caution.

There have been admirable efforts to incorporate more philosophy into the K-12 curriculum that I applaud.[21] Philosophy of most forms feeds the curious and trains capacities for imagination, abstraction, active questioning, justification, organization, and argumentation. For the purposes of civic education, though, some sorts of moral and political philosophy may be better on-ramps than others. For example, many are tempted to introduce students to philosophy through the Trolley Problem, moral dilemmas, or other puzzles and paradoxes.[22] I have four reservations about this approach, which I might characterize as an introduction to philosophy by way of difficult, improbable, high-stakes problems complemented by a stream of counterexamples to solutions.

First, part of what is appealing about the Trolley Problem is also a drawback, namely that the choice of who dies at the business side of a vehicle feels very much like making choices in a single-player video game. On the one hand, the game setup unrealistically inflates the agency of the protagonist. On the other hand, because the scenario is far-fetched, the stakes are both high and empty, removed from the reality of the reader's life and, specifically, removed from the recurring challenges citizens face and need to master.[23] Although philosophy is entertaining, there are hazards in pushing that trait as its leading feature. While we have been made vividly aware of the life-and-death stakes of our participation in collective behaviors like mask-wearing and social distancing, most of our individual decisions are not or should not be *difficult* choices about who lives and dies (and in which, no matter what, someone must die).

Second, the fact that the Trolley Problem involves an *individual* decision-maker making these lethal decisions renders the Problem (and its analogs) poor choices for civic education in particular. The Problem itself, in its setup and constraints, does not prime students to look for collective solutions to recurring issues or to cultivate the skills necessary to implement them, including understanding the needs and ideas of others and finding practicable consensus points. Its constraints are better suited to the training of a benevolent dictator with a penchant for micromanagement and an antiquated transportation system.

Third, introducing students to philosophical thinking by way of consulting intuitions[24] about wrenching problems and moral dilemmas without fully satisfying answers encourages a perspective on philosophical thinking as the domain of possibly unanswerable and therefore purely academic questions to be explored mainly by the most intrepid and indefatigable intellects. To be sure, philosophy may indeed be a refuge for (seemingly) intractable questions, but that is only one aspect of its brief and of its contributions to public life. By introducing students to the most difficult and possibly intractable questions at the outset, one risks pigeonholing philosophy in the minds of students in ways that diminish its perceived resources.

Finally, for related reasons, an early, immediate sense of dissatisfaction and irresolvability may also encourage premature conclusions of defeatism, intellectual skepticism, and relativism. To be sure, imparting a hefty sense of humility and open-mindedness to citizens is an important task. Further, education about the range of responses to disagreement and diverse thinking, including relativism, is important. There's a difference, though, between the quick relativism arrived at by way of frustration and the one earned after extended exposure to the strengths as well as the limits of philosophical thinking.

In sum, I worry that the introduction-by-trolley-problem approach fails to illustrate the resources and techniques of philosophical thinking, principles, and values important for the everyday life of democratic citizens and for understanding more commonplace problems and the norms, dispositions, collective behaviors, and institutions that address them.

What would the alternatives look like? The broad desiderata would involve exposing students to how values and principles may underlie collective actions and institutions, to the considerations and arguments underlying alternative principles, to how values and principles may extend to new situations, and to how role ethics and individual ethics interact with the ethical principles that structure institutions.

As an example, rather than starting with the Trolley Problem, one might start with arguments for equality and tracing out the arguments (and counterarguments) for deriving same-sex orientation equality from principles of gender equality and then asking what the further implications, if any, of traditionally conceived gender equality principles are for the treatment of transgender and nonbinary people. One could explore whether the activities of the Food and Drug Administration are best understood in terms of benevolent paternalism or a cooperative division of epistemic labor. A discussion of role responsibilities might be used to explore the different free speech freedoms and obligations of government actors, institutional actors, and individual citizens. As Brandon Terry's discussion in this volume powerfully details, one could use the history of interpretation and defiance of civil rights laws to illustrate both the transformative potential within our civil rights commitments as well as the ways in which that transformative potential may be perceived as a threat by elites, which in turn produces a counter-reaction of shallow, stilted, perverted, and reactionary counter-interpretations.[25]

One might also introduce students to what often feel to laypeople like esoteric areas of the law monopolized by elites, e.g., bankruptcy, taxation, contracts, or torts, and encourage them to identify the values that drive its structure and its gaps, to evaluate whether that structure is normatively coherent or sufficiently comprehensive, to consider alternatives, and to locate what role citizens play in supporting that structure, reforming it or both, as the case may be. For example, students may be asked to consider how society should manage the costs of accidents, what role law plays in nurturing personal responsibility, and whether personal responsibility and financial responsibility should be co-extensive in an economically unequal society. Or, students might be asked how they should approach contractual relations (from a standpoint of personal profit maximization, fairness between the parties, or broader social concerns), what degrees of legal freedom they should enjoy in contractual relations and why, and how their approach relates to their convictions about distributive justice, social justice, and climate change.

CONCLUSION

I have not yet touched directly on the specific topic of civic education in polarized times. Many of my judgments about it are probably already obvious. I find it difficult to shake the impression that ignorance, alienation, and a generalized distrust of government are major drivers in our current predicament, in addition to the persistent effects of injustice and the shame-based denial of them. For example, undifferentiated and unsubstantiated distrust in government and a failure to view oneself as a member of a mutually beneficial collective seem to be significant factors in vaccine hesitancy, mask resistance, and persistent inaccurate beliefs in widespread election fraud. Because I suspect that *some* of this entrenched ignorance may be traced to an inadequate investment in a broad-ranging civic education, I retain some optimism that, alongside governmental reform and greater progress toward justice, civic education could make some difference to forestalling repetitions of our unproductive divisions and to channeling disagreements toward more worthy, less lethal controversies.

Robert Tsai voices some reasonable skepticism regarding whether deeper civic education about the law could do much to address our social divisions without major social reform preceding it.[26] I entirely agree that civic education *alone* will do far too little and that major, transformative efforts are a necessary condition of a healthier civic culture. For the reasons I addressed, I am confident that a deeper civic education will be a necessary condition of maintaining a healthier civic culture, should we achieve it. I also suspect that a deeper civic education, one that, as Tsai describes,[27] exposes students to the sorts of achievements and commitments that are possible through law, its purposive interpretation, and its imaginative implementation, may play a crucial role in enabling social reform, establishing the expectations that underlie demands for reform, and stoking the hope that it is possible.

In particular, incorporating a deeper knowledge of laws and their purposes might play a salutary role in at least two ways. First, understanding the specifics of our legal structure and its values may do work to prevent generalized, unsubstantiated distrust from gaining a foothold in the psyche of the citizenry. To be sure, there are sound reasons for targeted, substantiated distrust of government given its historical and ongoing treatment of many populations, the potential for abuse in any concentration of power, and, in particular, the behavior of the last administration. Targeted distrust may also supply, as Terry powerfully describes, reasons for civil disobedience, rather than compliance.[28] Although our emphases in our chapters differ, our positions are not (I think) substantially in opposition. Noncompliance with injustice as protest and as political leverage work within the same spirit as deliberative compliance with democratic law.

Targeted distrust, however, is consistent with discrete forms of engagement. When coupled with transparent protections, it is not inconsistent with a willingness to participate and cooperate (even if only in rigidly delineated and discrete settings).

It is also capable of being rationally overcome—whether through supplying evidence that it is misplaced or that it has become misplaced because of thorough change and substantial progress toward justice. Whereas, undifferentiated distrust is more insidious. It can prove more resistant to evidence and to sincere efforts at change because it is an attitude that discredits counterevidence from the outset. It also generates a feedback loop that recruits, reinforces, and feeds off of a sense of alienation, distance, and a profound hesitance to cooperate with all but the most stalwart allies. Equipping students with a deeper understanding of government and the potential for a constructive, egalitarian role in its operation would, I hope, inoculate them against susceptibility to those who would instill the sort of undifferentiated distrust that stymies coordinated progress toward the achievement and maintenance of justice.

Second, learning more about the what and the why of democratic law, rather than predominantly the origin story of how it came to be, may, if nothing else, help to nurture in students a sense of ownership and entitlement over the system (whether positive, critical, or both), a sense of shared agency and responsibility for the content and success of democratic law, and a sense of identification with the common condition of its members.

Notes

I'm grateful to the editors and to Elyse Meyers for help with the manuscript; to Robert Tsai and Brandon Terry for our exchange and their important contributions; to Steve Shiffrin and Barbara Herman, as ever, for good advice; and to Isabella Chestney, Sean St. Charles, and Julia D'Errico for excellent research assistance.

1 This argument is developed at length in a companion paper, "Democratic Representation as Duty-Delegation," Presidential Address, *Proceedings of the American Philosophical Association* (2022). www.apaonline.org.

2 Substantive law makes an even rarer appearance in popular culture and it is prone to the same treatment, where it often becomes a signifier of political conflict or triumph. The Broadway musical *Hamilton* makes an initial stab at explaining the stakes of the debate about the National Bank Act, but then quickly pivots to depicting the statute as the site of a skirmish between Thomas Jefferson and Alexander Hamilton. See *Hamilton* (d. Lin-Manuel Miranda) (2016): Cabinet Battle #1.

3 See my longer discussion in *Democratic Law* (Oxford: Oxford University Press, 2021), ch. 2. See also Robert Hughes, "Responsive Government and Duties of Conscience," *Jurisprudence* 5 (2014): 244–264. For a nuanced discussion of the strengths and hazards of the use of custom in intellectual property law, see Jennifer E. Rothman, "Copyright, Custom, and Lessons from the Common Law," in *Intellectual Property and the Common Law*, ed. Shyamkrishna Balganesh (Cambridge: Cambridge University Press, 2013).

4 I elaborate on this point in *Democratic Law*, ch. 7.

5 See also Robert C. Hughes, "Law and the Entitlement to Coerce," in *Philosophical Foundations of the Nature of Law*, ed. Wil Waluchow and Stefan Sciaraffa (Oxford: Oxford University Press, 2013), 183–206.

6 I have in mind tactics like misrepresentation about the law's content, levels or consequences of enforcement, and misrepresentation about the law's aims. (For selective advocacy of the latter, see Michael D. Gilbert, "Insincere Rules," *Virginia Law Review* 101 (2015): 2185–2223.) Such misrepresentation by the state is inconsistent with democratic engagement and endorsement and, also, with freedom.

7 This is also one way to interpret the animating idea of "efficiency wages," which offer workers compensation higher than market clearing levels to incentivize higher quality work and self-supervision, and thereby to reduce the need for external monitoring and supervision. See, e.g., Harvey Leibenstein, *Economic Growth and Economic Backwardness* (New York: Wiley, 1957), 62–76; Samuel Bowles, "The Production Process in a Competitive Economy: Walrasian, Neo-Hobbesian, and Marxian Models," *American Economic Review* 75, no. 1 (1985): 16–36 at 25–26.

8 See David Luban, "Misplaced Fidelity," *Texas Law Review* 90 (2012): 668, 688 (reviewing W. Bradley Wendel, *Lawyers and Fidelity to Law* (Princeton, NJ: Princeton University Press, 2010), emphasis added.

9 An interesting study in Ontario, Canada, documented reduced learning outcomes in elementary school students when teachers, implementing work to rule, only performed the duties specified in their contracts but ceased to perform other cooperative activities such as running extracurricular activities, meeting with parents, and attending administrative meetings. See, e.g., David R. Johnson, "Do Strikes and Work-To-Rule Campaigns Change Elementary School Assessment Results?," *Canadian Public Policy* 37, no. 4 (2011): 479, 492–493.

10 Thus, my understanding of the mechanisms and lessons of work to rule is importantly more expansive than the account offered by Jessica Bulman-Pozen and David Pozen in their important article. Jessica Bulman-Pozen and David E. Pozen, "Uncivil Obedience," *Columbia Law Review* 115, no. 4 (2015): 809–872 (defining, analyzing, and critiquing uncivil obedience, defined as protests characterized by rigorous and disruptive adherence to formal rules in an unprecedented or unexpected way). They focus on situations in which work to rule and its civic analogs serve as protests of the (explicit) rules themselves and, in particular, of some overbearing or unreasonable feature of the (explicit) rules themselves when they are read literally and applied without exception. On their model, the primary force of complying to code is either to highlight the unreasonableness of a 55 mph speed limit or purportedly over-finicky safety rules or to highlight the importance of selective (non)application of these rules. The emphasis on such situations underplays the significance of cases like the Ontario teachers in Johnson, "Do Strikes and Work-To-Rule Campaigns Change Elementary School Assessment Results?," in which work-to-rule actions put into relief the positive contribution of supplementary discretion, judgment, and initiative, as opposed to highlighting the overbearing directions of certain regulations.

11 James Alm, "Designing Alternative Strategies to Reduce Tax Evasion," in *Tax Evasion and the Shadow Economy*, ed. Michael Pickhardt and Aloys Prinz (Cheltenham, UK: Edward Elgar, 2012), 13–32, 15; Benno Torgler, "Speaking to Theorists and Searching for Facts: Tax Morale and Tax Compliance in Experiments," *Journal of Economic Surveys* 16, no. 5 (2002): 657–683; James Andreoni, Brian Erard, and Jonathan Feinstein, "Tax Compliance," *Journal of Economic Literature* 36, no. 2 (1998): 818–860.

12 See my longer discussion in "Inducing Deliberation: On the Occasional Merits of Fog," *Harvard Law Review* 123 (2010): 1214–1246.

13 For an inspiring story of how a jury foreperson used her knowledge of emerging practices in internet privacy to lead a jury to think about what was necessary for sexual consent in the absence of a statutory definition, see Graham Bowley, "For One Cosby Juror, the Work Continues," *New York Times*, Arts, p. 1 (October 11, 2021).

14 I develop the relationship between the development of the thinker and the First Amendment in "A Thinker-Based Approach to Freedom of Speech," *Constitutional Commentary* 27, no. 2 (2011): 283–307, and further, in *Speech Matters: On Lying, Morality, and the Law* (Princeton, NJ: Princeton University Press, 2014), ch. 3.

15 *United States v. Alvarez*, 567 U.S. 709, 719, 730 (2012). For criticism of the *Alvarez* decision, see Seana Valentine Shiffrin, *Speech Matters: On Lying Morality and the Law*, ch. 4.

16 *Snyder v. Phelps*, 562 U.S. 443, 461 (2011).

17 See e.g., *Snyder v. Phelps*, 562 U.S. 443, 461 (2011); *R.A.V. v. City of St. Paul, Minnesota*, 505 U.S. 377, 396 (1992); *Virginia v. Black*, 538 U.S. 343, 367 (2003).

18 See also my discussion in *Speech Matters: On Lying, Morality and the Law*, 164–167, of some instances of legal forbearance as a valuable form of compassionate recognition and accommodation of human imperfection.

19 Unsurprisingly, I am not alone in this conviction. In particular, I applaud the vision and the detailed plans offered by the Educating for American Democracy Project. www.educatingforamericandemocracy.org. That vision advocates for a substantial reinvestment in civic education through all thirteen years of primary education and a curriculum that emphasizes knowledge of government, the cultivation of civic virtues such as civic friendship and civil disagreement, and a deeper understanding of our shared history. The country will be better if the project is implemented. This essay may be seen as a complement to it, making the case for a greater educational focus on substantive law, its purposes, and methods of interpretation and implementation.

20 See also Jack Balkin, *Living Originalism* (Cambridge, MA: Harvard University Press, 2011).

21 Promising initiatives are discussed in Lauren Bialystok, Trevor Norris, and Laura Elizabeth Pinto, "Teaching and Learning Philosophy in Ontario High Schools," *Journal of Curriculum Studies* 51, no. 5 (2019): 678–697, and various articles in Maughn Rollins Gregory, Joanna Haynes, and Karin Murris, *The Routledge International Handbook of Philosophy for Children* (New York: Routledge, 2017).

22 See, e.g., Sean M. Lennon, Jeffrey M. Byford, and J. T. Cox, "An Ethical Exercise for the Social Studies Classroom: The Trolley Dilemma," *The Clearing House: A Journal of Educational Strategies, Issues and Ideas* 88, no. 6 (2015): 178–181; Vaughn Bryan Baltzly, "Trolleyology as First Philosophy: A Puzzle-Centered Approach to Introducing the Discipline," *Teaching Philosophy* 44, no. 4 (2021).

23 See also Laura Martena, "Thinking Inside the Box: Concerns about Trolley Problems in the Ethics Classroom," *Teaching Philosophy* 41, no. 4

(2018): 381–406 at 390–392 for a discussion of other objectionable artificial features of the Trolley Problem, including its acontextuality.

24 If one regarded moral intuitions as valuable guides to moral thinking when and because they encapsulate the lessons wrought from years of moral experience and deliberation, one might question whether adolescents have the relevant experience that would make their intuitions worthy touchstones.

25 Brandon Terry, "Civic Education and Polarized Politics," chapter 2 of this volume.

26 Robert Tsai, "Civic Education and Democracy's Flaws," chapter 3 of this volume.

27 Tsai, "Civic Education and Democracy's Flaws."

28 Terry, "Civic Education and Polarized Politics."

2

CIVIC EDUCATION AND
POLARIZED POLITICS

TRANSITION, CRITIQUE, AND DISSENT

BRANDON M. TERRY

To address the aims and ambitions of democratic civic education in "polarized times" is to give an account of both the purposes of civic education and the problem of polarization, as well as what prompts political philosophy to treat their collision as a dilemma. At least two avenues of approach suggest themselves.

The first, and most familiar to professional political philosophy, *begins* by providing an ideal account of civic education in a properly just democratic society. Armed with this ideal, the philosopher aims to diagnose the shortcomings of what presently passes for civic education with clarity and systematicity. Any such account will entail views about the proper aims, reasonable expectations, and—lest we forget—the key *pedagogical agents* of ideally constituted practices of civic education.[1] From this vantage, when political polarization is raised as a problem, the shape in which the problem appears will be constrained by ideal theoretic aims. Polarization, therefore, will be treated principally as an *obstacle* to achieving reasonable consensus around civic ideals (including educational ones), or as a *consequence* of the collective failure to achieve such ideals. If the theory of civic education such a view generates aspires to be especially action-guiding, it will likely look for ways that implementing this ideal civic educational arrangement will ameliorate "polarization," targeting it as a sociopolitical *pathology*.

An alternative approach starts from a different, "non-ideal" or "transitional" direction. Instead of beginning with the attempt to model an ideal society and its civic educational arrangements, it instead generates a richly contextual account of the constituent elements offered as evidence of "polarization." It provides not just explanatory and descriptive analysis of obstacles to particular courses of action, but also a genealogical and discursive analysis of the keywords and concepts popularly used to construe the problem itself (including the idea of polarization)—*how* the historical inheritances, conceptual sediment, and other motivations lead us to think of the problem-space of polarization in particular ways.[2]

This interrogative practice is inspired by a fundamental question—what consequences do these dynamics have for injustice? Political theory is called upon to offer a *diagnosis* of how or whether the alleged dynamics of polarization and polarization-talk relate to existing forms of injustice. Evaluative and practical, this method foregrounds the related tasks of identifying those *responsible* for injustice, *critiquing* ideologically corrupted descriptions of the social realm that mystify injustice, and mapping *ethically defensible* and *practically efficacious* forms of resistance to injustice (along with the agents who might carry it out).[3]

When the question of civic education is raised from this perspective, how it appears is substantially different. Theorizing civic education *in medias res*, we are more concerned with critiquing existing ideals or practices of civic education that are, or threaten to become, *ideological* in the pejorative sense. Second, and relatedly, there is no defaulting to mainstream civic authorities as the legitimate, privileged, or most generative sites of "civic education." Beginning with a comprehensive account of the social bases of injustice compels us to think intensively about the agents of injustice and the obstacles they have erected to remedying it. We may also identify alternative practices that lay claim to the tasks of civic education as embodied in existing acts of resistance or in historical memory. The political theorist can reflect imminently on the ideals and practical claims of justice advanced through such dissenting practices. We can thus contribute to the "self-clarification" of emancipatory struggles as well as provide conceptual and evaluative insights toward more defensible conceptions of the just society and civic education.[4]

In what follows, I will flesh out the stakes of these two approaches to civic education in polarized times, taking in part as my occasion Seana Shriffrin's characteristically incisive chapter. Ultimately, I pursue and defend a version of the "non-ideal" or "transitional"-focused approach, arguing that it allows us to better apprehend how much of our existing discourse about polarization is objectionably ideological, while avoiding important problems with the conventional philosophical impulse toward "reconciliation" in our contemporary moment.[5] Using the history of race and American education to highlight the practical consequences of these concerns, I draw on exemplary instances of African American dissent to theorize what justice-oriented civic education demands in the present: pedagogical resistance to untimely and unjust appeals to reconciliation that obscure serious threats to democratic life.

IDEAL THEORY AND CIVIC EDUCATION

The "ideal-first" approach is consonant with the dominant way of thinking through the tasks of political philosophy in its leading professional guilds. John Rawls, for instance, influentially argued that one of the most important roles that political philosophy may play as part of the public political culture in a democratic society (or an *aspirationally* democratic society) is a "practical" one. Yet, by this Rawls means something quite particular: that political philosophy should attempt, in the midst of "divisive political conflict," to "focus on deeply disputed questions and to see whether, despite appearances, some underlying basis of philosophical and moral agreement can be uncovered, or differences narrowed, so that social cooperation on a footing of mutual respect among citizens can still be maintained."[6] Treating reasonable agreement as a regulative ideal and political telos, this conception of political philosophy endeavors to produce portraits of an ideally just democratic society (and its constitutive forms of civic education) that even as pictures prove *therapeutic* and *reconciliatory* in the midst of conflict.

I take it to be a clear implication of this approach to political philosophy that it aims to guide civic education, broadly construed.[7] Rawls contends that philosophy can educate our judgment, and help teach us the appropriate orientation toward civic matters, one that entails thinking from the vantage and purposes of our political and social institutions *as a whole*, and of ourselves *as citizens*, rather than "as individuals, or as members of families and associations."[8] In contrast with a cascade of identities he treats as likely partial, conflictual, and distorting (at least on matters of justice), Rawls sees this imagined civic identity as the position from which polity members might most effectively and defensibly reason toward principled agreement around political ideals and principles of justice, disclosing more favorable terrain upon which to adjudicate or safely bracket political disputes. Where such consensus proves stable, Rawls hopes to keep the centrifugal force of political disagreements in check while bolstering, over time, our faith that cooperative efforts to build a just democratic society remain worthwhile.

Learning this orientation may require, it seems, a resilient commitment to *reconciliation* as well. Rawls argues that political philosophy, at least in a democratic society, should "try to calm our frustration and rage against our society and its history by showing us the way in which its institutions, when properly understood, from a philosophical point of view, are rational, and developed over time as they did to attain their present, rational form."[9] Take, for example, the longing for "community," by which Rawls means a "body of persons united in affirming the same comprehensive, or partially comprehensive, doctrine." I do not think it too strong to say that Rawls believes a reconciliatory political philosophy can usefully *discipline* such desires. While there are anxieties that a pluralistic, complex society may induce or intensify, one task of political philosophy—and the civic education that issues from it—is to *reconcile* us to intractable social facts (e.g., that our judgments are burdened rather than perfect, or that liberty breeds reasonable pluralism) and better *disclose* or *describe* the goods that flow from a form of life that responds appropriately to such facts. In the right light, perhaps we can be taught not only to simply *tolerate* our fellows or *endure* our shared sociopolitical arrangement, but to *affirm* our interdependent situation as valuable and our institutions as worthy of continued allegiance, cooperation, and reform.[10]

Against the backdrop of this philosophical self-conception, it is hard to imagine a more perfectly cast villain than polarization. The highly emotive and expansive sorting of political society into mutually suspicious and antagonistic camps appears to call us back to our fundamental vocational tasks as political philosophers. We should feel compelled, on this view, to plumb the depths of underlying consensus beneath disagreement, and discipline the frustration of our interlocutors to teach them, and the broader citizenry they threaten, of the rational kernels of our institutions and forms of life.

These preoccupations are an important strand in Seana Shiffrin's "Democratic Civic Education and Democratic Law," which argues for a fundamental reorientation toward a more participatory conception of democratic citizenship. Incorporating this ideal model of democratic society into the processes by which we learn the constitutive expectations and virtues of civic life, we can refocus our atrophied appreciation of how our participatory and cooperative powers are always already at work in forging the substantive law we live under together.[11] With a form of civic education that brings our underappreciated capability to collectively make and remake the law out of concealment, Shriffrin hopes to perform some measure of reconciliation in the face of present-day polarization. On Shriffrin's view, such an education can "do work to prevent" a central source of polarization: when various frustrations, ignorant judgments, and legitimate complaints consolidate into "generalized, unsubstantiated distrust." This generalized distrust not only "*feeds* off of a sense of alienation, distance, and a profound hesitance to cooperate and participate with all but the most stalwart allies," but intensifies it as well, raising the specter of a nihilistic spiral.[12]

RECONCILIATION, IDEOLOGY, AND CIVIC EDUCATION

Despite the power and pedigree of this approach, it is important to remember that the project of reconciliation elicited worry even from its most eloquent proponents. Rawls, for example, expressed concern that tying political philosophy's educative role to reconciliatory hopes could become *ideological* in the traditionally Marxist and pejorative sense of a belief system or set of practices that provide false justification or legitimacy to "an unjust and unworthy status quo."[13] There are, in fact, times when we *should* refuse what he otherwise laudably describes as the task to "calm our frustration and rage," and instead recognize that such emotions (and the judgments they entail) are appropriate responses to the intolerable and irrational condition of our society.[14] Moreover, there are times when the insistence underlying the Rawlsian conception of "orientation"—namely, that agreement may lie productively below seemingly intractable controversies—similarly misapprehends the noxious condition of our political culture or the ability of organized ideological factions to prevent legitimate claims and claimants from achieving standing within it.[15] If, in *these* conditions, our practice of political philosophy and our dominant forms of civic education insist nevertheless on proceeding in pursuit of reconciliation, we likely find ourselves confronting philosophy and pedagogy that is, or is swiftly becoming, ideological.

To charge civic education with being *ideological* is to claim that teaching about civic matters wrongly furthers and legitimates practices of domination and social pathologies (e.g., by naturalizing them, stigmatizing legitimate objections or alternative forms of life, habituating us to perform roles that uphold or acquiesce to relations of oppression).[16] Where civic education is expansively colonized by ideology, it will leave members of the polity profoundly *disoriented* in the exercise of judgments about how best to conceive of their society, fulfill civic and other duties to one another, or—as Shiffrin rightly emphasizes—understand and relate to the legal order. In its deformed state, ideological civic education will offer vocabularies that mystify injustice, propagate concepts and practices that are self-undermining for political analysis and judgment, and amplify narratives of political peoplehood that are unjustifiably exclusionary or inferiorizing.[17] Ideological civic education may also constitute, and be constituted by, rituals, scripts, habits, and practices that sort and mold people to conform to roles that reproduce domination and acquiescence.[18]

Beyond a general worry about ideological deformations arising from philosophy's tasks of orientation and reconciliation, I want to express a more specific concern that the discourse of "polarization" is uniquely prone to going awry in this direction. This is especially true when polarization is treated as an idealized abstraction and modeled as a general social phenomenon without specific reference to the concrete historical-sociological development of the competing "poles" or the ethical content of their antagonisms.[19] To speak in sweepingly abstract terms about polarization, and presume, in an idealized fashion, that the task of philosophy is to ameliorate or overcome the divisions conjured by the term, seems to invite the minimization of historical and social scientific accounts of specific political conflicts and (mis)orient the philosopher toward drawing false political equivalences between factions.[20] The worry, in other words, is that if polarization talk in political philosophy becomes both unmoored from social reality and yet reflexively preoccupied with reconciliation and consensus as its "action-guiding" prescriptions, even the philosopher aiming toward justice and emancipation may end up mobilizing unjustified suspicion against the discord and dissensus meant to clarify political problems and effectively struggle for democratic renewal. Where this kind of disposition prevails, the polarization concept can be easily used to defame principled dissent, disagreement, and disobedience as constitutive of democracy's core *problem* rather than as a warranted response to its *deformation*.

This insight is among Martin Luther King Jr.'s many contributions to public philosophy.[21] In his 1963 "Letter from Birmingham City Jail," King responded to a group of religious critics who accused him and other civil rights activists in Birmingham of fomenting unwarranted chaos and division by critically redescribing their "peaceful" status quo as an "obnoxious negative peace." Narrating a brief history of the conflict over segregation, King insisted that "we who engage in nonviolent direct action are not the creators of tension. We merely bring to the surface the hidden tension that is already alive. We bring it out in the open where it can be seen and dealt with . . . with all of the tension its exposing creates, to the light of human conscience and the air of national opinion before it can be cured."[22] The failure of his critics, King argued, was that their paeans to "peace" and grievances regarding "tension" proceeded without a *critical* inquiry into such keywords, a *historical* accounting of said tension, or an *ethical* evaluation of the sides at conflict. Uncritical lamentations over division, King warned, can lead us unwittingly to produce noxious ideologies and enforce undue obedience by treating the task of "restoring" comity or "discovering" consensus as a self-evident and pressing good. King worried that without a more incisive kind of critical sensibility, prominent demands for reconciliation would leave us misoriented toward what democratic redemption and justice require.

Dwelling on King's reflections helps illuminate two broader problems about the relationship of contemporary political philosophy to history and social theory, both of which are subjects of an important recent essay by Katrina Forrester.[23] When philosophers and political theorists advance normative principles or defend ideal sociopolitical arrangements, Forrester argues, they should not treat the social problems and situations to which such interventions are meant to respond as if they are in a "black box." Without more systematic and self-conscious theorization of social life and historical processes (for her this includes the "political unconscious"), normative theory can end up in a kind of dead end, offering ideals that are inadequate, inapposite, or even self-undermining when questions of transitional justice are squarely faced.[24]

The second contention is that contemporary political philosophy and political science (at least in the Anglo-American academy) are haunted by one *particular* picture of the social and political world, namely, what Forrester describes as "an idealized vision of postwar liberalism." She goes on to urge us to recognize "there is no golden age of postwar affluence and equality to which we can return," and I suspect would be sympathetic to the view that the contemporary discourse of polarization, with its penchant for *declension* narratives from a mid-twentieth century "age of consensus," reflects one more instance of this broader phenomenon of historical romanticization.[25] As Michael Dawson has persuasively argued, American intellectuals' stubborn mythologizing of postwar "consensus" relies upon a bewildering blindness about the interpretive and evaluative problems raised by historical public opinion data, congressional voting patterns, and elite discourse analysis in a political order shaped by the repressive impact of McCarthyism, the violent authoritarianism of Jim Crow, and the sweeping marginalization of women, sexual minorities, and nonwhite members of the polity in the mainstream public sphere.[26] Bringing these repressed forms of domination and marginalization out of concealment, as King argued, helps to draw attention to the ways that power relations shaped and continue to shape what issues and constituencies *appear* as objects of legitimate and actionable political identification and contestation.[27]

Civic Education in Polarized Times:
Rethinking Our Angle of Approach

In light of these worries, an alternative philosophical approach to the challenge of civic education in polarized times can begin by demanding, first, a thicker account of the "polarized times" in which we find ourselves. If by the concept of polarization we mean partisan sorting across political positions, the intense political salience of attitudes about social groups, and strong in- and out-group affects, it is not clear that we should treat this phenomenon as always entailing a *universal* degradation of the capacities necessary for civic participation and self-government, or a *presumptive* obligation for us to seek reconciliation. In cases where our resort to the language of polarization is meant to capture especially contentious, affectively vicious, and mutually suspicious forms of sorting into hostile political camps, I want to suggest that, on occasion, these dynamics may actually be morally significant clues to the *depth* of our disagreements over the demands of justice and the content of competing civic ideals.[28]

Former president Barack Obama, for example, recently implored gubernatorial voters in Virginia to transcend the contemporary battles being waged over so-called critical race theory and gender ideology, which he derided as "phony trumped-up culture wars" and "fake outrage the right-wing media peddles to juice their ratings," and instead focus on giving kids a "world-class" education and "keeping our communities safe."[29] Yet this demand seems to fall short of the diagnosis. After all, the question is why, if more serious problems are so self-evident and deeper consensus so readily available, huge swaths of Americans remain so easily and intensely mobilized by these particular specters? Even the most cynical propaganda must plant its seeds in favorable soil to bear fruit.

If such reconciliatory transcendence is not on hand, perhaps philosophy needs to focus instead on the refinement of histories, hermeneutic strategies, and concepts that help us find surer footing within the conceptual space of polarization, so that we might effectively calibrate our responses according to the distinctions we draw between its different iterations. By theorizing the nature of the polarization at issue and its relation to pressing concerns of justice and democracy, this type of investigation seeks to understand more clearly not only what *dangers,* but also what *opportunities* the sociopolitical dynamics of polarization entail for the promotion and persistence of democratic ideals and practical strivings toward justice. Thinking from this standpoint emphasizes that, as in the discourse of physics from which the metaphor is derived, polarization *as such* is under-descriptive.[30] Understanding the stakes of our inquiry requires adjudicating between different kinds of polarization, identifying their central patterns, animating forces, and moral-political quandaries. While this angle of approach is more immanent and responsive, entangling more empirical social science with political theory, it raises at least four fundamental problems for political philosophic approaches to the problem of civic education in polarized times.

The first is whether reconciliation should be the presumptive task of political philosophy given the *specific* form of polarization that prevails and the dynamics (including revealed patterns of human reasoning) that structure it. The second concerns the relationship between learning and unlearning. The field of civic education is always *in media res*, so any theory of civic education must not imagine that reform entails not only *learning* "ideal" civic responsibilities and identities, as if against a blank slate, but must confront that civic education requires *unlearning* habits and orientations deeply entrenched within the broader (unjust) political culture and upheld by both organized political constituencies and diffuse affective attachments. On this view, civic education is treated as a contentious field of pedagogical practices through which competing constituencies exercise power and persuasion in hopes of crafting the ideals, knowledge, dispositions, and habits that members of the polity will deploy when performing their duties or exercising their judgment qua citizens.[31] The third problem follows from the second. Where might we find effective agents of change (including alternative sites and enactments of civic education) when in polarized times many exercises of state authority or popular political culture serve to repress, distort, or otherwise unduly constrain the forms of civic pedagogy necessary to cultivate authentically democratic dispositions and habits? Last and relatedly, what is the ethos that should govern these alternative and insurgent practices of civic education, especially where they involve some measure of disobedience or noncompliance?

On American Polarization

In what remains of this chapter, I will sketch some answers to these questions, beginning, as I insist we must, with judgments about the most morally and politically important features of contemporary American polarization. Three seem particularly notable given their consequences for civic standing and participatory parity:[32]

1. The severe racialization of partisanship and policy disputes in a society culturally and politically structured by a history of white supremacist ideology and rule
2. The entrenchment of highly negative forms of political affect (e.g., conspiratorial distrust and hostility) that often do not map neatly onto public policy disagreements
3. The growing popularity of political violence and repression, as well as rearguard defenses of the most anti-democratic features of the American political order to wield against the opposing faction

Race and Racialization

The key question for theorists of American polarization is not simply how did political parties become more ideologically homogenous, but why measures of racial resentment and racial attitudes have become such reliable predictors of party affiliation and hostile sentiments.

This was not always the case. The Democratic Party of the 1930s included both large populations of African American migrants to northern cities *and* the most ardent defenders of Jim Crow segregation and disenfranchisement in the white South, while major civil rights legislation relied upon the support of Republican moderates. The political scientist Eric Schickler carefully demonstrates that a major realignment was under way in the 1930s and '40s, with northern Democrats at the local and state levels becoming more racially liberal with the incorporation and influence of black constituents, a small group of black and racially progressive elected officials, and the powerful and interracialist Congress of Industrial Organizations (CIO).[33] National Democratic leadership tried to hold this New Deal coalition together, but as Doug McAdam and Karina Kloos argue, "the sustained pressure of the resurgent civil rights struggle . . . made the Democrats' grudging, cautious stance on the issue [of racial justice] ultimately untenable."[34]

As the Kennedy and Johnson administrations threw their support more openly behind civil rights legislation, the organized white supremacist coalition once led by Strom Thurmond and the Dixiecrats moved toward the center of mainstream Republican Party politics with George Wallace's insurgent presidential bid and Barry Goldwater's electoral success in the formerly Democratic "Solid South."[35] With Nixon's embrace of the infamous "southern strategy" and demonization of the ghetto poor, racial conservatism and hostility toward black reparative justice claims became a prime mover of voters toward the Republican Party, setting in motion a process that trended during these decades toward more ideologically uniform, politically polarized, and racially identified political parties.[36]

The successive presidencies of Barack Obama and Donald Trump, as well as dramatic demographic changes caused by the post-1968 waves of American immigration, intensified these trends.[37] Some of this stems from the highly valent Obama presidency and the extent to which its racial symbolism increased the extent to which one's attitudes about race could predict evaluations of political leaders, voting patterns, partisan attachments, policy preferences (e.g., the Affordable Care Act), and even profoundly unrelated cultural tastes (e.g., the popularity of Portuguese water dogs, one of which the Obamas adopted).[38] Crucially, during the Obama era, racial conservatives became, to an unprecedented degree, not only more Republican and more hostile to Democratic policy proposals, but also more supportive of congressional obstruction, partisan disenfranchisement, and extralegal methods of securing elected office, all key practices in any discussion of American polarization. In response, it appears that self-identified liberals, especially white liberals, have reversed a decades-long trend, becoming *more* progressive in opinions on racial justice questions.[39]

This attitudinal shift reflects a broader fracturing and reconfiguration of the meaning and significance of white identity and white solidarity. Not only did the era of neoliberal political economy erode the economic mobility and stability once more reliably associated with white American identity in the mid-twentieth century, but a once-palpable sense of "white" cultural normativity and status hierarchy has also suffered profound dislocation. Blanketing American politics, therefore, is an anxiety-ridden battle that we describe as "racial conflict," but is actually to a great extent a struggle over the future of "whiteness" between partisans of, and opposition to, the imposition of white "ethnonationalism" and its attendant gradations of citizenship on the polity.[40] Strident resistance to such efforts would perhaps constitute polarization, but would nevertheless be imperatives of justice.

Social Identity and Affect Mobilization

One way of understanding these racial dynamics is, as Lilliana Mason has influentially argued, that attempts to mobilize voters based on social identity categories have entangled partisanship *itself* with social identity and group-based sentiments. Her central evidence for this view is that Americans show "increased levels of partisanship and polarized behavior, including partisan bias, activism, and anger"—and even an expressed desire not to marry or live near members of the opposing party—even where disagreement over *policy issues* does not appear to map onto these extreme attitudes. "The passion and prejudice with which we approach politics," she and her co-authors write, "is driven not only by what we think, but also powerfully by who we think we are."[41] A wide range of identifications, cultural tastes, and political preferences seem to have collapsed into each other.

Especially noteworthy, and raising even more intense worries about white ethnonationalism, is that Mason and her colleagues show that support for Trump can be predicted (even among non-Republicans) by the *hostility* of one's feelings expressed prior to the campaign about African Americans, Latinos, Muslims, and LGBTQ-identified people (not simply warm feelings for one's own in-group).[42] Given their findings, they convey a worry that is worth quoting at length:

> [G]iven Trump's success, future candidates may attempt to create a winning coalition based on activating group-based animosities through the explicit use of anti-out-group rhetoric. Without

these kinds of explicit connections, citizens are left to merely infer whether their own out-group sentiments actually map onto elites' own sentiments. In that case, out-group sentiments may only be weakly related to support for elites who avoid explicit outgroup rhetoric . . . However, as both mainstream and social media amplify outrage, relatively unknown politicians might make a national brand for themselves by publicly issuing combative group-based statements. In doing so, they can provoke outrage within the mainstream media and the political left, further satisfying the psychological needs of constituents harboring group-based prejudice.

One consequence of this cyclical dynamic is that even Obama-esque calls for parties to try to moderate polarization by speaking to popular issues of public policy remain exceptionally vulnerable to hijacking. Effective political entrepreneurs will strive to reframe a wide range of public policy questions in ways that provoke out-group animosity and resentment (e.g., critical race theory, crime panics, migrant caravans), availing themselves of hyperpartisan media, targeted internet communication, and the abetment of other elites who seem increasingly willing to tolerate mass deception in service of political power.

While recent research has cast some doubt on a broadly *causal* link between strong affective polarization and support for political violence and repression, it strikes me that conclusions in this direction should be advanced with great care. Not only might affective polarization play its most important role in anti-democratic practices by weakening the resistance to their use by elites to hold on to power or distracting the citizenry from matters of basic democratic equality, but its relationship to social identities like race is more complicated than it seems is appreciated among social scientists.

A missing term might be the concept of "group position." Group identities are not simply related to partisan identities, but understood in widely known, often hierarchical relations of status between each other. Rather than understand group-based hostility as adequately captured in positive or negative feelings, the sociologist Herbert Blumer argued that the "feelings of competition and hostility" that we are interested in are structured by "historically and collectively developed judgments about the positions in the social order that in-group members should rightfully occupy relative to members of an out-group."[43] In other words, the group-based sentiments so central to the study of polarization are nested within a broader ecosystem of views about the supposed "qualities" of groups, imagined degrees of behavioral and cultural difference, claims to privileges, opportunities, and advantages, and anxieties about competing groups' desires to usurp other positions in the status hierarchy.[44] History, in particular, plays an enormous role here. Lawrence Bobo and Vincent Hutchings argue that these views are derived "from the long-term experiences and conditions that members of a racial group have faced" and are shaped by "an on-going process of collective social definition that cannot be reduced to the current status of individuals."[45] Therefore, "the longer the history of relations between dominant and subordinate group members [exists], the more fully crystallized is the sense of relative group position."[46]

The undertheorized connection between affective polarization by group identities and group position theory is that people's judgments about their hostility to various groups involve, in part, notions that the normative ordering of groups is under threat or transformation. We should not be surprised that there exists explosive anxiety and resentment caused by highly symbolic events that suggest the erosion of group hierarchy (e.g., the Obama election), at least on the Blumer model. Yet, what seems to have gone undertheorized is the idea that if group position ideology is as powerful as some of the polarization data suggest, then the "spillover" effect may create, in and of itself, a legitimation crisis in democracy.

Anti-Democratic Practices and Violence

To put the point more bluntly, a political coalition that holds a very strongly hierarchical sense of group position based on social identity may judge a political system that permits the erosion of its hierarchies as de facto illegitimate. To the extent that group position instability is taken as prima facie evidence of decadence or corruption by a large swath of the population, political demagogues and cynical elites have political dynamite at their disposal. To grasp at power, they can appeal to these sentiments in order to justify strategies of anti-democratic maneuvers (e.g., gerrymandering, voter disenfranchisement and intimidation, dark money campaign financing, violence, etc.) or violate cooperative norms.[47]

As previous waves of highly racialized forms of political polarization sparked by white identitarian backlash in the United States (e.g., post-Reconstruction) show, rights-based constraints and democratic norms are not always reliable bulwarks against such hostilities. A recurring feature of a highly racialized, affectively intense, and policy-unmoored partisan sorting in the United States is the temptation to tolerate and even outright champion uses of violence, political repression, and anti-democratic maneuvers against groups perceived to be in violation of traditional hierarchy—often using substantive law and federalist dispersal to pursue these ends or rule certain regions (e.g., the Jim Crow South) as "authoritarian enclaves."[48]

Civic education, moreover, is an especially disclosive site for these dynamics. Across the United States, for example, hysteria over critical race theory in education has led to literally hundreds of proposed and enacted measures by state legislatures, municipalities, school boards, and attorneys general to *ban* efforts to teach the history of white supremacy in the United States or bring to bear conceptual tools developed by critical philosophers and theorists of racial injustice (e.g., "structural" or "institutional" racism) in the classroom.[49] While not political violence, these efforts are still *repressive* and *ideological* in important ways. They aim to give largely white administrators and lawmakers arbitrary and intolerable power to police racially egalitarian speech and to enforce an ideological worldview hostile to reparative justice and anti-discrimination claims. Most insidiously, they claim the rhetorical mantle of "reconciliation" and target (largely) minority and left scholars and teachers as principally concerned with *ressentiment* or *subversion* rather than truth claims and the renewal of democratic norms. The telos of this politics is a political landscape antithetical to the First Amendment culture that Shiffrin compellingly discusses in this volume, and is reflected in the swift movement, for example, from the highly targeted attack on the *New York Times*' "1619 Project" to the proliferation of book ban proposals that threaten to exclude even texts like Toni Morrison's *Beloved* or Ta-Nehisi Coates's *Between the World and Me*.

The goal of these polices (and agitation for them) is not simply to silence or impose a chilling effect on progressive discourse about race where possible, but also to cultivate epistemic norms and interpretive orientations that make such speech presumptively illegitimate, incoherent, or illicit. The rhetoric of reconciliation and "divisiveness" or "polarization" is critical here. Frustratingly, many critics on the academic left do not seem to grasp this point, focusing instead on the obvious theoretical and political shortcomings of various popular intellectuals and educational constituencies who claim the mantle of "anti-racism." The excesses and shortcomings of liberal anti-racism *are* important to debate, and leftists have reasonable concerns that in some educational settings, poorly conceived "anti-racist" approaches have been at odds with cultivating independence of mind or genuine reasoning. A more fundamental challenge, however, is the question of state repression, where the violence and economic sanction of the state are in play. This is what is unfolding across our federated educational system while national media and urbane progressives, given their focus on large city school systems and elite private schools, exhaustively debate so-called wokeness and its discontents.

It is tempting to minimize the critical race theory panic as minor cultural war hysteria, especially when compared to something as spectacularly brazen as the riot at the US Capitol on January 6, 2021. Yet the battle over civic education and national history has important consequences. W. E. B. Du Bois, in his monumental *Black Reconstruction in America* (1935), argued that the reign of post–Civil War white nationalism was built, ideologically, upon rhetoric of sectional reconciliation and the racist "Dunning School" historiography that served to justify it. Du Bois understood the compulsion toward reconciliation, noting how "war and especially civil strife have terrible wounds" and declaring it "the duty of humanity to heal them." Yet, as Du Bois argued, this compulsion toward "consensus" took the form of judging it "neither wise nor patriotic to speak of all the causes of strife and the terrible results to which sectional differences in the United States had led," leading historians and public figures alike to minimize the *causal* significance of slavery and racial injustice in explaining the outbreak of war or judging its meaning.[50] The usurpation enabled by reconciliation rhetoric was so thoroughgoing that the moral significance of

Reconstruction's experiment in multiracial democracy was subject to mockery for decades. Rather than functioning as a touchstone for democratic ideals and critical insight, it was mobilized in textbooks and popular culture as *negative exemplar,* a "tragic" mistake said to reveal the fool's errand of racial equality.[51]

While ideas from the polarization discourse may help us to understand some of how these dynamics unfold, we should be wary of the ways that the moral valence attached to consensus and polarization can transform them into mystifying concepts that mischaracterize attempts to resist this repressive, anti-democratic pole of a recurrent conflict. Coming down into this morass from the heights of abstraction, it seems a crucial function of civic education in a society with *this* history and sociology, to train our judgment to recognize these patterns when they emerge. This is key to theorizing democratically redemptive forms of dissent to resist them and pursue transitional justice.

CIVIC EDUCATION IN POLARIZED TIMES

As I have argued throughout, one major difficulty of theorizing civic education as a contentious practice within the political context outlined above is that struggles over educational ideals and projects invite not just heated disagreement, but illegitimate repression and cultural stigma. Worse, such responses often proceed under the ideological cover of law, bureaucratic reason, or the cultural-philosophic norm of reconciliation, mystifying and legitimizing their practice. Indeed, insofar as the discourse on civic education inevitably involves defining what *counts* as privileged sites or agents of civic pedagogy, one surreptitious feature of ideology may be the *narrowness* with which we conceive of the sites and practices that are, and historically have been, constitutive of genuinely emancipatory and democratic civic learning in contentious political cultures. In certain conditions, an aspirationally democratic civic education may need to be less concerned with reconciliation than reconstruction, and take the form of noncompliance rather than obedience, to use Shiffrin's helpful distinction.

If this is so, the agents from which we might learn the most about civic education in polarized times, including the appropriate relation to the law, may often be engaged in forms of pedagogically oriented noncompliance with the law, or withdrawal from state-based instruction, rather than the state-sanctioned education inevitably foregrounded on a liberal ideal theoretic model. In other work, I have emphasized the *pedagogical* character of black protest, especially in reference to complex configurations of law and social power.[52] Political philosophy needs to develop receptive ways of recognizing and reading such praxis, and in the spirit of building this capacity, let me conclude with two examples drawn from the archive of African American political thought and praxis, which I find especially generative here given its preoccupation with forms of resistance in highly repressive political conditions marked by the kinds of hostilities we associate with polarization.

I share Shiffrin's civic educational concerns with "legal literacy about the substantive content and the normative underpinnings of law," but want to emphasize the *critical* function of this literacy and the ways that such "literacy" can be embedded, learned, and extended in the *praxis of resistance* to oppression and injustice. Activists like Martin Luther King and Huey Newton, for instance, sought to unmask the ideological content and oppressive practice of extant legal authorities, modeling how what Shiffrin describes as "skills of interpretation, analogous reasoning, critical evaluation, and cross-contextual, imaginative extension of principles to new situations" were necessary to recognize and resist forms of racial oppression that operated under the cover of substantive law.[53]

While King's "Letter from a Birmingham Jail" is probably most well-known for its invocation of the natural law tradition's distinction between a just law and an unjust law, he also expounds at length about laws becoming unjust through their *application*. In other words, facially neutral statutes can conceal the discriminatory and unjust application of substantive and procedural laws, constituting a legal order that is tyrannical and estranging. For King, the way for the oppressed to overcome this estrangement and recover the democratic power of collective lawmaking was, paradoxically, to *break* the law in collective action. By withdrawing cooperation with the unjust application of legal rules, King argued that the oppressed could force a series of public and procedural conflicts over the meaning and method of law. Crucially, King thought that his practice of civil disobedience should be informed by an ethos of *agape* love and a willingness to accept punishment.

This served at least two functions germane to the preceding discussion. First, it tried to perform the pedagogical work of contextual critique, revealing King's opponents to be the true violators of legitimate, democratic legal authority. The acceptance of punishment, King thought, showed sincere fidelity to the ideal of a genuinely cooperative rule of law among equals and not the kind of self-exemption from reciprocity or self-binding to the legal order he saw as characteristic of segregationists. Second, King criticized the way that labels of "extremism" were conventionally used to compel reconciliation to legalized injustice. While King admitted an initial disappointment in being categorized as an extremist responsible for unnecessary division, he eventually came to see that being considered extremist could, in certain circumstances and when indexed to justice, be a badge of honor. "The question is not whether we will be extremist," King argued while invoking Lincoln, Jesus, and a series of prophetic Christian figures, "but what kind of extremist will we be?"[54]

In addition to questions about the political ethics of noncompliance, therefore, the encounter with King also raises the question of the *ethos* that should inform civic education in an age of polarization more broadly. Is there, as King surmised, a route that arrives at a more just society, while avoiding the intensification of mutual hostility and distrust? Might a transcendent concept like love, rather than the familiar philosophical vocabulary of duties, norms, and democracy, provide a way of reconfiguring the affects and identities driving polarization without acquiescing to premature reconciliation? And if an atmosphere is marked, as ours is, by polarization *and* severe injustice, what kind of disobedience or noncompliance is required? If it has pedagogical aims to compel us to rethink civic ideals and identities, or our relation to the legal order, must it be conducted openly, lovingly, and with a willingness to accept punishment?[55]

The historian Jarvis Givens, in his pathbreaking *Fugitive Pedagogy*, gives us some reason to be hesitant about these prescriptions. Under Jim Crow, black teachers were widely required to teach from textbooks and school standards that endorsed white supremacy, systematically misrepresented and marginalized African American history, and brought glaringly racist images and tropes into the classroom. Not only were black teachers subject to discriminatory pay scales, substandard schools, and other precarious work conditions, but they were also heavily surveilled by white school officials (and their black allies) to ensure compliance. Like other forms of Jim Crow repression, violation of these rules and norms could invite severe personal and political sanctions, up to and including physical violence.

What Givens shows us, through archival material and the refracted testimony of black students, is that, while a number of black teachers *performed* compliance with these unjust restrictions, many also engaged in what he calls "fugitive pedagogy." In other words, they practiced pedagogical disobedience that "explicitly critiqued and negated white supremacy and antiblack protocols of domination, but . . . often did so in discreet or partially concealed fashion" so as to elude surveillance and sanction by hostile authorities.[56] Struggling against the epistemic injustice of American schooling, they tried to equip their students with the historical knowledge and critical disposition to effectively criticize racist ideology and resist absorbing it into their self-conception. Fighting to maintain their students' self-respect, these fugitive pedagogues smuggled in alternative texts, redesigned curricula, and conducted their own original research to develop an insurgent practice of anti-racist civic education arrayed to battle with the civic ideals of white supremacy.

Arguably most fascinating in Givens's reconstruction (and most productively dissonant with the prevailing anarchistic discourse of fugitivity in Black Studies) is that this wide range of fugitive pedagogical practices were connected through a larger *institutional network* of black educators organized through the eminent Association for the Study of Negro Life and History (ASNLH) and other groups (i.e., Colored Teachers' Associations). Especially important to this fugitive culture was the eminent Harvard-trained historian and philosopher of education, Carter G. Woodson. His writings and organizing efforts did the most to "name how school curriculum cultivated antiblackness and racism as a social competence among students . . . thus pulling it out into the open and making it accountable to critique."[57]

Givens's captivating retrieval of this past leads me to a set of final questions, which dovetail with the transitional approach to the problem of civic education in polarized times that I have tried to pursue throughout this chapter. Crucially, in raising the problem of "agents of change," this angle of approach allows us to ask more clearly *how* we should understand the disjuncture between the norms required of *official educational systems* in the United States and *the ethical responsibility of teachers within?* When the former reflects deep societal injustice and imposes objectionable ideological constraints, what sorts of dissent are permissible for individual teachers or networks of teachers? Any persuasive answer to this question must balance sincere political convictions and compelling claims about how CRT bans represent a threat to basic democratic freedoms with other ethical-prudential concerns, including teachers' custodial duties toward minors, students' vulnerability to high-stakes tests and meritocratic contests that currently prevail in society, and the fact that any disobedience or dissent must navigate a national education discourse awash in propaganda. Indeed, it would be a missed opportunity for political theorists and philosophers seeking to show solidarity with teachers to refuse to enter into this conversation about "fugitive pedagogy" and its institutional bases with insights gleaned from work on two philosophical traditions not usually associated with educational ethics.

The first is the rich literature on contentious dissent by state officials and the ethics of civil and uncivil disobedience. As repression intensifies, many educators may feel compelled, by vocational, civic, or moral duty, to turn to subterfuge and dissemblance to ensure that anti-racism is a constitutive part of civic education. Such disobedients argue that students need exposure to critical thinking about race to have interpretive patterns they can draw upon to understand America's history, civic life, and current democratic disfigurations. This, in part, reflects a realism about the irrationalism, conflict, and affective states constitutive of contemporary American politics. But, as the best work on realist civil disobedience shows, such dynamics do not absolve the disobedient of producing compelling normative arguments (at least to their potential cooperators) informed by the best of the tradition of civil resistance.[58] More work in educational ethics demands to be done in this arena.

The other tradition that needs to be brought to bear is the philosophical conversation on black nationalism and black communitarianism. There is an important set of arguments advanced by Woodson, Du Bois, and a host of organizers and educators from

the Black Power movement, influenced by this tradition, that argue
for the parallel development of black and anti-racist educational
practices outside of state authority when the society might reasonably be considered hostile to such pedagogy. Du Bois, for example,
despite never abandoning the moral imperative of a racially integrated society, nevertheless offered a dismal survey of the prospects for education in hostile, nominally integrated school systems
at the dawn of the 1960s. In a little-studied essay, "Whither Now
and Why?," Du Bois argued in defense of pedagogical disobedience against racist and Red Scare repression, imploring teachers
"to teach the truth as they see it even if they lose their jobs."[59] But
Du Bois also argues for great effort and resources to be put into
developing alternative educational spaces as well:

> Negro parents and Negro Parent-Teacher Associations at least tem-
> porarily will have to take on and carry the burden which they have
> hitherto left to [all-black, segregated] public schools. The child in
> the family, in specific organizations, or in social life must learn what
> he will not learn in school until the public schools vastly improve.
> Negro history must be taught for many critical years by parents, in
> clubs by lecture courses, by a new Negro literature. This must be
> done systematically . . . This is going to take time and money and is
> going to call for racial organizations.[60]

Du Bois view is too complicated to patiently reconstruct here, as it
involves a tangle of commitments to preserving putatively "black"
cultural identity, the critique of racist ideas, the cultivation of alternative values (e.g., anti-materialism), the promotion of black youth
self-esteem, and the teaching of African American history. I reference it just to underscore, a final time, the way that the most
favorable agents for defending civic education in an unjust society may themselves raise quandaries obscured by the rhetoric of
reconciliation: Are race-specific educational institutions (i.e.,
those run by churches, unions, neighborhood groups, nonprofit
groups, etc.) a defensible response to current curricular politics,
either temporarily or for the foreseeable future? Does it do further
justice to give such efforts our material aid, or are we ironically
deepening segregation and racial hostilities in ways at odds with
that goal? Should civic education efforts, hosted online or in civil

society organizations, be interracially organized around anti-racist principles rather than racial or cultural identities? Are there costs that would make us abandon integrationism as an ideal in such spaces? And what should be the stance of these parallel organizations toward state-based civic education, especially the fate of those teachers who do disobey the edicts of school systems that seek to repress the kind of education they have organized to defend?

I can only pose more questions than answers here, but if the preceding analysis is persuasive, a central obstacle to our judgment is clear. Abstract invocations of "polarization" will throw off more heat than light, leaving us grasping at shadows in dark times that demand more.

NOTES

1 Sometimes these contentions, especially about the ideal agents of education, will be implicit (usually state-authorized public school teachers). It also seems to follow that any theory of mass civic education will entail (or at least presuppose) views about the mind, cognition, and learning as well. At least one way these presuppositions become more explicit is when one confronts radically egalitarian or inegalitarian philosophies of education. See, for example, Jacques Rancière, *The Ignorant Schoolmaster,* trans. Kristin Ross (Stanford, CA: Stanford University Press, 1991).

2 This conception of a critically self-reflexive and problem-focused approach to political philosophy draws on Rahel Jaeggi, *Critique of Forms of Life,* trans. Ciaran Cronin (Cambridge, MA: Belknap Press of Harvard University Press, 2018), esp. ch. 5. For an exemplar of genealogical and discursive analysis of a crucial keyword of a political moment, see Nancy Fraser and Linda Gordon, "A Genealogy of Dependency: Tracing a Keyword of the US Welfare State," *Signs: Journal of Women in Culture and Society* 19, no. 2 (1994): 309–336.

3 I have been inspired in this account by Ben Laurence, *Agents of Change: Political Philosophy in Practice* (Cambridge, MA: Harvard University Press, 2021), especially chs. 3–4.

4 On critical theory as the self-clarification of the struggles of the age, see Nancy Fraser, "What's Critical about Critical Theory? The Case of Habermas and Gender," *New German Critique,* no. 35 (1985): 97–131. Fraser draws on Karl Marx, "For a Ruthless Criticism of Everything Existing (Marx to Arnold Ruge)," in Karl Marx and Friedrich Engels, *The Marx-Engels Reader,* 2nd ed., ed. Robert C. Tucker (New York: W. W. Norton, 1978), 12–15.

5 This continues a larger critique of the preoccupation with reconciliation as the task of political philosophy that I have developed across a
range of writings, most recently Brandon M. Terry, "Conscription and the
Color Line: Rawls, Race and Vietnam," *Modern Intellectual History* 18, no. 4
(2021): 960–983.

6 John Rawls, *Lectures on the History of Political Philosophy*, ed. Samuel Free-
man (Cambridge, MA: Belknap Press of Harvard University Press, 2007), 10.

7 It is important to note that, in Rawls's treatment, "civic education" is
not something that happens simply in schools, but is also enacted in forums
where political officials articulate reasons for decisions and judgments. Judicial opinions from higher courts are especially important on this conception.

8 Rawls, *Lectures on the History of Political Philosophy*, 10.

9 Rawls, *Lectures on the History of Political Philosophy*, 10.

10 For a powerful argument that toleration is a normative ideal that
should not be diminished by appellations like "mere," or the longing for
thicker forms of mutual affirmation and recognition, see Teresa M. Bejan,
Mere Civility: Disagreement and the Limits of Toleration (Cambridge, MA: Harvard University Press, 2017).

11 Shiffrin, "Democratic Civic Education and Democratic Law," in this
volume.

12 Shiffrin, "Democratic Civic Education and Democratic Law," in this
volume.

13 For Rawls on Marx on ideology, see Rawls, *Lectures on the History of
Political Philosophy*, 10, 359–362.

14 The value of rage is stridently defended in Myisha Cherry, *The Case
for Rage: Why Anger Is Essential to Anti-Racist Struggle* (Oxford: Oxford University Press, 2021).

15 Stanley Cavell, *Conditions Handsome and Unhandsome: The Constitution of Emersonian Perfectionism: The Carus Lectures, 1988* (Chicago: University of Chicago Press, 2018), 101–126.

16 See, for example, Louis Althusser, *On the Reproduction of Capitalism:
Ideology and Ideological State Apparatuses* (Brooklyn, NY: Verso, 2014), 51.
On ideology generally, see Tommie Shelby, "Ideology, Racism, and Criti-
cal Social Theory," *Philosophical Forum* 34, no. 2 (2003): 153–188.

17 On the idea of political peoplehood, see Rogers M. Smith, *Political
Peoplehood: The Roles of Values, Interests, and Identities* (Chicago: University of
Chicago Press, 2015). On the critique of vocabularies, see Charles Taylor,
"Interpretation and the Sciences of Man," *Review of Metaphysics* 25, no. 1
(1971). On ideological "justification narratives," see Rainer Forst, *Norma-
tivity and Power: Analyzing Social Orders of Justification*, trans. Ciaran Cronin
(Oxford: Oxford University Press, 2017).

18 This was central to W. E. B. Du Bois' critique of the racial politics of education. See his essay, "The Immortal Child," in W. E. B. Du Bois, *Darkwater: Voices from within the Veil, The Oxford W. E. B. Du Bois* (New York: Oxford University Press, 2007), 95–106. For an elegant analysis of how the habituation of domination and acquiescence works in civic life, see Danielle S. Allen, *Talking to Strangers: Anxieties of Citizenship after* Brown v. Board of Education (Chicago: University of Chicago Press, 2004).

19 Onora O'Neill, "Abstraction, Idealization and Ideology in Ethics," *Royal Institute of Philosophy Supplements* 22 (1987): 55–69.

20 See the excellent discussions about the dangers of polarization talk in Thomas Zimmer, "Reflections on the Challenges of Writing a (Pre-) History of the 'Polarized' Present," *Modern American History* 2, no. 3 (2019): 403–408.

21 S. Jonathan Bass, *Blessed Are the Peacemakers: Martin Luther King, Jr., Eight White Religious Leaders, and the "Letter from Birmingham Jail"* (Baton Rouge: Louisiana State University Press, 2001).

22 Martin Luther King, "Letter from Birmingham City Jail," in *A Testament of Hope: The Essential Writings of Martin Luther King, Jr.* (San Francisco: Harper & Row, 1986), 295.

23 Katrina Forrester, "Liberalism and Social Theory after John Rawls," *Analyse & Kritik* 44, no. 1 (2022), 1–22.

24 The idea of a "black box" problem in social theory is from Nancy Fraser and Rachel Jaeggi, *Capitalism: A Conversation in Critical Theory,* ed. Brian Milstein (Medford, MA: Polity, 2018), 4–8. Fraser and Jaeggi are principally concerned with a critique of liberal egalitarianism's evasion of political economy in their practice of normative theory, but surely one can treat as a "black box" any manner of complex social problems with similar deleterious effects.

25 Forrester, "Liberalism and Social Theory after John Rawls."

26 Michael C. Dawson, *Black Visions: The Roots of Contemporary African-American Political Ideologies* (Chicago: University of Chicago Press, 2001), ch. 1.

27 This question was one of the central themes of the literature on "faces of power." See, for example, John Gaventa, *Power and Powerlessness: Quiescence and Rebellion in an Appalachian Valley* (Urbana: University of Illinois Press, 1980); Steven Lukes, *Power: A Radical View,* 2nd ed. (Houndmills, Basingstoke, Hampshire New York: Palgrave Macmillan, 2004).

28 Rogers M. Smith, *Civic Ideals: Conflicting Visions of Citizenship in U.S. History* (New Haven, CT: Yale University Press, 1997).

29 Ryan Teague Beckwith, "Obama Attacks GOP Candidate's 'Phony Culture Wars' in Virginia," *Bloomberg News* (New York), October 23, 2021, www.bloomberg.com; Gregory S. Schneider and Laura Vozzella, "Obama

Casts the Virginia Election As Historic, but Will His Energy Spark Democrats to Vote?," *Washington Post*, October 23, 2021, www.washingtonpost.com.

30 Aaron Bramson, Patrick Grim, Daniel J. Singer, William J. Berger, Graham Sack, Steven Fisher, Carissa Flocken, and Bennett Holman, "Understanding Polarization: Meanings, Measures, and Model Evaluation," *Philosophy of Science* 84, no. 1 (2017): 116–117.

31 On problems with the ideal and deviation as the presupposition of social theoretic critique, see Charles W. Mills, "'Ideal Theory' as Ideology," *Hypatia* 20, no. 3 (2005): 167.

32 On participatory parity, see Nancy Fraser, "Social Justice in the Age of Identity Politics: Redistribution, Recognition, and Participation," in *Redistribution or Recognition?: A Political-Philosophical Exchange*, ed. Nancy Fraser and Axel Honneth (New York: Verso, 2003), 26–47.

33 Eric Schickler, *Racial Realignment: The Transformation of American Liberalism, 1932–1965* (Princeton, NJ: Princeton University Press, 2016).

34 Doug McAdam and Karina Kloos, *Deeply Divided: Racial Politics and Social Movements in Postwar America* (Oxford: Oxford University Press, 2014), 23.

35 McAdam and Kloos, *Deeply Divided*, 24.

36 Delia Baldassarri and Andrew Gelman, "Partisans Without Constraint: Political Polarization and Trends in American Public Opinion," *American Journal of Sociology* 114, no. 2 (2008). Also, see Ashley Jardina and Trent Ollerenshaw, "The Polls—Trends: The Polarization of White Racial Attitudes and Support for Racial Equality in the US," *Public Opinion Quarterly* 86, S1 (2022): 576–587.

37 Ashley Jardina, *White Identity Politics* (New York: Cambridge University Press, 2019).

38 Michael Tesler, *Post-Racial or Most-Racial?: Race and Politics in the Obama Era* (Chicago: University of Chicago Press, 2016).

39 Robert Griffin et al., "Racing Apart: Partisan Shifts on Racial Attitudes Over the Last Decade," Democracy Fund Voter Study Group (October 2021), www.voterstudygroup.org.

40 For a relatively early attempt to map these dynamics, see Joel Olson, "Whiteness and the Polarization of American Politics," *Political Research Quarterly* 61, no. 4 (2008): 704–718.

41 Lilliana Mason, "'I disrespectfully agree': The Differential Effects of Partisan Sorting on Social and Issue Polarization," *American Journal of Political Science* 59, no. 1 (2015): 128–145.

42 Lilliana Mason, Julie Wronski, and John V. Kane, "Activating Animus: The Uniquely Social Roots of Trump Support," *American Political Science Review* 115, no. 4 (2021): 1508–1516.

43 Lawrence Bobo and Vincent Hutchings, "Perceptions of Racial Group Competition: Extending Blumer's Theory of Group Position to a Multiracial Social Context, *American Sociological Review* 61, no. 6 (December 1996): 955. For the original statement, see Herbert Blumer, "Race Prejudice as a Sense of Group Position," *Pacific Sociological Review* 1 no. 1 (1958): 3–7.

44 Bobo and Hutchings, "Perceptions of Racial Group Competition," 956.

45 Bobo and Hutchings, "Perceptions of Racial Group Competition," 956–957.

46 Bobo and Hutchings, "Perceptions of Racial Group Competition," 957.

47 These are all pressing pathologies characteristic of our democratic crisis. See Carol Anderson, *One Person, No Vote: How Voter Suppression Is Destroying Our Democracy* (New York: Bloomsbury, 2018); Ryan D. Doerfler and Samuel Moyn, "Democratizing the Supreme Court," *California Law Review* 109 (2021): 1703–1772; Jane Mayer, *Dark Money: The Hidden History of the Billionaires Behind the Rise of the Radical Right*, 1st ed. (New York: Doubleday, 2016).

48 Robert Waite Mickey, *Paths Out of Dixie: The Democratization of Authoritarian Enclaves in America's Deep South, 1944–1972* (Princeton, NJ: Princeton University Press, 2015).

49 Taifha Natalee Alexander, LaToya Baldwin Clark, Isabel Flores-Ganley, Cheryl Harris, Jasleen Kohli, Lynn McLelland, Paton Moody, Nicole Powell, Milan Smith, and Noah Zatz, "CRT Forward Tracking Project," UCLA School of Law Critical Race Studies Program. Accessed November 22, 2022. www.crtforward.law.ucla.edu. Also see Hannah Natanson, "Her Students Reported Her for a Lesson on Race. Can She Trust Them Again?," *Washington Post*, September 18, 2023. www.washingtonpost.com.

50 W. E. B. Du Bois, *Black Reconstruction: An Essay Toward a History of the Part Which Black Folk Played in the Attempt to Reconstruct Democracy in America, 1860–1880*, 1st ed. (New York: Harcourt, Brace & Co., 1935), 713–714.

51 Henry Louis Gates, *Stony the Road: Reconstruction, White Supremacy, and the Rise of Jim Crow* (New York: Penguin Press, 2019); Donald Yacovone, *Teaching White Supremacy: America's Democratic Ordeal and the Forging of Our National Identity*, 1st ed. (New York: Pantheon Books, 2022).

52 Brandon M. Terry, "After Ferguson," in Jon Baskin and Anastasia Berg, eds., *The Opening of the American Mind: Ten Years of the Point* (Chicago: University of Chicago Press, 2020), 117–138.

53 The "Panther Patrols," started by Huey P. Newton and Bobby Seale in Oakland, California, to conduct armed surveillance of police and pre-

vent brutality are a fascinating example of insurgent, street-level civic education regarding substantive law. While popular memory of the Panther
patrols focuses primarily on the Panthers' weapons, the autobiographical,
first-person accounts are equally fixated on the fact that the Panthers—
and especially Newton—openly cited and read from the California legal
code to inform any persons detained of their rights, train the witnessing
crowds of their legal rights, and challenge police power where it overstepped its legal authority. While they sought to prefigure a wildly different legal order, Panther patrols were emphatically *not* forms of civil
disobedience; they took great care to dramatically perform compliance
with the law. Yet, their dramatic, theatrical insistence on their possession
of rights enumerated in California law—especially concerning treatment
by police, rights to bearing arms, and rights to participate in public safety by observing police—enacted a popular, street-level civic pedagogy of
such resounding and enduring effect that even the recent waves of citizen
witnessing to police brutality in the Black Lives Matter movement draw
explicitly on their exemplarity. Huey P. Newton, *Revolutionary Suicide*, ed.
J. Herman Blake, Penguin classics deluxe edition (New York: Penguin
Books, 2009), 120–135.

54 Martin Luther King Jr., "Letter from Birmingham City Jail," in *A
Testament of Hope: The Essential Writings of Martin Luther King, Jr*, ed. James
Melvin Washington (San Francisco: Harper & Row, 1986), 297–298.

55 King Jr., "Letter from Birmingham City Jail," 294.

56 Jarvis R. Givens, *Fugitive Pedagogy: Carter G. Woodson and the Art of
Black Teaching* (Cambridge, MA: Harvard University Press, 2021), 5–6.

57 Givens, *Fugitive Pedagogy*, 18.

58 For a wonderful overview of the civil disobedience literature in
philosophy, see Candice Delmas and Kimberley Brownlee, "Civil Disobedience," *The Stanford Encyclopedia of Philosophy* (Winter 2021 edition), ed.
Edward N. Zalta, https://plato.stanford.edu. On the question of realism
and civil disobedience, see Andrew Sabl, "Realist Disobedience," in *The
Cambridge Companion to Civil Disobedience*, ed. William Scheuerman (Cambridge: Cambridge University Press, 2021), 153–177, and Karuna Mante-
na, "Another Realism: The Politics of Gandhian Nonviolence," *American
Political Science Review* 106, no. 2 (2012): 455–470.

59 W. E. B. Du Bois, "Whither Now and Why," in *The Education of Black
People: Ten Critiques, 1906-1960*, ed. Herbert Aptheker (New York: Monthly
Review Press, 2001), 203.

60 Du Bois, "Whither Now and Why," 196–197.

3

CIVIC EDUCATION AND DEMOCRACY'S FLAWS

ROBERT L. TSAI

If I could talk with all my white fellow-countrymen on this subject, I would say to them, in the language of Scripture: "Come and let us reason together."
— Frederick Douglass, "The Color Line," *North American Review,* June 1881

Today, liberalism and democracy are beset by competitors that seek to return power to religious traditionalists or partisans masquerading as civic republicans.[1] In such an environment, can civic education do some good, and even help bridge our society's deepening divides?

Seana Shiffrin has characteristically brought deep learning and penetrating insight to the project of civic education in a modern democracy. Against a "dominant" model of citizenship in which "citizens vote and hand over power to their representatives"—which she believes encourages the people to maintain an unhealthy distance from government—she proposes a richer account of political community in which people see their role as "fellow duty-holders." To facilitate this vision of legal order, Shiffrin proposes greater societal investment in developing "skills of interpretation, analogous reasoning, critical evaluation, and extension of principles to new situations."

I begin with the conviction that democracy in the United States remains worth defending, despite a constitutional tradition that originally treated broad citizen participation in public affairs with

suspicion. I also agree heartily that civic education is indispensable to the survival of democracy—not just as a technocratic enterprise, but rather as a way of life. Any disagreements I have with
Shiffrin concern the level at which theory can ensure the quality
of civic learning necessary to keep the American experiment alive.
There's a limit to how much philosophy can guarantee the utility
of education—the rest is a matter of pedagogy and the openness of
the people to self-correction.

I shall begin by briefly summarizing Shiffrin's key arguments
while emphasizing that much of the success of her proposal
depends on the substance of what is taught and how political
know-how is conveyed. Her analysis largely stays at a high level of
abstraction, content with sketching models, attitudes, and habits
to be reproduced or avoided. But I contend that what's missing is
also essential to any civic education project: honest confrontation
with democracy's deficits. Thus, while Shiffrin's theory of democratic citizenship is admirably thicker than what many proponents
of legal liberalism allow, her account of education at present may
be too incomplete to equip the citizen to tackle the problems facing an aging political order. Instead, I shall suggest that what would
make a meaningful impact at this historical moment is a form of
education that teaches citizens the ability to diagnose democracy's
shortcomings and the capacity to reason from injustice.

Preferring Thick Citizenship in Polarized Times

Proponents of thin liberalism emphasize awareness of basic rights
and institutions, but Shiffrin is correct that such models of citizenship fail to foster robust connections of obligation, cooperation,
and sacrifice.[2] At the same time, they render citizens overly passive, providing elected officials and employers more power than
they deserve and robbing citizens themselves of the benefits of
fulsome participation. As she frankly acknowledges, her theory of
a person's proper place within the political order "requires both
oversight and a developed sense of judgment about what the duty
requires."

I'm going to put aside the low-hanging objections that proponents of thin citizenship would surely raise, such as that too dense
a notion of citizenship inevitably smuggles in substantive visions of

the good about which we are deeply divided or that, as an empirical matter, Shiffrin's account of citizenship is overly demanding of the typical person and instructor to be implemented successfully. I agree with her that we need a vision of community and power that is more meaningful and interactive than the thin gruel of rights-based liberalism so often ladled into our bowls.

Certainly, robust conceptions of citizenship are compatible with the tradition of civic republicanism and popular sovereignty in the United States, as well as one's intuitive sense that roles of all sorts arise from social experience.[3] Moreover, as Shiffrin's account suggests, a political community is, at its essence, a collective moral project rather than merely a framework for the fulfillment of individual desires. As a result, habits for living together, as well as a commitment to and knowledge of the "minimal conditions of justice," are paramount expectations of the polity's members.

The additional complication that we live in a nation experiencing unprecedented cultural heterogeneity and ideological polarization should nudge us toward a deeper vision of citizenship rather than more tenuous ones. A multiplicity of identities and belief systems, along with a growing pile of unmet grievances, can act as centrifugal forces that accelerate trend lines of democratic decline and loss of faith in the rule of law. Inclusive terms for political membership, such as birthright citizenship, which are predicated on the accident of birthplace, must be accompanied by more.[4] Yet when heartier notions of autonomy, respect, and collective enterprise are not available or cannot reach average citizens, the vacuum will be filled with visions of community that are more coercive, nostalgic, and parochial in order to satisfy the longing for meaning and place. People who cannot bear to live together any longer begin dreaming of ways to live apart; they also begin to disintegrate as a people in the political sense.[5]

From this vantage point, it is worth wondering whether a model of citizenship that rests primarily upon "deeper exposure to a band of the substantive law" is sufficient to meet the moment. Shiffrin contends that a more accurate, earlier, understanding of "how the legal infrastructure facilitates daily living" may "generate more substantive and affective grounds for the general compliance with law and democratic participation."[6] But in a time of fractured identities and experiences, will exposure to more law do the trick?

The democratic habits emphasized by Shiffrin include listening actively, speaking with sincerity, toleration, open-mindedness. These are indeed valuable characteristics worth instilling in the citizenry. Yet other traits are arguably even more desperately needed among the populace at this moment: a capacity for righteous outrage, the ability to make wise decisions among our portfolio of identities and agendas, fear of role reversal, charity in engagement, an instinct for forgiveness. All of these are necessary to develop a sense of justice in each citizen as well as the practical skills to realize it in this world.

For the moment, I'll focus on the connection between civic equality and role reversal. Much has been made of the importance of empathy, i.e., the capacity to recognize the suffering of others.[7] But teaching compassion has not necessarily translated into a noticeable increase in benevolent politics, and one reason may be that socioeconomic differences and their attendant consciousnesses and habits have increasingly calcified. If that is the case, then we might turn to a critical idea occasionally presented in literature and the arts: role reversal.[8]

The genesis of role reversal can be found in the Black community under slavery and later segregation, when African Americans repeatedly denied equal dignity struggled mightily to persuade fellow citizens of the inhumanity of racial inequality. As Frederick Douglass reminds, "[t]he doctrine of human equality is the bitterest yet taught by the abolitionists."[9] Writers and artists dreamed of ways to depict the gulf between the white and Black communities and prick the collective democratic conscience. One vivid example of role reversal (as well as poetic, if not legal, justice) can be found in Langston Hughes's writings, where he imagines Governor Faubus forced by judicial decree to go back to school and endure segregation. Along the way, Hughes poses the tantalizing question: How might legal justice differ from existing jurisprudence if the US Supreme Court was populated entirely by African Americans?[10]

Role reversal as an approach to learning civic lessons rests on the insight that appeals to equal respect are insufficient when those who belong to the dominant majority feel secure in their old ways. Something must destabilize the political imagination. Neither self-reflection nor equal justice is possible until those who enjoy power and the fruits of material inequality have their sensibilities shaken, even temporarily. Thus, civic education that reveals the fragility of communal relations and the sudden impact of loss of status, political influence, or material opportunity can foster receptivity to learning about the virtues of equality. A sense of imagined loss may engender not merely principled anger at injustice, but also a willingness to cheer on others' efforts to gain legal satisfaction and to play a part in reconciliation. Role reversal can thus stimulate one's moral sensibility and break the circuit of seeing every social dispute as a zero-sum game.

As just one example, in a course I teach on mass inequality and social trauma, I expose students to the reversal of fortune experienced by loyal Japanese Americans evacuated and interned after Pearl Harbor. They believed that they were real citizens all along, chasing the American Dream like everyone else, but being a productive member of the economy was not enough. Nor did earning a law degree, as Minori Yasui discovered, save a person of Japanese ancestry from being reduced to their race. It took mobilizing for reparations by their children and grandchildren to reverse the process of internalized shame, begin intergenerational reconciliation, and bring some public vindication of the importance of equal respect.[11] Similarly, we investigate the gains in economic and political power wielded by free Black people during Reconstruction. The visible exercise of this newfound status and influence subsequently led to white majoritarian backlash, efforts to restore racialized forms of governance, and a turning away from multiracial democracy. These, too, offer hard lessons about how the rule of law and democracy can facilitate injustice when neither is underwritten by a deep commitment to equal respect.

Deep dives into other incidents like these can also acclimate students to the fact that citizenship is not simply an abstract ideal or bundle of rights; rather, the concept of citizenship is rendered meaningful through struggles over material opportunity and political status. They also teach that democracy itself has flaws, that the rule of law (and even theoretical existence of rights) is not enough to ensure justice, and that many injustices enjoy widespread support. That central dilemma—we need democracy and the rule of law in order to live together well, but both institutions have contributed to immense suffering—must guide civic education into the future.

The Content of Civic Education

Turning to the content of democratic education, Shiffrin singles out the common law method, which she believes will present a realistic account of a judge's interpretive authority as well as an empowering portrait of "citizens' roles in the development and articulation of law through their instigation and participation in common law cases." As she also has argued elsewhere, the common law makes a "special contribution" to the law by "generating a continuous, morally articulate body of law and establish[ing] a baseline moral culture and identity."[12]

It's true that enhanced exposure to the common law would demonstrate how judges decide cases, teach the value of a precedent-based system of dispute resolution, as well as the true range of policymaking involved in the judicial function. So, too, citizens would learn to appreciate the values that are often associated with the law, including notice, predictability, integrity, transparency, and fair play. Of course, citizens also need to carefully probe inspiring accounts of individuals who overcome great odds and join together to successfully advance the cause of liberty or equality.[13]

Still, a few cautionary notes might be sounded. First is the risk that stressing the common law method simply presents a judge-centered account of the legal process. Reading Brandeis, Cardozo, or Holmes, for instance, can easily leave the impression of the judge as master craftsman and focal point of the legal universe, rather than presenting an inspiring and complete account of citizen efforts to create and reform institutions or resist legal domination and entrenchment of oligarchy through judge-made law. This is often the misimpression left in the nation's law schools. The unfortunate dynamic could well be replicated if an attempt is made to teach the common law in more scaled-down fashion at the secondary and primary school levels.

To ensure that political agency is not lost or demoralization worsened through immersion in the common law, one must also convey that judges have deployed unobjectionable concepts such as property, self-defense, and even trespass to justify subordination, exclusion, and even expulsion. In other words, one must convey the lesson that the common law is one way of doing justice, but that it has also been a potent engine of injustice. In the name of justice, common law outcomes have had to be repudiated, replaced by statutes, or subverted—often through alternative methods.

A second concern in a divided nation is the possibility that gaining a rudimentary comprehension of institutions, practices, and ideals still leaves citizens ill-equipped to deal with the reality of political engagement. I concur with Shiffrin that citizens should be better equipped to engage in public debate. Yet they will still need to be taught that progress comes in different forms at different historical moments, and all of this requires making hard choices between short- and long-term goals. It also requires enormous creativity when trying to build counterweights to oppressive practices and rectify unvirtuous conduct.

This brings us to a third point: Civic education today must respond to widespread political demoralization—both a cause and by-product of polarization. Being told one has legal duties, and even receiving training in legal form, will not generate democratic affection if the law remains alien and impotent to everyday existence. Whatever their background or vision of the good life, many individuals suffer from a crisis of faith when they learn that powerful groups and corporations bend the law to their selfish ends, while neither democracy nor law affords the poor or sick much relief from material deprivation.

Shiffrin distinguishes between "unsubstantiated distrust" and "targeted, substantiated distrust of government," positing that more sophisticated knowledge of the law "may do work to prevent" the former from "gaining a foothold in the psyche of the citizenry." But this still seems to rest on a diagnosis that insufficient legal know-how is the problem rather than something else. It is not at all apparent that the causes of distrust are limited by such fine distinctions, or will respond to solutions calibrated this way. After all, both kinds of disaffection she describes can be found in people who share the same ecosystem. When tweaks in education are compared with a significant investment in educational resources, an increase in formal influence, improvement in material well-being, or amelioration of structural roadblocks, these other solutions will surely have a greater effect in reducing political alienation.

But let us stay on topic. Because so much about improving civic education will depend on what is taught and how it is taught, let me add a few words on that subject. I applaud Shiffrin's view that "history and literature can offer philosophical lessons." Additionally, the curriculum will have to be less Plato's *Republic* or the Hart-Fuller debate, and more Machiavelli's *Discourses* and *The Prince* or Robert Cover's *Justice Accused*.

One lesson that must be imparted is law's limits. Even well-intended laws depend on virtuous human beings to enforce them, and social groups in competition predictably turn the law to their own ends. For instance, we learn from Machiavelli that Athens was awash in laws, and yet the "insolence of the nobles and the license of the populace" helped pave the way for the tyranny of Peisistratus. Laws are often broken, ignored, or deployed for indirect effects even in less order-shaking circumstances, and the causes of such dynamics must be confronted or else cynicism will be the likely outcome of civic learning rather than political empowerment.

Second, laws are not good or bad by virtue of their sources or based on some other universal criteria. Instead, the "rule of law" is weak or strong, good or evil, stable or disuniting, depending on the nature of the people writing and enforcing the laws. Again, as Machiavelli points out, in a society that has become corrupt, the laws and institutions appear the same but what has changed is that "the virtuous and deserving" are no longer actively engaged in government. Instead, as in Athens, "only the powerful proposed laws, not for the common good and liberty of all, but for the increase of their own power."[14] What happens then is that citizens themselves are "by force and fraud made to resolve upon their own ruin."

A third lesson about the law is that contestation over terminology, concepts, and background values is part and parcel of the legal process (as it is of democracy generally). As Machiavelli famously put it, "all the laws that are favorable to liberty result from the opposition of these parties [nobles and the people] to each other."[15] Here, Robert Cover's insights are most valuable in promoting the epistemological skepticism necessary to foster autonomous and engaged participation in democracy. First, there is Cover's admonition that enforcement of the rule of law presents a dominant vision of social order while simultaneously trying to suppress alternative visions of power and community. We must constantly wonder what is being left off-stage, kept out of sight.[16] Second, as far as the judicial process is concerned, judges in hard cases must confront what Cover called the "moral-formal" dilemma—whether to choose to embrace substantive moral values that pull at a judge's conscience on the one hand, or to vindicate the "interests and values served by fidelity to the formal system" when doing so will block expression of the moral proposition.[17] Judges continue to face such quandaries when, for instance, they are asked by a death row inmate to overlook his lawyer's procedural failure to object to a constitutional violation (say, using race to pick jurors) or instead to allow a state to execute him for his attorney's mistake.

When judges choose to do the latter, they turn to such strategies as elevating the formal stakes of a dispute over moral stakes (at least for them), retreat to "mechanistic formalism," or ascribe moral responsibility to other parties and away from themselves.[18] But, as Cover reminds us, these are still exercises of discretion and involve particular rhetorical strategies of dealing with external political dynamics as well as a decision-maker's personal sense of role fidelity and willingness to innovate within that role. It's important that our civic education does not merely generate citizens who are good at order-reproducing, but also (as I'm certain Shiffrin agrees) capable of order-questioning and order-changing behavior.

While Shiffrin envisions democracy and the rule of law as largely compatible practices, in fact deep tensions between the two are routinely exploited. Problems of malapportionment, antiquated design choices, and failures of information and mobilization, as well as misplaced faith in particular leaders and organizations, can nevertheless lead to the creation of legitimate laws and seeming compliance with democracy's minimal standards, at least in a formal sense. But such formally legitimate laws or practices fall short when we apply some broader criteria for evaluating the justness of a regime or course of action. If the rule of law is understood as containing these minimal conditions for justice, then at times democratic processes and outcomes will stand in deep tension with, and sometimes even violate, the rule of law. By the same token, if the rule of law is understood primarily as fidelity to preexisting methods or rules, mechanistic enforcement of the law may contravene what we think of a properly functioning democracy. Complete escape from the moral-formal dilemma may not be possible given the existence of judicial discretion, but we should understand how and why choosing one or the other in particular situations may aid liberation or perpetuate injustice.

Reasoning from Injustice: Another Way?

All of this brings us to the possibility that what might be most beneficial in an aging democracy is inculcating an entirely different way of thinking about problems of democratic justice: Not simply as a project of political design or maintenance of social harmony but instead through an immersion in what Judith Shklar called "everyday injustice."[19] As Shklar suggests, this can be a fruitful supplemental method of identifying the causes of complicity in violence and indignity (an obstacle to justice Douglass termed "cold-blooded indifference"[20]), as well as recognizing the distinctive and recurring forms of injustice. The goals would be explicitly reformative and remedial and seek to untangle the cluster of causes, motivations, policies, beliefs, and effects.

While this isn't the place for a full accounting of the skills required to execute this method of imparting civic knowledge, it is possible to identify a few aspects of this alternative approach.[21] First, unlike the democratic law-based approach articulated by Shiffrin, reasoning from injustice does not proceed from the assumption that existing institutions, doctrines, or methods are neutral, stable, or even that they promote justice. Certainly, they are all part of a legal tradition—long-standing ways of doing things—but these methods may or may not still be defensible today. To imbue them with a coherent moral dimension as she does, rather than merely the promise of predictable relations, may be doing too much. For if democracy's flaws have caused injustice, then a substantial number of citizens will reject the law's moral claim and be suspicious of the peculiar "social-moral intuitions" associated with dominant modes of analysis. In that sense, reasoning from injustice fosters a way of seeing democracy and the rule of law not as givens, but as practices that themselves must be constantly challenged, defended, and improved.

Second, reasoning from injustice entails emphasizing the distance between legal ideals and material reality, as well as the gaps in the law that are exploited, and spending quality time in the distance between government and citizens that so troubles Shiffrin. Doing so promotes deeper reflection on the possible causes of persistent failures to achieve a political community's aspirations. Douglass offers us a role model in how to immerse oneself in the empirical conditions of injustice when he invites us to consider the horrifying, historical sweep of Black inequality. He says that "of all the races and varieties of men which have suffered" from race prejudice, "the colored people of this country have endured most." The phenomenon has met them "at the workshop and factory . . . the church, at the hotel at the ballot-box, and worst of all, it meets them in the jury-box." Reflecting on those material deprivations, he says that even after slavery's end, laws are "well calculated to repress his manly ambition, paralyze his energies, and make him a dejected and spiritless man . . . fit to prey upon."[22]

Third, rather than emphasizing legal continuity, the approach prods citizens to pay particularly close attention to empirical inconsistencies, doctrinal discontinuities (including reversal of precedent), and moments of political rupture. Consideration of these imperfections can promote the widest sense of what is possible because it is during these moments that existing methods are questioned and legal creativity is necessary to communal survival rather than perceived as a threat to legal order. But investigation of how a legal phenomenon like ordinary discrimination or an entire social system such as segregation actually operates can yield valuable civic insights. Douglass offers a glimpse of this potential when he invites readers to probe the notion of "prejudice against color," which he says does not exist "in the abstract." When we examine how people have treated others differently on account of race, he argues, we notice "inconsistencies" and "contradictions" that reveal the truth that "most men . . . want to have something under them."[23] In other words, he argues that appeals to racial difference are not about something intrinsic to any human being, but instead about hierarchy, status, and control.

Together, these three aspects of civic learning, grounded in peo-ple's actual experiences in the law, may point us toward a better way of relating to one another and rekindle interest in democratic self-government. There is some risk, of course, that any curriculum that casts a nation's history and tradition in less than an adoring light can generate unproductive feelings of guilt and shut down learning. But the truth is almost always uncomfortable, and the risks of counterproductive effects can be reduced through effec-tive pedagogy—for instance, by carefully choosing tragedies and triumphs across a broad spectrum of experiences. The incidences explored might encompass not just the Chinese migrants chased out of West Coast towns, but also the Irish poor prevented from disembarking ships and accused of being public charges. Not only the creative litigation efforts that led to the dismantling of legal segregation, but also the incredible efforts by activists and politi-cians to enact landmark civil rights statutes. Attention to language and purpose, such as avoiding unnecessarily partisan rhetoric or that which unwittingly reifies one group's experience, can further avoid exacerbating the sense of unbroachable division or the para-lyzing feeling that all of our futures are already written and there's nothing to be gained from participating in democratic life.

But let us finish by returning to where we started. Shiffrin rightly laments the dilute sense of duty and authority encouraged by rights-based models of participation. For most citizens, there is no escape from one another. The only question is whether we are suf-ficiently invested in living together that we are willing to learn what we owe to one another.

NOTES

My thanks to Seana Shiffrin and Brandon Terry for being generous interlocutors. Any mistakes are mine alone.

1 See Adrian Vermeule, *Common Good Constitutionalism* (Cambridge, UK and Medford, MA: Polity, 2022); Patrick Deneen, *Why Liberalism Failed* (New Haven, CT: Yale University Press, 2018).

2 Another recent defense of legal liberalism that emphasizes mutual duties can be found in James E. Fleming and Linda C. McClain, *Ordered Liberty: Rights, Responsibilities, and Virtues* (Cambridge, MA: Harvard Uni-versity Press, 2013).

3 See Michael Sandel, *Liberalism and the Limits of Justice* (Cambridge: Cambridge University Press, 1982).

4 There may be good reasons to favor inclusive terms for political membership, and I mostly agree with them, but there's no denying that the boundaries of community affect the general character and conditions of the polity itself.

5 See Timothy Waters, *Boxing Pandora: Rethinking Borders, States, and Secession* (New Haven, CT: Yale University Press, 2020); Robert L. Tsai, *America's Forgotten Constitutions: Defiant Visions of Power and Community* (Cambridge, MA: Harvard University Press, 2014).

6 This insight might be further elaborated by treating citizenship as (in part) an identity-producing phenomenon, and seeing that the role of citizen is one among many in a portfolio of roles that every individual plays (albeit a very important one), each with its own spheres, responsibilities, and powers (whether legal or cultural).

7 Martha C. Nussbaum, *From Disgust to Humanity: Sexual Orientation and Constitutional Law* (New York: Oxford University Press, 2010).

8 Robert L. Tsai, "Simple Takes on the Supreme Court," *Alabama Journal of Civil Rights and Civil Liberties* 5 (2013): 35–75; Robert L. Tsai, "The Ethics of Melancholy Citizenship," *Oregon Law Review* 89 (2010): 557–580.

9 Frederick Douglass, "Prejudice Against Color," *The North Star*, June 13, 1850, reprinted in John Stauffer and Henry Louis Gates Jr. (eds.), *The Portable Frederick Douglass* (New York: Penguin Classics, 2016), 424.

10 Poetic justice entails an appeal to ordinary or mainstream sources, such as intuitive notions of fairness or religious texts that might stand in tension with the trajectory of secular law, in order to critique the state of legal justice. The move asks what a wrongdoer deserves as just desserts if ordinary constraints on the political imagination and legal force did not obtain.

11 Yasuko I. Takezawa, *Breaking the Silence: Redress and Japanese American Ethnicity* (Ithaca, NY: Cornell University Press, 1995).

12 Seana Valentine Shiffrin, *Democratic Law* (New York: Oxford University Press, 2021), 87–88.

13 In *Practical Equality: Forging Justice in a Divided Nation* (New York: W. W. Norton, 2019), I show how judges (and others) found ways to promote the interests of equality—sometimes doing so indirectly by turning to other principles such as fair play, free speech, or anti-cruelty—when they ran into doctrinal or ideological roadblocks. Grounded in the necessity of collective action and principled compromise, the account falls within the spirit of the "imaginative application of principles" that Shiffrin hopes to inspire.

14 Machiavelli, *Discourses*, Ch. 18.

15 Machiavelli, *Discourses*, Ch. 4.

16 Robert M. Cover, "Violence and the Word," *Yale Law Journal* 95 (1986): 1601–1629; Robert M. Cover, "Nomos and Narrative," *Harvard Law Review* 97 (1983–84): 4–68.

17 Robert M. Cover, *Justice Accused: Antislavery and the Judicial Process* (New Haven, CT: Yale University Press, 1975), 197.

18 Cover, *Justice Accused*, 198–199.

19 Judith Shklar, *The Faces of Injustice* (New Haven, CT: Yale University Press, 1990). For a critique of plan-based definitions of justice, see Amartya Sen, *The Idea of Justice* (Cambridge, MA: Belknap Press, 2009).

20 Frederick Douglass, "Prejudice Against Color," in Stauffer and Gates, *The Portable Frederick Douglass*, 421.

21 Robert L. Tsai, "Reasoning from Injustice," working paper.

22 Douglass, "The Color Line," *North American Review*, June 1881, in Stauffer and Gates, *The Portable Frederick Douglass*, 503.

23 Douglass, "The Color Line," 510–511.

4

CIVIC EDUCATION, STUDENTS' RIGHTS, AND THE SUPREME COURT

JUSTIN DRIVER

Toward the end of every year, in a practice that dates back decades, the Chief Justice of the United States has released a document titled the "Year-End Report on the Federal Judiciary."[1] Despite their New Year's Eve timing, these reports consistently elicit less celebration than somnolence. Standard fare includes the stagnant salaries of Article III judges and how many cases the Justices decided during the term that concluded a few months prior—items painstakingly illustrated with bar graphs and the occasional chart.[2] Even among the closest of Supreme Court watchers, these annual reports seldom garner sustained attention, as they seem deliberately designed to evade notice.[3] More often than not, they realize their modest ambitions. As one journalist who covers the Supreme Court and its intricacies noted with considerable understatement: "The year-end report is usually devoid of anything controversial."[4]

In 2019, however, as the United States descended further into its era of political polarization, Chief Justice John G. Roberts Jr. issued that rarest of items: a year-end report that actually proved momentous. That unusual report explored the judiciary's myriad connections to civic education. Among other intersections, Roberts contended that the American judiciary can be construed as intrinsically promoting awareness of the nation's foundational legal commitments and thereby fostering civic education. "By virtue of their judicial responsibilities, judges are necessarily engaged in civic education," Roberts wrote.[5] "When judges render their judgments through written opinions that explain their reasoning, they advance public understanding of the law."[6] The Supreme Court's iconic decision invalidating school segregation in *Brown v. Board of Education*,[7] Roberts noted, could helpfully be viewed through this prism. Chief Justice Earl Warren saw to it that the *Brown* opinion would be sufficiently concise—running only eleven pages—so that it could be reprinted in newspapers around the nation.[8] *Brown*, Roberts wrote, thus vividly exemplifies "the power of a judicial decision as a teaching tool," as it provided "every citizen [an opportunity to] understand the Court's rationale."[9] But Roberts did not content himself by basking in *Brown*'s reflected glory. Rather, he also delivered a sobering assessment of the nation's disregard for democratic ideals and the attendant decline of civic education. "[W]e have come to take democracy for granted," Roberts lamented, "and civic education has fallen by the wayside."[10]

Since Roberts issued this cri de coeur in 2019, these concerns regarding democracy and civic education have only intensified. Most prominently, of course, the atrocities committed at the US Capitol on January 6, 2021, represented the starkest repudiation of democracy on American soil in decades. That insurrection has been termed "a sputnik moment for an ambitious revival of civics instruction."[11] As divisions over race, gender, and immigration have deepened, controversies involving civic education have become a salient, persistent topic of national controversy over the last few years. In 2019, the *New York Times* released its 1619 Project, which emphasized the nation's deep connections to race-based chattel slavery and the ongoing legacy of that odious institution.[12] In response, President Donald Trump formed the 1776 Commission with an eye toward attacking and displacing the 1619 Project's slavery-based narrative.[13] The ensuing report undertook precisely that mission.[14]

My concern is not to relitigate the merits and demerits of these competing reports. Those debates have already received ample airtime.[15] I do, however, wish to make two observations. First, although the documents were not widely understood in this fashion at the time, both the 1619 Project and the 1776 Report expressly conceived of themselves as tools of civic education. Each document contemplated how schools could implement their animating ideas, and various educators across the nation have in fact done just that.[16] Second, the competing reports, which hotly dispute the nation's true origins, embody the profound polarization that currently afflicts American society.[17] As a nation, our two dominant political tribes appear perilously close to singing in unison: "You say 1619. I say 1776. Let's call the whole thing off."[18] Ronald Dworkin memorably captured the problems of American polarization that were already apparent at the start of the twenty-first century:

> American politics are in an appalling state. We disagree, fiercely, about almost everything. We disagree about terror and security, social justice, religion in politics, who is fit to be a judge, and what democracy is. These are not civil disagreements: each side has no respect for the other. We are no longer partners in self-government; our politics are rather a form of war.[19]

Dworkin offered this evaluation way back in 2006. From today's vantage point, that time resembles nothing less than the halcyon days of American political consensus.[20] In addition to the salient disagreements that Dworkin identified—which have only grown more hostile with the passage of time—Democrats and Republicans have also adopted ferociously conflicting positions on a pandemic.[21]

It sometimes seems that agreeing to disagree (often angrily) is the only thing that Blue America and Red America can agree upon. Yet the nation would be well served by attempting to identify some common ground on the question of civic education. Rather than fighting exclusively about what should *not* be taught in the nation's public schools, it seems far more profitable to expend at least some intellectual energy contemplating approaches to civic education that could plausibly garner widespread support.

Even in our intensely polarized era, it is important to realize that there is broad, bipartisan agreement that the current state of civic education is lacking. In March 2021, Senator Chris Coons, a Democrat from Delaware, and Senator John Cornyn, a Republican from Texas, co-sponsored a bill called the "Civics Secures Democracy Act."[22] That measure would have appropriated roughly $6 billion over the course of six years to foster civic education.[23] Supreme Court Justices from across the ideological spectrum have also joined forces on this cause. Justice Neil Gorsuch and Justice Sonia Sotomayor, who often disagree in high-profile cases, have made joint appearances touting the need to deepen student comprehension of our basic civic structures.[24] On such occasions, Justice Gorsuch has spoken powerfully about how the state of civic education poses a national security crisis, and noted that political and cultural polarization forms an important part of the crisis: "How can the democracy function if we can't talk to one another, and if we can't disagree, kindly, with respect for one another's differences and different points of view?"[25] For her part, Justice Sotomayor has also dedicated significant time to promoting iCivics, an organization founded and formerly chaired by Justice Sandra Day O'Connor, which seeks to capitalize on youngsters' fascination with video games to spark their interest in learning about US government.[26]

Concerns regarding civic education are not the product of an illogical panic but instead are well founded, as the state of civic comprehension in the United States is—in a word—grim. The leading national method for assessing civic education found that less than 25 percent of American students attain proficiency in the subject.[27] Consider only one egregious indicator of students' lack of knowledge, even about a signal event in American history: Fewer than one-third of eighth graders could successfully identify why the Founders adopted the Declaration of Independence.[28] Nor does the situation magically improve when minors reach the age of majority. In 2016, one survey determined that only about one in four Americans could name all three branches of government.[29]

Basic civic understanding is shoddy in many areas—including about the judiciary. The Annenberg Public Policy Center has found in recent years that: nearly one-third of American adults thought that Supreme Court opinions can be appealed; fewer than half of American adults understood that when the Supreme Court issues a decision by a 5–4 margin the majority opinion holds the same formal status as does a unanimous opinion; 23 percent of American adults responded that when the Court issues a 5–4 decision, Congress ultimately resolves the dispute, and an additional 16 percent thought that the lower courts settle the matter.[30] Predictably, adults who took a civic-education course in high school demonstrated a stronger grasp of our constitutional order.[31]

Chief Justice Roberts's year-end report identified several ways that the judiciary is connected to civic education. In addition to judicial opinions, Roberts highlighted—among others—how a New

York program brings students into a federal courthouse to better understand the judicial system, and how an esteemed judge on the US Court of Appeals for the District of Columbia Circuit dedicated time to tutoring students at a local, underprivileged elementary school.[32]

In this essay, I aim to amplify Chief Justice Roberts's call for connecting the judiciary to civic education, but perhaps in a different register and more loudly than he ever envisioned. I seek to promote what I label a "student-centered approach to civic education"—an approach that could find widespread support even in polarized times.[33] Of course, virtually all advocates of civic education in elementary- and secondary-school settings would readily assert that their preferred models center the concerns of students. Exactly no one boasts of *teacher*-centered civic education, or—even more improbably—*principal*-centered civic education. But student-centered civic education differs from many approaches by centering the historic struggles for students' constitutional rights as the very touchstone of civic education.[34] The approach foregrounds the major Supreme Court decisions that have shaped the everyday lives of students across the nation, but also uses these decisions as a springboard for discussing the broader issues, arguments, and student activism that fueled those controversies. It is simultaneously retrospective and prospective; teaching students about the hard-fought constitutional struggles that young people waged yesteryear, and encouraging them to evaluate critically the contours of their rights in the context of today's civic society. A student-centered approach to civic education thus not only frames students as active participants in shaping our constitutional order, but it also positions them well to become engaged, able stewards of our constitutional democracy. I begin by describing the numerous salutary developments that the student-centered approach may offer (including the less obvious second-order effects), then engage with objections to this approach, and close by proposing how advocates might best pursue the urgent task of civic-education reform.

* * *

A chief virtue of a student-centered approach to civic education is that it undertakes comprehending conflicts over political values, and the relationships between the people and their government in a way that is tangibly, palpably connected to the daily lives of adolescents. Many, perhaps even most, high school students view relatively abstract constitutional concepts—like federalism, the separation of powers, executive authority, and the amendment process—as being utterly disconnected from the matters about which they care most.[35] But highlighting constitutional conflicts involving students and the limitations that judicial opinions have placed on school authority hits young people where they spend vast portions of their waking hours. The schoolhouse occupies a concomitantly large share of students' mental energy. Many of the nation's fifty million public school students, like people generally, will find it easier to gain traction on a subject matter if they begin by clearly understanding how the subject matter is relevant to their lives.[36]

The facts of leading cases involving students' constitutional rights will fascinate and captivate students in a visceral fashion that no other civic-education topic can match. Should schools be able to force students who participate in extracurricular activities to provide urine samples for drug testing even if educators have no individualized suspicion of wrongdoing on students' parts?[37] Should schools be able to punish students for not following directions or for talking in class by striking them forcefully with a two-foot-long wooden paddle twenty times?[38] Should schools be able to strip-search students in an effort to locate ibuprofen tablets—an item educators have defined as contraband—even when there is no reason to believe that students have secreted the forbidden pain relievers in their undergarments?[39] Should schools be permitted to ban unauthorized immigrants from obtaining elementary and secondary educations?[40] Should schools be able to suspend a cheerleader from the junior-varsity squad for an entire year who posts a vulgarity on social media—off-campus on a weekend afternoon—to vent her frustration about failing to make varsity?[41] These are but a few of the many scintillating questions presented by actual Supreme Court opinions involving constitutional rights in schools. These questions would engage even the most jaded students enrolled in a civic-education course.

The student-centered approach to civic education also drives home the important lesson that young people have made invaluable contributions to our current constitutional order. Sometimes, young people mistakenly believe that civic affairs are the exclusive domain of adults. But when students today read about teenagers John Tinker and Mary Beth Tinker wearing black armbands to school in the 1960s over the objections of school authorities in Des Moines, Iowa,[42] they can see that citizens' constitutional rights do not simply materialize out of thin air or are always willingly handed over to them by government authorities. Rather, the Tinkers—by daring to protest the Vietnam War on school grounds—sacrificed a tremendous amount and drew scorn from many Iowans to make students' First Amendment rights a reality.[43] Thus, *Tinker v. Des Moines Independent Community School District* drives home the point that young people of prior generations have successfully stood up for constitutional rights and thus played a pivotal role in creating modern civic society.[44] This realization instructs today's students that they, too, have an indispensable role to play in bequeathing a constitutional tradition to subsequent generations.

Another virtue of student-centered civic education is that it offers young Americans an opportunity to gain deeper understanding and respect for long-standing constitutional values at a time when some of those values have come under attack. It is no secret, for example, that many young people today—particularly on the left—harbor grave skepticism about the First Amendment's utility.[45] Free expression, left-leaning critics maintain, is used as either a shield to protect the powerful or a cudgel to bash the powerless. But if students learned at a formative age how young people have successfully harnessed the power of free speech in schools—including not just *Tinker*'s protection of antiwar speech,[46] but other judicial precedents such as one vindicating the ability of civil rights activists in Mississippi to promote racial equality[47]—it would be difficult to maintain that the First Amendment *invariably* oppresses marginalized groups.

The nation's universities have in recent years witnessed numerous, high-profile conflagrations where students have evinced precious little respect for free speech.[48] Commentators on the left and on the right have expressed great alarm that our institutions of higher education—where intellectual exchange on contentious topics is supposed to be prized—sometimes appear to hold free speech in such low regard.[49] Too few of those commentators have noted, alas, that college students may well disdain freedom of expression in no small part because they did not meaningfully encounter the concept in elementary or secondary school. Waiting to cultivate respect for free speech until a student reaches college is, of course, a little late in the day for such a momentous intervention. That process should have been initiated long before students even step foot on campus, something that a student-centered civic education would prioritize.

Student-centered civic education would not have pupils simply learn about judicial decisions involving their constitutional rights in a passive manner. To the contrary, the material lends itself to active debate among the students about the appropriate scope of constitutional rights in school. After students learn the basic contours of, say, free speech in schools, teachers should offer novel factual scenarios in mock hearings that are designed to test the limits of permissible student speech by assigning half of the class to act as lawyers for the student and the other half of the class to act as lawyers for the school board. These mock disputes would thus encourage students to disagree with each others' constitutional views respectfully, and thereby aid our ailing democratic experiment.[50] If students do not begin learning how to disagree with their peers in the relatively safe school context, disagreements in nonschool settings will increasingly escalate into the ad hominem attacks that are already a disconcerting staple of both our politics and our broader culture.[51]

Ideally, in these mock settings, teachers would often assign students to defend a legal position that runs counter to the students' own expressed viewpoints. (Contrary to popular belief, students do not always espouse the "pro-student" position on constitutional controversies in school.) When students advocate a legal position that they do not actually hold, it requires them to contemplate and voice the most compelling arguments on the other side. This exercise of walking in the shoes of one's opponents encourages a measure of empathy for people with whom we might often disagree. This empathic understanding could play some meaningful role in helping to reduce political polarization. It is often difficult to demonize people on the other side of an issue when you have taken their views seriously, and even articulated them.[52]

One theme that students ought to explore in a student-centered civic-education course is how the Supreme Court itself has construed schools as shaping citizens. Some of the most significant opinions assessing students' constitutional rights have expressly emphasized the citizen-formation aspect of the nation's public schools.[53] In *Brown v. Board of Education*, Chief Justice Warren famously contended in 1954: "[E]ducation is perhaps the most important function of state and local governments. . . . It is the very foundation of good citizenship."[54] Eighteen years later, when assessing a Free Exercise Clause objection to a compulsory education law in 1972, the Supreme Court returned to this theme: "[E]ducation is necessary to prepare citizens to participate effectively and intelligently in our open political system if we are to preserve freedom and independence."[55] One decade later, when the Supreme Court invalidated a Texas measure that sought to exclude unauthorized immigrants from public schools, Justice William Brennan's majority opinion noted that excluding young people from education "den[ies] them the ability to live within the structure of our civic institutions."[56] In 2021, Justice Stephen Breyer's opinion for the Court in *Mahanoy Area School District v. B.L.*, a case involving off-campus student speech, noted that public schools themselves have an interest in protecting students' free expression because doing so preserves our democratic society. "America's public schools are the nurseries of democracy," Justice Breyer contended. "Our representative democracy only works if we protect the marketplace of ideas."[57]

The Supreme Court has also repeatedly suggested that it bears a special responsibility for safeguarding constitutional rights in the school context, lest students draw incorrect lessons about citizenship. Justice Robert Jackson stated this point for the Court most powerfully in 1943, when he led the Court's invalidation of a state measure that required students to salute the American flag in *West Virginia State Board of Education v. Barnette*. "That [public schools] are educating the young for citizenship is reason for scrupulous protection of Constitutional freedoms of the individual," Justice Jackson wrote, "if we are not to strangle the free mind at its source and teach youth to discount important principles of our government as mere platitudes."[58] In 1960, the Supreme Court reiterated this idea that the public school is a preeminent site of constitutional interpretation: "The vigilant protection of constitutional freedoms is nowhere more vital than in the community of American schools."[59]

In exploring the Supreme Court's conceptualization of public schools as institutions that form citizens, it is important for students to appreciate that various Justices hold sharply divergent views of what citizenship entails, particularly for young people in school settings. Some Justices have embraced a robust conception of citizenship for students, suggesting that schools ought to permit and foster wide-ranging, spirited debates on the contentious questions of the day. This notion of citizenship suggests that the culture of American schools should resemble the larger clamorous nation of which they are a part. Writing for the Court in *Tinker*, Justice Abe Fortas espoused this robust notion of citizenship:

> Any word spoken, in class, in the lunchroom, or on the campus, that deviates from the views of another person may start an argument or cause a disturbance. But our Constitution says we must take this risk, and our history says that it is this sort of hazardous freedom— this kind of openness—that is the basis of our national strength and of the independence and vigor of Americans who grow up and live in this relatively permissive, often disputatious, society.[60]

Other Supreme Court Justices, in contrast, have offered a thin, even anemic conception of citizenship for students. On this view, schools should not host free-wheeling debates but should instead concentrate on imposing order and discipline on students. This notion of citizenship is what might be termed "Report Card Citizenship," with a nod toward the grade for behavior that some elementary schools use to evaluate students based on their willingness to exhibit deference, follow directions, and play nicely with others. Justice Hugo Black, dissenting in *Tinker*, has advanced the leading articulation of Report Card Citizenship. "School discipline . . . is an integral and important part of training our children to be good citizens—to be better citizens," he contended.[61]

Although Justice Black dissented in *Tinker*, the thin conception of citizenship has seen its stock fluctuate dramatically in Supreme Court opinions during subsequent decades. The Court at times seemed to endorse Report Card Citizenship with enthusiasm during the 1980s. In assessing a school district's ability to punish a high school student for a lewd speech at a school assembly, the Supreme Court emphasized the school's duty to "inculcate the habits and manners of civility" and to "teach by example the shared values of a civilized social order."[62] But the Supreme Court's most recent decision involving student speech rebuked Report Card Citizenship. Justice Breyer's opinion for the Court in *Mahanoy Area School District v. B.L.*, like Justice Fortas's opinion in *Tinker*, made clear that schools cannot act as roving censors who punish students for dissident speech without immeasurably harming our democracy.[63] Pupils enrolled in student-centered civic-education courses should be encouraged to evaluate critically these sharply divergent conceptions of citizenship.

* * *

One subtle, second-order virtue of the student-centered approach to civic education is that the diffusion of knowledge regarding students' constitutional rights would help to prevent schools from committing some of the more egregious violations of those rights in the first instance. A teacher who leads a classroom discussion on *Barnette*,[64] for instance, will be far less likely to suspend students for refusing to salute the American flag. Such conflicts are, alas, distressingly common in American schools even though *Barnette* decisively repudiated mandatory flag salutes eight decades ago.[65]

Teachers of a student-centered civic curriculum would, moreover, not only help to honor constitutional rights within their own classrooms, but they could also become invaluable resources for an entire school. It seems unrealistic in the extreme to believe that busy math and science teachers are going to become intimately familiar with the minutia of the Supreme Court's doctrine governing schools. Yet, when algebra and chemistry teachers confront scenarios potentially touching upon students' constitutional rights, instructors with expertise in the area could provide guidance to their colleagues about constitutional protections. In addition to helping colleagues, these same instructors could serve as valuable sounding boards for school administrators contemplating thorny constitutional questions, as it is often difficult to obtain advice from school-board attorneys on an urgent question in the midst of a hectic school day. Such informal consultations mean that the existence of even one teacher trained in student-centered civic education could well help to increase respect for students' constitutional rights within the community.

While diminishing flagrant constitutional violations would be laudable in its own right, this diminution would also help to tamp down a significant, underappreciated source of political polarization. It seems that the Culture Wars—to borrow a phrase from the 1990s[66]—are increasingly being waged on the terrain of our nation's public schools, and these disputes often involve infringements of students' constitutional rights.[67] Our media outlets routinely highlight instances where school authorities have overstepped their constitutional authority. But our deeply divided media—a product doubtless of our deeply divided nation—do not seize upon and then showcase the same violations. Instead, left-leaning media companies elevate one set of school-based constitutional conflicts with a particular political valence, and right-leaning media companies elevate a different set of constitutional conflicts with a very different political valance. The consumers of these varied, highly clickable reports are left to conclude that the nation's public schools are systemically attacking their most cherished values, thereby intensifying our nation's political polarization.

Consider two recent high-profile constitutional controversies that arose when public schools erroneously censored students' First Amendment rights—the first involving speech associated with liberals and the second involving speech associated with conservatives. In 2021, two Black elementary school students in Ardmore, Oklahoma, wore T-shirts reading: "Black Lives Matter."[68] For this seemingly innocuous action, the students were ejected from their classrooms and forced to sit in an administrative office until the end of the day.[69] One school official justified these disciplinary actions by stating that—in the wake of George Floyd's killing—political statements would no longer be permitted at school.[70] The school district superintendent suggested that he applied this broad policy to statements from across the political spectrum: "I don't want my kids wearing MAGA hats or Trump shirts to school either because it just creates, in this emotionally charged environment, anxiety and issues that I don't want our kids to deal with."[71] After this controversy appeared in the *New York Times*, the school district expressly updated its policy to prohibit clothing "items [displaying] social or political content."[72]

The second scenario arose when a high school senior in Franklinton, Louisiana, decided to have his parking space at school painted over with a portrait of President Trump wearing a bandana and aviator sunglasses, both of which featured images of the American flag.[73] The portrait was part of an official school policy that permitted seniors to decorate their spaces in exchange for a modest fee.[74] Although the policy prohibited designs from including either vulgar language or another student's name, it did not prohibit political statements.[75] Nevertheless, shortly after the portrait of President Trump appeared, school officials painted over the image because they deemed it excessively political.[76] A federal district court judge overrode the school's decision, holding that it plainly violated *Tinker*'s foundational protection for student speech.[77] As one might predict, these events received no mention in the *New York Times*, but were trumpeted by Fox News.[78]

Many other examples of this polarizing phenomenon could easily be adduced. Consider only two more, both arising from high school valedictorian speeches that were delivered at graduation ceremonies in 2021. A valedictorian in Voorhees Township, New Jersey, wished to discuss how his queer identity had shaped his high school experience and to deliver a message of pride regarding his sexual orientation.[79] Another valedictorian in Westland, Michigan, wished to discuss how her Christian identity had provided meaning to her life, and to suggest that faith could be helpful in overcoming the adversity that life sometimes delivers.[80] Both valedictorians encountered sustained efforts from school administrators to squelch their preferred messages, even though the First Amendment—properly understood—affords both students protection.[81] It will come as no surprise that the *New York Times* featured the queer valedictorian's ordeal,[82] and Fox News (quite extensively) featured the Christian valedictorian's ordeal.[83] But neither outlet mentioned the other student's regrettable encounters with high school censors.

These local stories of constitutional conflict reverberate across the nation for two primary reasons. First, they have extremely low barriers to entry and are therefore instantly legible to even the most casual news consumers. Whereas a story about tax policy or the latest armed conflict in the Middle East may be hard to understand without considerable knowledge on those topics, virtually everyone in the United States attended school for some time and many of us at some point encountered a school official we deemed overzealous. These stories, moreover, involve young people, over-reaching government authority, and the future of our nation—and those topics often prove irresistible. Second, and related, these stories tend to elicit strong normative assessments from readers. These stories of constitutional conflict in schools are hardly designed to instill a sense of complexity or nuance, but rather to spark a deep emotional reaction. Given that readers carefully curate their own, personalized media landscapes and that those landscapes reinforce their ideological inclinations,[84] it should not be surprising that the dominant emotions generated are anger and outrage.[85]

* * *

Some readers may well believe that the uncommonly potent combination of qualities in these stories of constitutional conflict suggests that society should figure out a way to regulate or even eliminate their distribution. If these articles inflame people and further polarize our deeply fractious nation, according to this theory, then we should cut off this producer of civic discord at the source. While such a view would have been fringe until quite recently, declining reverence for First Amendment principles[86] and widespread skepticism about social media[87] render this impulse increasingly cognizable. For my own part, though, I vehemently reject any slide toward censorship that would entertain such proposals. Rather than concentrating on the distributional problem, we should instead concentrate on the manufacturing problem. We should, that is, dedicate ourselves to preventing public schools from systematically trampling students' constitutional rights in the first instance. If constitutional violations of students' rights were not so flagrant and so prevalent, there would be no need for controlling their distribution. Adopting a student-centered approach to civic education would treat the underlying disease, rather than simply suppress the distressing symptoms.

Other readers may lodge an even more fundamental objection, one that questions student-based civic education altogether. On this view, students ought not learn about their own constitutional rights because they should not in fact be understood to possess such rights. The reason that such incredibly divisive newspaper articles exist, this objection runs, is because the federal courts have repeatedly erred by determining that schools can actually infringe the constitutional rights of the pupils whom they are charged with educating.[88] Educators, these critics would maintain, should be viewed as acting in loco parentis, meaning that they stand in the shoes of parents when students are in the school environment.[89] Accordingly, just as parents do not, say, violate the Fourth Amendment when they search their teenagers' rooms for narcotics, neither would educators be viewed as even potentially violating the constitutional rights of students. Supreme Court Justices have, on occasion, expressed some enthusiasm for versions of this in loco parentis idea.[90]

Extinguishing students' constitutional rights would, in my view, be profoundly misguided. As a preliminary matter, it is important to recognize that the Constitution now recognizes students' rights in a vast array of significant areas—including race, religion, immigration, speech, liberty, privacy, and criminal procedure.[91] Declaring public schools to be Constitution-free zones would thus require a radical assault on our American constitutional traditions. Some of our nation's most cherished constitutional opinions arose from the public school context,[92] and it will simply no longer suffice to assert blithely that judges are not teachers and that they therefore lack competence to identify constitutional violations in educational arenas.

Equally important, though, a judicial retreat from schools would send students a dangerous message about the limitless reach of government power. The sites of the nation's public schools are the first locations where most Americans have consistent exposure to any governmental entity. Those early, implicit lessons in civic affairs doubtless prove formative. Justice John Paul Stevens captured this idea astutely in a concurring opinion in 1985. "The schoolroom is the first opportunity most citizens have to experience the power of government," Stevens wrote. "Through it passes every citizen and public official, from schoolteachers to policemen and prison guards. The values they learn there, they take with them in life."[93] It would be surpassingly odd if a nation that prides itself on liberty permitted its young people to spend a large portion of their waking hours in a setting where they enjoyed no constitutional protections whatsoever. Ensuring that schools honor students' constitutional rights thus constitutes an invaluable civic lesson unto itself. Justice

Brennan conveyed this point more than four decades ago: "Schools cannot expect their students to learn the lessons of good citizenship when the school authorities themselves disregard the fundamental principles underpinning our constitutional freedoms."[94]

Still other readers may object to student-centered civic education on the ground that it neglects what should be the core mission. If the ultimate goal is to prepare students to engage responsibly in civic society for the long haul, this argument runs, it is foolish for civic education to focus on school rather than on the various spheres that they will soon occupy as adults.

Although this objection may initially seem plausible, perhaps even devastating, numerous difficulties undermine the critique. It overlooks the fact that there is often no sharp dividing line between the constitutional rights of minors, on the one hand, and the constitutional rights of adults, on the other. Instead, minors typically enjoy one set of constitutional rights in school, and then they enjoy what is sometimes misapprehended as the "adult set" of rights outside of school.[95] When students are in the public park after school, for example, they have traditionally been understood as enjoying robust First Amendment rights that bear a strong resemblance to adults' free speech rights. Extending this point, it is important to realize that a palpable relationship links the constitutional rights of students and the constitutional rights that protect people—minors and adults alike—in nonschool settings. In many areas of the law, students' rights can be viewed as diluted, "junior varsity" versions of the constitutional rights that exist beyond the schoolhouse gate.[96] For instance, although the Fourth Amendment prohibition on unreasonable searches and seizures typically requires "probable cause," the school context requires only the less demanding "reasonable suspicion" standard.[97] Learning about students' constitutional rights thus can be an effective bridge to learning about constitutional rights in nonschool settings.

More broadly, as noted above, student-centered civic education's effort to foreground opinions involving the constitutional rights of students does not mean that those opinions are the *only* content that would be covered in such a curriculum. To the contrary, the student-centered approach should ideally serve as a foundation from which to explore some of the more abstract concepts that form an important part of any comprehensive civic education.

Contemplate a few examples that illuminate how cases involving students' constitutional rights can lay the groundwork for examining adjacent concepts. Classroom discussion of *Barnette*'s prohibition on compulsory flag salutes in school tees up broader analysis of the government's ability to instill patriotism and to prohibit speech that is regarded as antipatriotic.[98] Those discussions logically lead to contemplating both state and federal legislative efforts to prohibit burning the American flag, and the two Supreme Court decisions that have invalidated such efforts.[99] Those decisions in turn present opportunities to teach students about federalism, separation of powers, congressional authority, and executive authority. Similarly, a classroom discussion about *Hazelwood School District v. Kuhlmeier*—which held that educators can typically regulate articles appearing in school newspapers without violating the First Amendment[100]—invites a larger discussion about the media's central role in maintaining democracy. Finally, analyzing *San Antonio Independent School District v. Rodriguez*—which refused to invalidate dramatically unequal school-financing schemes[101]—provides students with a valuable opportunity for reflecting upon how well a nation that extols providing opportunity to all lives up to that lofty ideal.

* * *

How should proponents of improving and redirecting civic education seek to achieve their goals? One possible answer—perhaps to be anticipated coming from a law professor—is through litigation. Pursuit of this potential avenue of reform is not merely a possibility, but a reality. Indeed, Professor Michael Rebell of Columbia University filed a high-profile federal lawsuit in Rhode Island a few years ago contending that the state's approach to civic education was so wanting that it violated students' constitutional rights.[102] This lawsuit asserted that by failing to provide pupils with the basic civic knowledge that they need to participate effectively in American society—including serving on juries, casting votes for elected officials, and exercising their First Amendment rights—Rhode Island does not provide even a minimally adequate education.[103] While the Supreme Court in *Rodriguez* in 1973 did not recognize that the Constitution protects a fundamental right to education,[104] the opinion did not completely foreclose the possibility that an education could be so woeful, so inadequate as to trigger a constitutional violation.[105] Rebell's lawsuit marshaled some disturbing realities in Rhode Island in an effort to capitalize upon this question left open by *Rodriguez*. For instance, the lead plaintiff in Rebell's lawsuit—Aleita Cook— never took a course that explored civic society or government structure during her four years in a Providence high school.[106]

In *A.C. v. Raimondo*, District Court Judge William Smith issued an opinion in 2020 rejecting the claim that Rhode Island's approach to civic education violated the Constitution.[107] Judge Smith, whom President George W. Bush nominated to the bench, reasoned that the Supreme Court's binding precedents prevented him from granting the relief that the plaintiffs sought.[108] He did, however, go to elaborate lengths to decry the sorry state of civic education and to sound alarms regarding the ominous threat it poses to American society. Observing that he was writing not long after President Trump floated the idea of postponing the upcoming 2020 presidential election,[109] Judge Smith adopted a searing, even apocalyptic tone, one highly uncommon in judicial opinions:

> This case . . . represent[s] . . . a cry for help from a generation of young people who are destined to inherit a country which we— the generation currently in charge—are not stewarding well. What these young people seem to recognize is that American democracy is in peril. Its survival, and their ability to reap the benefit of living in a country with robust freedoms and rights . . . is something that citizens must cherish, protect, and constantly work for. We would do well to pay attention to their plea.[110]

Judge Smith repeatedly construed the baleful state of civic education as posing nothing less than an existential danger to the nation: "This is what it all comes down to: we may choose to survive as a country by . . . educating our children on civics, the rule of law, and what it really means to be an American, and what America means. Or, we may ignore these things at our and their peril."[111] Judge Smith concluded his opinion by "commend[ing the plaintiffs] for bringing this case" because it "highlights a deep flaw in our national education priorities and policies," and by expressing his hope that "others who have the power to address this need will respond appropriately."[112]

I heartily applaud the creativity of Rebell's lawsuit, aiming as it does to forge a coalition of liberal and conservative jurists who are united in harboring deep concerns about the nation's deficiencies in providing civic education. Trying to locate common terrain in this highly contested area is, as I have suggested, a worthy project.[113] I also endorse Rebell's animating belief that litigation and the resulting judicial opinions have, at times, dramatically improved American society—particularly in the school context. In *Flunking Democracy*, where Rebell outlines the legal theories pursued in *A.C. v. Raimondo*, he contends: "Judicial declarations of rights and responsibilities and court orders can inspire and motivate state policy makers and educators to prepare their students to confront and surmount the serious challenges to democratic functioning that our students—and all Americans—face today."[114] This view of judicial opinions' potency, once prevalent, is now deeply unfashionable within the elite ranks of legal academia.[115] But it is a view that I nonetheless support.[116] I would add to Rebell's account, moreover, that even unsuccessful lawsuits can sometimes act to galvanize and mobilize support for a cause. Even when litigation loses in the courthouse, the underlying claim sometimes ultimately prevails in the statehouse.[117] Indeed, Judge Smith's bracing opinion in *A.C. v. Raimondo* is quite self-consciously designed to produce civic-education reform—even if he believes it is a nonjudicial entity that should grant relief.

Despite being based at a law school, I have grave reservations about relying primarily upon litigation to reform civic education. Rebell has stated that his largest ambition is that he "want[s] the federal courts, and ultimately the US Supreme Court, to declare there is a right to a basic quantity of education to prepare kids for capable citizenship."[118] Given the conservative composition of today's Supreme Court,[119] though, I can see no plausible scenario where that institution would grant Rebell's constitutional wish. The six Republican-appointed Justices on the current Court have demonstrated little to no appetite for interpreting the Constitution in a manner that would meaningfully reconstrue *Rodriguez*'s language involving a right to education.[120] Unlike some of my fellow liberals, I do not believe that it is altogether impossible for left-leaning Justices to identify areas of overlap with the Court's conservatives in the field of education law.[121] To the contrary, I have contended that liberals could find common cause with the libertarian-inflected vision of constitutional law that Republican-appointed Justices have occasionally endorsed to deliver significant victories involving students' constitutional rights.[122] That claim bore at least some fruit in 2021 when the Supreme Court declared that students typically enjoy more robust free speech protections when they are off campus rather than on campus.[123]

Nevertheless, even I recognize that it is one thing for the current Court to recognize students' free speech rights, and it is quite another to ask them to become involved in policing what constitutes the minimum permissible curricular offerings that a state must provide for civic education. The former can be viewed as falling into line with conservatives' general approach to constitutional interpretation (a receptivity to First Amendment claims that liberals sometimes view as excessive);[124] the latter would require them to expand notions of "substantive due process" (a bête noire in conservative constitutional thought for decades).[125]

A more promising approach to achieving widespread reform along the lines that I have sketched here would be to form a presidential commission on civic education. I realize that many readers may well almost reflexively assert that the road to hell—or, dread word, irrelevance—is paved with presidential commissions.[126] Sometimes such criticisms are doubtless deserved. But it is also essential to appreciate that at least occasionally presidential commissions and their ilk can serve an important signaling function. In the realm of education, for example, *A Nation at Risk* served as a significant focal point for reformers throughout much of the 1980s.[127]

Many private, public, and philanthropic organizations have dedicated attention to examining civic education over the years.[128] These organizations, though, pursue their various projects in something that too often resembles intellectual silos. While this centrifugal approach can possess some real value, we need—especially in these most polarized times—to find a way to come together by harnessing the centripetal energy. A presidential commission examining civic education could provide an excellent occasion for such a gathering, enabling communities to better understand which approaches work well and which do not. A commission that embraces student-centered civic education should include model lesson plans in an appendix. Such plans would distill relevant

Supreme Court opinions into portions that are easily digestible for students, offer hypothetical scenarios involving students that are designed to test the limits of those Supreme Court opinions, and offer concrete advice to teachers on how they might get students to engage with those topics. It is a maxim among teachers that they should "beg, borrow, and steal" from lesson plans that work.[129] The commission's appendix would ideally serve as one-stop shopping for teachers focusing on civic education. Of course, the commission would in no sense aim to mandate that public schools adopt a particular approach to civic education. Instead, building on the abundant existing resources in this domain, the commission would devise a model that teachers and local school districts would be welcome to adopt and to adapt.[130] The hope is that many school districts and teachers, from very different parts of the country, would feel comfortable implementing the framework because it would focus upon students learning the current contours of students' constitutional rights, and then encouraging them to actively, critically evaluate the content of those rights.

Forming a commission on civic education would also seem to be a sound political idea for President Joseph Biden. In one of his first moves after claiming the Oval Office in January 2021, President Biden swiftly rescinded the 1776 Commission Report.[131] Professor Michael Kazin, a sophisticated, insightful historian, argued in the *New York Times*: "Now that the 1776 Commission is deprived of federal authority, its influence will wane more quickly than that of the president who established it."[132] But Kazin's statement, alas, seems tantamount to wishful thinking about the supposedly vanishing influence of both President Trump and his 1776 Commission. Just as President Trump continues to cast a long shadow over the American political scene,[133] the contents of the 1776 Commission's Report can easily be accessed by anyone with a working internet connection.[134] Closing our eyes will not somehow magically make the 1776 Report disappear. Instead, President Biden should assemble a civically minded group from a range of ideological perspectives to offer an affirmative vision of civic education—one that should, in my view, highlight the struggle for students' constitutional rights. If President Biden seeks to dislodge the 1776 Report from our intellectual landscape, he must supply his own conception of civic education, and he should explicitly frame it in Justice

Gorsuch's terms of promoting a vital national security interest.[135] We too often construe national security threats as arising only from foreign lands, but our disastrous state of civic education presents a paradigmatic instance of a domestic national security crisis.

Prominent Republicans have not shied away from discussing civic education. In May 2020, Steve Bannon, the former advisor to President Trump, offered a remarkable statement about future political struggles: "The path to save the nation is very simple— it's going to go through the school boards."[136] In the aftermath of the 2020 election, it seems that some right-wing segments of the Republican Party have set out to implement what might be termed the "Bannon Playbook" by focusing on educational issues and getting elected to school boards. The most prominent tactic in this political strategy, of course, has been to transform and distort Critical Race Theory into an intellectual boogieman.[137] Prominent figures in the Democratic Party have largely remained silent on these high-profile cultural questions. But it is incumbent upon Democrats, I believe, to provide their own notions of civic education. As the old adage runs, "If you don't define yourself, someone else will do it for you."[138]

President Biden has consistently emphasized his desire to locate common ground with Republicans when possible—without, of course, sacrificing his core principles. Focusing on the content of students' constitutional rights as articulated by the Supreme Court—a struggle that dates back to the first half of the twentieth century—would enable Biden's commission to minimize some of the polarizing disputes that have proved insoluble during recent debates. Many Americans understand the profound need to improve missing, limited, or ineffective civic education as a way of bolstering our nation's foundational commitments. In 2018, for instance, one national survey found that the most popular approach to fortifying American democracy was a policy aimed at "ensur[ing] that schools make civic education a bigger part of the curriculum."[139] To underscore that the commission is truly dedicated to locating commonality on civic education for Americans of different political stripes, President Biden should make sure to tap high-profile people associated with the Republican Party to serve. Indeed, he could even consider selecting Chief Justice Roberts to chair, or co-chair, the civic-education commission.[140] In the event that the Chief Justice should resist efforts to conscript him, President Biden could nonetheless identify Roberts's year-end report from 2019 as an important inspiration for the group and even title the commission after a passage that Roberts wrote. Near the very end of his 2019 year-end report, Chief Justice John Roberts stated: "Civic education, like all education, is a continuing enterprise and conversation."[141] Biden's Presidential Commission on the Civic Enterprise has a nice ring to it, suggesting that civic education is a collaborative, difficult undertaking that demands considerable effort.[142]

The ideas that I have sketched here are sure to generate disagreement in certain quarters. Some readers may contend, as I suggested above, that "students' constitutional rights" is simply a contradiction in terms. Other readers may object that President Biden ought not tread—however carefully—on ground that quintessentially belongs to states and localities, not the federal government. Still other readers may find the student-centered civic-education approach to lavish far too much attention on judges, courts, and rights at the expense of material that they would deem more central. For my own part, I welcome such disagreements—and many others besides—because their existence would indicate that civic education is being actively debated in venues where such debates are all too rare. On this score, I cast my lot with Chief Justice Roberts. I have, to be sure, vehemently disagreed with plenty of Chief Justice Roberts's opinions over the years.[143] But I wholeheartedly endorse his conclusion that we must continue the civic-education conversation, as our nation's very vitality depends upon it.

* * *

Before closing, I should note that my interest in promoting the student-centered model of civic education is not purely intellectual and theoretical. Rather, it is inescapably informed by two significant sets of real-world experiences that occurred in my life, separated by more than two decades. Upon graduating from college in 1997, long before I ever dreamed of becoming a law professor, I enrolled in a one-year teacher-certification program at Duke University. As part of that program, I had the privilege of teaching a civic-education class to ninth graders at a public school in

Durham, North Carolina. I recall witnessing the students—some of whom had seemed largely uninterested in analyzing the differences among the three branches of government a few weeks earlier—come alive and engage deeply when we turned our attention to a unit on *Tinker*.[144] Perhaps the ninth graders responded so enthusiastically because they somehow sensed much better than I did at that time that my professional path would inexorably lead me to a career in legal academia, with a special focus on students' constitutional rights. On this account, I unknowingly did an effective job (or less ineffective than usual, anyway) of communicating the importance of judicial opinions involving education, and the students may have responded to my abundant energy. But I do not believe that is the case, for that view accords ninth graders much stronger powers of perception and responsiveness to their instructors' enthusiasms than I am conformable granting. Instead, I believe that the students engaged with *Tinker* deeply because they viewed themselves—at long last—as having some skin in the game. They viewed themselves, that is, as possessing genuine expertise about the regulation of students in schools. While it would perhaps be ideal if students immediately viewed themselves as having a personal stake in the separation of powers, it seems far more pedagogically profitable to meet students where they are at first, and then build outward from there.[145]

The second set of real-world experiences began in 2019, after I joined the faculty at Yale Law School. I have the great honor of serving as the faculty supervisor for a long-standing program that places law school students in New Haven's public schools and permits them to teach a student-centered civic-education course. The program is, in my view, admirable for many reasons, not least because it helps in some small, but meaningful way to bridge the staggeringly wide chasm that all too often separates elite, cloistered Yale from gritty, under-resourced New Haven. My role in the program is admittedly quite modest. The redoubtable, committed Yale Law students who participate in the program do virtually all of the work, including preparing their students for a city-wide oral-argument competition that occurs on Yale's campus every spring. I do occasionally sit in on a class, and I invariably find it an inspiring, rewarding experience. During my first year at Yale, I remember driving early one morning across town to a New Haven public school—one with a virtually all Black and Latino student population, a majority of whom are eligible for free lunch. After passing through the school's metal detectors, I managed to find my way to the correct classroom, where I witnessed students diligently preparing for their upcoming oral argument. The New Haven public school students sounded very much like young lawyers, using shorthand for case names to claim that the Supreme Court's precedents either required (or foreclosed) finding that a hypothetical principal violated a hypothetical student's First Amendment rights. These students plainly viewed themselves as the subjects of law, not the objects of law, and the class seemed to leave them feeling legally and civically empowered.[146] As the students began filing out after the invigorating class, I overheard one young Black woman say quietly to a classmate, "I want to be a judge when I grow up." It is my fervent hope that expanding the student-centered model will inspire young people around the country to endorse similar civically minded ambitions.

NOTES

1 Chief Justice Warren E. Burger appears to have inaugurated this tradition in 1970, though he used a slightly different title for the documents. See Chief Justice Burger, "The State of the Judiciary—1970," *American Bar Association Journal* 56, no. 10 (1970). Chief Justice William H. Rehnquist and Chief Justice John G. Roberts Jr. have continued the custom. See "Chief Justice's Year-End Reports on the Federal Judiciary," Supreme Court of the United States, accessed October 20, 2021, www.supremecourt.gov.

2 See, e.g., Chief Justice John G. Roberts Jr., "2006 Year-End Report on the Federal Judiciary," Supreme Court of the United States, January 1, 2007, www.supremecourt.gov.

3 See, e.g., Robert Barnes, "Roberts Praises District Judges in Year-End Report," *Washington Post*, January 1, 2018, A2 ("Chief Justice John G. Roberts Jr. continued to steer well clear of controversy in his year-end report issued Saturday.").

4 Mark Walsh, "Chief Justice Warns That 'Civic Education Has Fallen by the Wayside,'" *Education Week*, December 31, 2019, www.edweek.org.

5 Chief Justice John G. Roberts Jr., "2019 Year-End Report on the Federal Judiciary," 2, Supreme Court of the United States, December 31, 2019, www.supremecourt.gov.

6 Roberts, "2019 Year-End Report," 2.

7 347 U.S. 543 (1954).

8 Roberts, "2019 Year-End Report," 2.

9 Roberts, "2019 Year-End Report," 2.

10 Roberts, "2019 Year-End Report," 2.

11 Andrea Gabor, "Democracy Needs to Be Taught in School," *Bloomberg Opinion,* January 14, 2021, www.bloomberg.com.

12 "The 1619 Project," *New York Times Magazine,* August 14, 2019, www.nytimes.com.

13 See Nicole Gaudiano, "Trump Creates 1776 Commission to Promote 'Patriotic Education,'" *Politico,* November 2, 2020, www.politico.com.

14 See Michael Crowley and Jennifer Schuessler, "In Report, White House Tries to Revise U.S. History," *New York Times,* January 20, 2021, A16. The 1776 Report stated: "By turning to bitterness and judgment, distorted histories of those like Howard Zinn or the journalists behind the '1619 Project' have prevented their students from learning to think inductively with a rich repository of cultural, historical, and literary referents." The President's Advisory 1776 Commission, *The 1776 Report* (Washington, DC: The White House, 2021), 36.

15 See, e.g., Michael Kazin, "The 1776 Follies," *New York Times,* February 1, 2021, www.nytimes.com.

16 The *New York Times* 1619 Project devised a curriculum. Leslie M. Harris, "I Helped Fact-Check the 1619 Project. The *Times* Ignored Me," *Politico,* March 6, 2020, www.politico.com ("The *Times* [as part of the 1619 Project] produced not just a magazine, but podcasts, a newspaper section, and even a curriculum designed to inject a new version of American history into schools."). Many schools across the country have implemented aspects of the 1619 curriculum. See, e.g., Chantal Da Silva, "U.S. Schools Have Openly Taught the 1619 Project for Months," *Newsweek,* September 7, 2020, www.newsweek.com. President Trump stated that the goal of the 1776 Commission was to "restore patriotic education to our schools." President Donald J. Trump, "Remarks by President Trump at the White House Conference on American History" (speech, Washington, DC, September 17, 2020), Trump White House, https://trumpwhitehouse.archives.gov. Some schools have also adopted the 1776 curriculum. See, e.g., Julie Carr, "Dr. Matthew Spalding of Hillsdale College Talks 1776 Commission Curriculum and New Resources for K12 Parents," *Tennessee Star,* September 21, 2021, https://tennesseestar.com; see also Rob Way and Jared Kofsky, "SC Lawmakers May Use Trump's 1776 Report to Shape US History Curriculum," *WMBF News,* March 31, 2021, www.wmbfnews.com.

17 See generally Ezra Klein, *Why We're Polarized* (New York: Avid Reader Press, 2020).

18 The reference here, of course, is to the classic song: "Let's Call the Whole Thing Off." Fred Astaire with Johnny Green and His Orchestra, "Let's Call the Whole Thing Off," track 1 on *Let's Call the Whole Thing Off*, Brunswick Records, March 3, 1937.

19 Ronald Dworkin, *Is Democracy Possible Here? Principles for a New Political Debate* (Princeton, NJ: Princeton University Press, 2006), 1, quoted in Michael A. Rebell, *Flunking Democracy: Schools, Courts, and Civic Participation* (Chicago: University of Chicago Press, 2018), 2.

20 I should note, though, that I am highly skeptical that the term "consensus" accurately captures the complex dynamics that existed in American society during the 2000s, the 1950s, or any other decade. Conflict, rather than consensus, has always more accurately characterized American society, in my view. See Justin Driver, "The Consensus Constitution," *Texas Law Review* 89, no. 4 (2011).

21 See, e.g., John Kerr et al., "Political Polarization on COVID-19 Pandemic Response in the United States," *Personality and Individual Differences* 179 (September 2021), https://doi.org/10.1016/j.paid.2021.110892.

22 Senator Chris Coons and Senator John Cornyn, "The Civics Secures Democracy Act," Chris Coons, March 11, 2021, www.coons.senate.gov.

23 Coons and Cornyn, "The Civics Secures Democracy Act." The need for an increased federal monetary commitment to civic education seems undeniable. See Danielle Allen and Paul Carrese, "Opinion: Our Democracy Is Ailing. Civics Education Has to Be Part of the Cure," *Washington Post*, March 2, 2021, www.washingtonpost.com (noting that the nation spends about $50 per year educating each student in science, technology, engineering, and math, but only 5 cents per year educating each student in civic education).

24 John Fritze, "Three Supreme Court Justices Tackle U.S. Partisan Divisions in Public Remarks," *USA Today*, April 14, 2021, www.usatoday.com.

25 Fritze, "Three Supreme Court Justices."

26 See "Justice Sonia Sotomayor Sits Down with Soledad O'Brien to Talk Civic Education," *iCivics*, January 8, 2019, www.icivics.org. If my eighth-grade daughter, Claire, is a reliable indicator, iCivics has executed its mission with aplomb.

27 See, e.g., "NAEP Report Card: Civics," Nation's Report Card, accessed September 25, 2021, www.nationsreportcard.gov (noting that less than 25 percent of eighth graders demonstrated proficiency in the 2018 National Assessment of Educational Progress).

28 Rebell, *Flunking Democracy*, 18.

29 See Sarah Shapiro and Catherine Brown, "The State of Civics Education," Center for American Progress, February 21, 2018, www.americanprogress.org, citing "Americans' Knowledge of the Branches of Govern-

ment Is Declining," Annenberg Policy Center, September 13, 2016, www.annenbergpublicpolicycenter.org.

30 Kathleen Hall Jamieson, "The Challenges Facing Civic Education," *Dædalus* 142, no. 2 (Spring 2013): 74, https://doi.org/10.1162/DAED_a_00204, citing Kathleen Hall Jamieson and Bruce Hardy, "Will Public Ignorance and Partisan Election of Judges Undermine Public Trust in the Judiciary?," *Dædalus* 137, no. 4 (Fall 2008); Kathleen Hall Jamieson and Michael Hennessy, "Public Understanding of and Support for the Courts," *Georgetown Law Journal* 95, no. 4 (2007): 899–902.

31 Hall Jamieson, "The Challenges Facing Civic Education," 75.

32 Roberts, "2019 Year-End Report," 3. Judge Robert Katzmann initiated the New York program. See "About Us," *Justice for All*, accessed September 29, 2021, https://justiceforall.ca2.uscourts.gov. Then-Judge Merrick Garland tutored students at J.O. Wilson Elementary in Washington, DC, for decades. See Perry Stein, "Supreme Court Nominee Merrick Garland Has Tutored These D.C. Schoolkids for Years," *Washington Post*, March 19, 2016, www.washingtonpost.com.

33 This term has recently been used to refer to an approach where students engaging in civic-education activities receive minimal instruction from their teachers. See, e.g., Julia Marin Hellwege, "Left to Their Own Devices: A Student-Centered Approach to Civic Engagement," *Journal of Political Science Education* 15, no. 4 (2019), https://doi.org/10.1080/15512169.2018.1500917. But I have in mind a quite distinct concept. My version is "student-centered" not because students are primarily guiding their own educations, but because the student experience is centered—literally—in the civic-education curriculum itself.

34 See Elizabeth Beaumont, *The Civic Constitution: Civic Visions and Struggles in the Path Toward Constitutional Democracy* (New York: Oxford University Press, 2014), xvi ("[T]aking the Constitution seriously requires taking citizens' disputes over its essential commitments more seriously.").

35 See also Sylvia Rousseau and Scott Warren, "Civic Participation Begins in Schools," *Stanford Social Innovation Review*, March 20, 2018, https://ssir.org (noting that students tend to "discount democracy" because they perceive it to be "an abstract and ineffective concept").

36 See, e.g., Jeffrey R. Albrecht and Stuart A. Karabenick, "Relevance for Learning and Motivation in Education," *Journal of Experimental Education* 86, no. 1 (2018): 3, https://doi.org/10.1080/00220973.2017.1380593 ("Over the past few decades, the idea that education should be made relevant to students has been studied and endorsed by motivation researchers in education and psychology."); Margot Belet, "The Importance of Relevance to Student Lives: The Impact of Content and Media in Introduction to Sociology," *Teaching Sociology* 46, no. 3 (2017): 208, https://

doi.org/10.1177/0092055X17730113 (finding that students' "perceptions of . . . [a] course as relevant [is] associated with . . . course satisfaction and achievement").

37 See Bd. of Educ. v. Earls, 536 U.S. 822, 826 (2002).

38 See Ingraham v. Wright, 430 U.S. 651, 653–57 (1977).

39 See Safford Unified Sch. Dist. No. 1 v. Redding, 557 U.S. 364, 368–69 (2009).

40 See Plyler v. Doe, 457 U.S. 202, 205 (1982).

41 See Mahanoy Area Sch. Dist. v. B.L., 141 S. Ct. 2038, 2043 (2021).

42 Tinker v. Des Moines Indep. Cmty. Sch. Dist., 393 U.S. 503, 504 (1969).

43 For a brief overview of the Tinkers' tribulations, see Justin Driver, *The Schoolhouse Gate: Public Education, the Supreme Court, and the Battle for the American Mind* (New York: Vintage Books, 2018), 85–86.

44 See *Tinker*, 393 U.S. at 504–14.

45 Jonathan Zimmerman and Signe Wilkinson, *Free Speech: And Why You Should Give a Damn* (Buffalo, NY: New Idea Press, 2021), x (noting that younger Americans disproportionately agree that the First Amendment "goes too far" in protecting speech); David Cole, "Why We Must Still Defend Free Speech," *New York Review*, September 28, 2017, https://nybooks.com (noting and critiquing the diminished youth support for First Amendment protections).

46 *Tinker*, 393 U.S. at 504–14.

47 Burnside v. Byars, 363 F.2d 744, 748–49 (5th Cir. 1966).

48 See, e.g., Editorial, "Smothering Speech at Middlebury," *New York Times*, March 7, 2017, A26; Alina Tugend, "Challenging Free Speech," *New York Times*, June 6, 2018, L4.

49 See, e.g., Erwin Chemerinsky and Howard Gillman, *Free Speech on Campus* (New Haven, CT: Yale University Press, 2017); Sigal L. Ben-Porath, *Free Speech on Campus* (Philadelphia: University of Pennsylvania Press, 2017); George F. Will, "The Closed American Mind," *Washington Post*, December 2, 2012, A27.

50 For more on the importance of actively teaching democratic participation and debate in the classroom, see generally Amy Gutmann, *Democratic Education* (Princeton, NJ: Princeton University Press, 1987); Diana E. Hess and Paula McAvoy, *The Political Classroom: Evidence and Ethics in Democratic Education* (New York: Taylor & Francis, 2015); and Jonathan Zimmerman and Emily Robertson, *The Case for Contention: Teaching Controversial Issues in American Schools* (Chicago: University of Chicago Press, 2017). The student-centered model of civic education would thus in effect be an exercise in "deliberative democracy," which suggests that in a diverse democratic society it is essential for everyone to have reasoned discussions

with people whose commitments differ from their own. See Gutmann, *Democratic Education*, 51: "Children must learn not just to behave in accordance with authority but to think critically about authority if they are to live up to the democratic ideal of sharing political sovereignty as citizens."

51 See, e.g., Kevin Quealy, "The Complete List of Trump's Twitter Insults (2015–2021)," *New York Times*, January 19, 2021, www.nytimes.com.

52 See, e.g., Lee De-Wit et al., "What Are the Solutions to Political Polarization?," *Greater Good Magazine*, July 2, 2019, https://greatergood.berkeley.edu (endorsing "perspective taking" as a solution to polarization).

53 Many distinguished legal scholars have incisively probed the relationship between the Supreme Court's decisions and civic education. See, e.g., Anne C. Dailey, "Developing Citizens," *Iowa Law Review* 91, no. 2 (2006); Helen J. Knowles, "The Supreme Court as Civic Educator: Free Speech According to Justice Kennedy," *First Amendment Law Review* 6, no. 2 (2008); Betsy Levin, "Educating Youth for Citizenship: The Conflict Between Authority and Individual Rights in the Public School," *Yale Law Journal* 95, no. 8 (1986).

54 347 U.S. 483, 493 (1954).

55 Wisconsin v. Yoder, 406 U.S. 205, 221 (1972); see also Prince v. Massachusetts, 321 U.S. 158, 168 (1944) ("A democratic society rests, for its continuance, upon the healthy, well-rounded growth of young people into full maturity as citizens, with all that implies.").

56 Plyler v. Doe, 457 U.S. 202, 223 (1982).

57 141 S. Ct. 2038, 2046 (2021) (internal quotation marks omitted).

58 319 U.S. 624, 637 (1943).

59 Shelton v. Tucker, 364 U.S. 479, 487 (1960). For an elaboration of this theme, see Justin Driver, "The Public School as the Preeminent Site of Constitutional Law," *Nebraska Law Review* 98, no. 4 (2020).

60 Tinker v. Des Moines Indep. Cmty. Sch. Dist., 393 U.S. 503, 508–09 (1969) (internal citation omitted).

61 *Tinker v. Des Moines*, 524 (Black, J., dissenting). I have previously explored the competing conceptions of citizenship offered by various Supreme Court Justices. See Driver, *The Schoolhouse Gate*, 78–79; Justin Driver, "Two Cheers for a Free Speech Ruling," *New York Times*, June 25, 2021, A23.

62 Bethel Sch. Dist. No. 403 v. Fraser, 478 U.S. 675, 681 (1986).

63 141 S. Ct. 2038, 2046 (2021) ("This free exchange [of ideas] facilitates an informed public opinion, which, when transmitted to lawmakers, helps produce laws that reflect the People's will. That protection [of the marketplace of ideas] must include the protection of unpopular ideas, for popular ideas have less need for protection.").

64 W. Va. State Bd. of Educ. v. Barnette, 319 U.S. 624 (1943).

65 See, e.g., Christine Hauser, "High Schools Threaten to Punish Students Who Kneel During Anthem," *New York Times*, September 29, 2017, www.nytimes.com. In one particularly distressing confrontation, a sixth-grade student in Florida was arrested by police officers in 2019 following his refusal to participate in saluting the American flag. Christine Hauser and Matthew Haag, "Florida Student, 11, Arrested After Dispute over His Refusal to Say Pledge of Allegiance," *New York Times*, February 19, 2019, www.nytimes.com.

66 See James Davison Hunter, *Culture Wars: The Struggle to Define America* (New York: Basic Books, 1991).

67 See Jonathan Zimmerman, *Whose America? Culture Wars in the Public Schools* (Cambridge, MA: Harvard University Press, 2001); Driver, *The Schoolhouse Gate*, 9–13 (noting that the cultural conflicts that divide American society often appear in the nation's public schools). For a recent article pursuing this theme in the context of rules regarding masks during the COVID era, see Michelle Cottle, "Chaos at the School Board Meeting," *New York Times*, September 8, 2021, A22.

68 Jesus Jiménez, "2 Oklahoma Boys Pulled from Class for 'Black Lives Matter' T-Shirts," *New York Times*, May 9, 2021, www.nytimes.com.

69 Jiménez, "2 Oklahoma Boys."

70 Jiménez, "2 Oklahoma Boys."

71 Jiménez, "2 Oklahoma Boys."

72 Michael D. Smith, "Ardmore School Dress Code Quietly Updated, Prohibits Social Content at Elementary Schools," *Daily Ardmoreite* (Ardmore, OK), May 27, 2021, www.ardmoreite.com.

73 John Simerman, "Louisiana Teen Told No Trump Painting in School Parking Lot, But Federal Judge OKs It," *Times-Picayune / New Orleans Advocate*, October 10, 2020, https://www.nola.com.

74 Simerman, "Louisiana Teen."

75 Simerman, "Louisiana Teen."

76 Simerman, "Louisiana Teen."

77 Thomas v. Varnado, 511 F. Supp. 3d 761, 767–70 (E.D. La. 2020) (citing Tinker v. Des Moines Indep. Cmty. Sch. Dist., 393 U.S. 503 (1969)).

78 Bob D'Angelo, "Federal Judge Rules Louisiana Teen Can Keep Trump Painting in School Parking Space," *FOX23 News*, October 10, 2020, www.fox23.com.

79 Alyssa Lukpat, "When a Valedictorian Spoke of His Queer Identity, the Principal Cut Off His Speech," *New York Times*, June 28, 2021, www.nytimes.com.

80 Sam Dorman, "Michigan Valedictorian's Speech Censored, Criticized As 'Very Christianized': Complaint," *Fox News*, June 1, 2021, www.foxnews.com.

81 See *Tinker*, 393 U.S. at 508 ("[I]n our [constitutional] system, undifferentiated fear or apprehension of disturbance is not enough to overcome the right to freedom of expression."); see also Santa Fe Indep. Sch. Dist. v. Doe, 530 U.S. 290, 302 (2000) ("[T]here is a crucial difference between *government* speech endorsing religion, which the Establishment Clause forbids, and private speech endorsing religion, which the Free Speech and Free Exercise Clauses protect.") (quoting Bd. of Educ. v. Mergens, 496 U.S. 226, 250 (1990) (opinion of O'Connor, J.)).

82 Lukpat, "When a Valedictorian Spoke."

83 Dorman, "Michigan Valedictorian's Speech Censored"; Sam Dorman, "Michigan High School Violates Federal Law by Opposing Religious Language in Grad Speech: Complaint," *Fox News*, May 26, 2021, www.foxnews.com; Sam Dorman, "Michigan High School Reverses After Opposing Religious Language in Valedictorian Speech," *Fox News*, May 28, 2021, www.foxnews.com.

84 See Cass R. Sunstein, *Republic.com* (Princeton, NJ: Princeton University Press, 2001), 3–22 (describing the idea of the "Daily Me").

85 See Margaret O'Mara, "Why the Social Media Rage Machine Won't Stop," *New York Times*, November 3, 2020, www.nytimes.com.

86 See, e.g., Cole, "Why We Must Still Defend Free Speech."

87 See, e.g., Jamelle Bouie, "Facebook Has Been a Disaster for the World," *New York Times*, September 18, 2020, www.nytimes.com.

88 For arguments expressing deep skepticism about the wisdom of protecting students' constitutional rights, see Richard Arum, *Judging School Discipline: The Crisis of Moral Authority* (Cambridge, MA: Harvard University Press, 2003); Anne Proffitt Dupre, *Speaking Up: The Unintended Costs of Free Speech in Public Schools* (Cambridge, MA: Harvard University Press, 2009); and Anne Proffitt Dupre, "Should Students Have Constitutional Rights? Keeping Order in the Public Schools," *George Washington Law Review* 65, no. 1 (November 1996).

89 See *Black's Law Dictionary*, 11th ed. (St. Paul, MN: Thomas Reuters, 2019), s.v. "In Loco Parentis."

90 See, e.g., Vernonia Sch. Dist. 47J v. Acton, 515 U.S. 646, 654–55 (1995) (expressing enthusiasm for in loco parentis doctrine in a Fourth Amendment decision); Bd. of Educ. v. Earls, 536 U.S. 822, 840 (2002) (Breyer, J., concurring) (same); Mahanoy Area Sch. Dist. v. B.L., 141 S. Ct. 2038, 2046 (2021) (acknowledging the in loco parentis doctrine in the context of placing some limitations on the ability of schools to punish students for off-campus speech). For a warning about the dangers of viewing educators as standing in loco parentis, see Justin Driver, "Two Cheers."

91 See, e.g., Brown v. Bd. of Educ., 347 U.S. 483, 493–95 (1954) (prohibiting racial segregation in schools); Lee v. Weisman, 505 U.S. 577,

586–99 (1992) (prohibiting school-sponsored prayers at public school graduation ceremonies); Plyler v. Doe, 457 U.S. 202, 216–30 (1982) (invalidating a Texas statute that sought to exclude unauthorized immigrants from schools); Tinker v. Des Moines Indep. Cmty. Sch. Dist., 393 U.S. 503, 505–14 (1969) (protecting student speech); Goss v. Lopez, 419 U.S. 565, 572–76 (1975) (recognizing that students possess due-process protections regarding school suspensions); Safford Unified Sch. Dist. v. Redding, 557 U.S. 364, 374–77 (2009) (holding that educators violated a student's constitutional rights by subjecting her to a strip search in an effort to find ibuprofen tablets); J.D.B. v. North Carolina, 564 U.S. 261, 271–81 (2011) (determining—in a case arising from a school setting—that if police officers are aware that a criminal suspect is a minor, that awareness is relevant for determining whether *Miranda* warnings must be issued).

92 See, e.g., *Brown*, 347 U.S. 483.

93 New Jersey v. T.L.O., 469 U.S. 325, 385–86 (1985) (Stevens, J., concurring in part). Justice Stevens also stated: "Schools are places where we inculcate the values essential to the meaningful exercise of rights and responsibilities by a self-governing citizenry." *T.L.O.*, 373.

94 Doe v. Renfrow, 451 U.S. 1022, 1027–28 (1981) (Brennan, J., dissenting from denial of certiorari).

95 I do not suggest, of course, that the legal rights of minors are *always* coextensive with legal rights of adults when they are in nonschool settings. Minors cannot vote for elected officials, nor can they be conscripted, among other significant differences.

96 Justin Driver, "Three Hail Marys; *Carson, Kennedy,* and the Fractured Détente over Religion and Education," *Harvard Law Review* 136, no. 1 (2022): 208, 213 (exploring the notion of students possessing "junior varsity" rights).

97 *T.L.O.*, 469 U.S. at 341–43 (applying the reasonable-suspicion standard, and disavowing probable cause in school settings).

98 W. Va. State Bd. of Educ. v. Barnette, 319 U.S. 624, 638–42 (1943).

99 Texas v. Johnson, 491 U.S. 397, 410–20 (1989); United States v. Eichman, 496 U.S. 310, 313–19 (1990).

100   484 U.S. 260, 266–73 (1988).

101   411 U.S. 1, 56–59 (1973).

102   Class Action Complaint at 2–6, A.C. v. Raimondo, 494 F. Supp. 3d 170 (D.R.I. 2020) (No. 18-cv-645).

103   "Class Action Complaint." For insightful newspaper coverage of this lawsuit, see Dana Goldstein, "Lawsuit Says Rhode Island Failed to Teach Students to Be Good Citizens," *New York Times*, November 29, 2018, A18.

104   *Rodriguez*, 411 U.S. at 29–39.

105   *Rodriguez*, 411 U.S. at 36–37. *Plyler v. Doe*, 457 U.S. 202, 218–23, 230 (1982), makes clear that completely denying an education to young persons can violate the Constitution. See also Papasan v. Allain, 478 U.S. 265, 285 (1986) ("As *Rodriguez* and *Plyler* indicate, this Court has not yet definitively settled the question [of] whether a minimally adequate education is a fundamental right.").

106   "Class Action Complaint," 22; Goldstein, "Rhode Island Failed to Teach Students."

107   *A.C.*, 494 F. Supp. 3d at 184–97.

108   *A.C.*, 494 F. Supp. 3d at 184–97.

109   *A.C.*, 494 F. Supp. 3d at 176–77.

110   *A.C.*, 494 F. Supp. 3d at 175.

111   *A.C.*, 494 F. Supp. 3d at 181.

112   *A.C.*, 494 F. Supp. 3d at 197.

113   I made this point in contemporaneous press coverage of *A.C. v. Raimondo*. See Alia Wong, "The Students Suing for a Constitutional Right to Education," *The Atlantic*, November 28, 2018, www.theatlantic.com.

114   Rebell, *Flunking Democracy*, 33.

115   For works expressing this pessimistic view, see, for example, Michael J. Klarman, *From Jim Crow to Civil Rights: The Supreme Court and the Struggle for Racial Equality* (New York: Oxford University Press, 2004); and Gerald N. Rosenberg, *The Hollow Hope: Can Courts Bring About Social Change?* (Chicago: University of Chicago Press, 1991).

116   See Driver, *The Schoolhouse Gate*, 22 ("[T]he Court is neither omnipotent nor impotent, but, simply, unambiguously potent.").

117   See generally Douglas NeJaime, "Winning Through Losing," *Iowa Law Review* 96, no. 3 (2011).

118   Leslie Brody, "Students Press Unusual Argument in Court: A Constitutional Right to Civics," *Wall Street Journal*, December 5, 2019, www.wsj.com.

119   See Laura Bronner and Elena Mejía, "The Supreme Court's Conservative Supermajority Is Just Beginning to Flex Its Muscles," *FiveThirtyEight*, July 2, 2021, https://fivethirtyeight.com.

120   Lower federal courts share this lack of appetite. See, e.g., *Gary B. v. Whitmer*, 958 F.3d 1216 (6th Cir. 2020) (en banc) (vacating a panel decision holding that Detroit public schools fell below the minimum adequate education that *Rodriguez* suggested the Constitution may require).

121   For a claim that *The Schoolhouse Gate* evinces undue optimism about the prospects for the current Supreme Court delivering education law opinions that liberals can celebrate, see Joseph Fishkin, "This Court Doesn't Deserve This Book: A Reflection on Justin Driver's *The Schoolhouse Gate*," *Boston University Law Review Online* 100 (2020).

122   See Driver, *The Schoolhouse Gate*, 23.

123   See Mahanoy Area Sch. Dist. v. B.L, 141 S. Ct. 2038, 2046 (2021).

124   See, e.g., Adam Liptak, "Is a Cheerleader's Vulgar Post Protected Speech?," *New York Times*, December 29, 2020, A14 (noting that Chief Justice Roberts has called himself "probably the most aggressive defender of the First Amendment on the court now"). For a decision that many liberals construed as the Supreme Court becoming exceedingly solicitous of First Amendment claims, see *Janus v. American Federation of State, County, and Municipal Employees, Council 31*, 138 S. Ct. 2448, 2486 (2018), which held that public-sector unions cannot require nonmember employees to pay agency fees, even if nonmember employees benefit from the union's collective bargaining. See also *Janus*, 138 S. Ct. at 2501 (Kagan, J., dissenting) (critiquing conservatives for "weaponizing the First Amendment").

125   See Jamal Greene, "The Meming of Substantive Due Process," *Constitutional Commentary* 31, no. 2 (Summer 2016) (identifying and critiquing how the phenomenon of substantive due process became demonized in legal circles).

126   For the inspiration of this verbal formulation, see Alexander Bickel, *The Supreme Court and the Idea of Progress* (New York: Harper & Row, 1970), 151, which declared that "*Brown v. Board of Education*, with emphasis on the education part of the title, may be headed for—dread word—irrelevance."

127   National Commission on Excellence in Education, *A Nation at Risk: The Imperative for Educational Reform* (Washington, DC: US Government Printing Office, 1983). President Reagan's Education Secretary, Terrel H. Bell, issued the major report that shook the nation with its bleak assessment of public schools' performance and sparked years of policy discussions by offering numerous recommendations to improve public education. See Valerie Strauss, "'A Nation at Risk' Demanded Education Reform 35 Years Ago. Here's How It's Been Bungled Ever Since," *Washington Post*, April 26, 2018, www.washingtonpost.com.

128   See, e.g., Michael Hansen et al., "The 2018 Brown Center Report on American Education: How Well Are American Students Learning?," Brown Center on Education Policy, June 27, 2018, www.brookings.edu.

129   See, e.g., "Harry Wong Addresses National Conference," *Education World*, November 2, 2000, www.educationworld.com.

130   One particularly valuable resource that deserves a special salute is Jamin B. Raskin, *We the Students: Supreme Court Cases for and About Students*, 3rd ed. (Washington, DC: CQ Press, 2008). For a more theoretical approach aimed at teachers, see Hess and McAvoy, *The Political Classroom*. The presidential commission could also produce a list of recommended readings. If schools were to implement a student-centered approach to

civic education, my book exploring students' constitutional rights could prove helpful to some audiences. See generally Driver, *The Schoolhouse Gate.* Indeed, *The Schoolhouse Gate* might be used in lieu of a textbook in a class focusing upon students' constitutional rights for some high school classes.

131 Bryan Pietsch, "The Biden Administration Quickly Revamped the White House Website. Here's How," *New York Times,* January 20, 2021, www.nytimes.com. It is true that in April 2021, the Department of Education published its "Proposed Priorities—American History and Civics Education" in the *Federal Register.* "Proposed Priorities—American History and Civics Education," *Federal Register* 83, no. 73 (April 19, 2021): 20348. But this measure flew under the radar and does not, in my estimation, constitute anything like a full-throated, affirmative response to the 1776 Commission.

132 Kazin, "The 1776 Follies."

133 See, e.g., Lisa Lerer, "Trump Keeps an Iron Grip on the G.O.P.," *New York Times,* May 9, 2021, A1.

134 See The President's Advisory 1776 Commission, *The 1776 Report.*

135 See Fritze, "Three Supreme Court Justices."

136 Jonathan Zimmerman, "Why the Culture Wars in Schools Are Worse Than Ever Before," *Politico,* September 19, 2021, www.politico.com.

137 See Lauren Jackson, "What Is Critical Race Theory?," *New York Times,* August 18, 2021, www.nytimes.com (noting conservative efforts to contend that schools teach students Critical Race Theory as a method of political mobilization).

138 This adage paraphrases Audre Lorde, "Learning from the 60s," in *Sister Outsider: Essays and Speeches* (Trumansburg, NY: The Crossing Press, 1984), 131.

139 Michael J. Abramowitz, Antony Blinken, and Holly Kuzmich, *Reversing a Crisis of Confidence* (Washington, DC: The Democracy Project, 2018), 9–10.

140 Although this arrangement might be thought to raise separation-of-powers concerns, it is important to note that President Lyndon B. Johnson selected Chief Justice Earl Warren to chair the governmental group that investigated the death of President John F. Kennedy, colloquially known as the Warren Commission. See Associated Press, "Warren Panel Reports to Johnson Thursday," *New York Times,* September 22, 1964, A26.

141 Roberts, "2019 Year-End Report," 4.

142 Oxford English Dictionary defines "enterprise" as "[a]n undertaking, task, or project; (usually) *spec.* one which is bold, difficult, or important; a venture, an endeavour." Oxford English Dictionary, 3rd ed. (Oxford: Oxford University Press, 2018), s.v. "Enterprise."

143   For only two major opinions written by Chief Justice Roberts—both arising from the education realm—with which I sharply disagree, consider *Parents Involved in Community Schools v. Seattle School District No. 1*, 551 U.S. 701, 720–48 (2007) (plurality opinion), and *Morse v. Frederick*, 551 U.S. 393, 403–10 (2007). For my evaluations of those opinions, see Driver, *The Schoolhouse Gate*, 115–124, 293–308.

144   Tinker v. Des Moines Indep. Cmty. Sch. Dist., 393 U.S. 503 (1969).

145   See Roberts, "2019 Year-End Report," 3 ("[T]o reach people you have to meet them where they are.").

146   This statement suggests that student-centered civic education could help to close what Meira Levinson has insightfully termed the "civic empowerment gap." See Meira Levinson, *No Citizen Left Behind* (Cambridge, MA: Harvard University Press, 2012), 56 ("Elimination of the civic empowerment gap, and education for civic empowerment more generally, necessitates a shift in focus from distant heroes and their accomplishments to more ordinary role models and their specific techniques of civic engagement, especially of collective action.").

5

CAN DRIVER'S CIVIC EDUCATION MODEL CIRCUMVENT PARTISANSHIP?

JENNIFER MORTON

We find ourselves in a politically fractured historical moment. In the United States, partisans disagree not just about policy but fundamental facts. Few of us understand or agree on the basic tenets of government. This lack of mutual understanding and civic knowledge has predictably damaged our political community. The pandemic has exacerbated the bitterness of the divide—debates about masking, vaccines, and school reopenings have turned those with whom we disagree into villains. We need to rebuild common ground—to get clear about the terms under which we live together and relearn the importance of civic discourse across political boundaries. As Justin Driver argues, civic education is well-poised to help us do both. Driver's solution is brilliant not only because it has a legitimate claim to bipartisanship (in these times, that is no easy feat!), but also because it is pedagogically incisive.

As many of us know, students are more likely to engage with material that centers the experiences of young people like themselves. Driver's student-centered approach to civic education would do just that by having students read and discuss US Supreme Court cases in which students are the focus or protagonists. This is an intrinsically engaging and pedagogically rich entry point into civic knowledge. Students would learn about the Constitution, the judicial process, their rights, and how these have changed over time. These debates—in cases such as *Tinker* or *Brown*—are beautifully described in Driver's *The Schoolhouse Gate*. Reading that book, one understands how considering even one of these Supreme Court

134

opinions would give students a rich, nuanced, and deep understanding of the American legal and political framework within which we live.

I fear, however, that when we think through this proposal in practice, we will not avoid the kind of bitter partisan divides that Driver seeks to circumvent. More problematically, this approach seems to be in tension with another critical aim of civic education—enabling students to reimagine the terms on which our society is built, including the Constitution and the legal process it enshrines. By taking Supreme Court opinions as the launching pad for a civics course, we tether civic education too closely to our institutions as they are, rather than offering students the tools to think about how these institutions ought to be. It might be possible to take an approach like the one proposed by Driver and use it as a "trojan horse" toward a more radical vision of civic education. This would involve interrogating the fundamental premises that a more conservative approach to the same course would take for granted. It is unlikely, however, that we could reach bipartisan agreement around such an approach. Instead, we would seem to be caught anew in the grips of a partisan battle. In my conclusion, I will suggest that Driver's model might still be the best we can do in our current political climate. Even if we find the bipartisan middle in an anemic, little "c" conservative approach to these topics, this will still constitute progress. However, such a limited approach should be seen not as an ideal model for civic education, but rather as a reflection of how far we are from a well-functioning civic society.

THE CRITICAL IMPULSE

Civic education aims to equip students with the tools they need to participate effectively in our political system. This goal can be construed narrowly—understanding how government works, the basics of the Constitution, the rights and obligations of citizens—or, more broadly—instilling the knowledge, reasoning, and other civic skills that allow students to become the kind of citizens who improve on our existing social compact.[1] Schools are the battleground between the first, more conservative understanding of civic education and the latter, more progressive one. Could Driver's proposal thread that needle?

In the spirit of Driver's pedagogically sensitive approach, let us start with the classroom. I often teach political philosophy. In these classes, we discuss what I see as the central issue of civics—the terms under which we can live together as a political community. Students who are new to philosophy will often approach the course tentatively, unsure of what counts as a good argument or what qualifies as evidence for a claim in this domain. These are legitimate concerns that I hope to allay as we do philosophy together. Inevitably, a few students will offer arguments by putting forward claims like this: X is right because the Constitution protects X (or X is wrong because the Constitution forbids X). These are not good philosophical arguments, but they stem from an understandable confusion about the difference between the normative standing of the legal framework in which they live and the critical questions I am asking them to consider about its justification.

This example helps us see a broader range of gaps in three key areas of civic education: factual institutional knowledge, critical thinking about political and legal institutions, and the capacity for creative and imaginative political thinking. First, students' understanding of the Constitution is lackluster, to say the least. As Driver notes, students arrive on college campuses without a good grasp of how the First Amendment—the one students tend to most readily cite in my courses—has been used in practice. They appeal to it in making arguments, but they do not understand its power. Second, too many students graduate from high school not having had the opportunity to think critically about the political and legal institutions in which they live. To be clear, they often have these conversations outside the classroom, with their friends, or on social media. Students certainly have many political opinions. What they don't have is much experience thinking about the assumptions they make critically and systemically in the context of a classroom where they are encouraged to engage with other viewpoints.[2] Posting a tweet about Black Lives Matter is a far cry from thinking critically about the history of racial domination in this country and how it infects all our institutions, even those in which students may unwittingly participate.[3] Finally, students are rarely given the opportunity to think creatively about how our political, legal, and social institutions could be better and different than they are. Too often, they take as necessary features of our system that are anything but. All of these are civic deficits, and the latter two are at least as problematic as the gaps in historical and institutional knowledge that Driver emphasizes.

Driver's student-centered approach to civic education has the potential to make some important inroads here. First, students who learn about *Tinker*, for example, would develop a deeper understanding of the First Amendment and its deployment in historically critical moments. As Driver notes, this would teach students about their First Amendment rights and help them start to see themselves as having agency in the political domain. Understanding a case like *Tinker* can also allow students to think critically about the educational institutions through which they move. The drive that motivated those students to don black armbands is a critical, political one. Learning about these students can validate that same motivation in today's students. However, it is with respect to the third goal—rethinking the terms of our political project—that the limitations of Driver's approach are evident.

One way of understanding a case like *Tinker* is that it shows us the power of the First Amendment to protect the rights of students. In so doing, it enshrines the Constitution's powerful ideal of free speech and sets the debate's limits. Using Diana Hess's and Paula McAvoy's language here, it takes the Constitution's authority to be a closed question.[4] A different approach would encourage students to consider the Constitution's authority an open question. In the age of social media, one might ask whether the Constitution is limited in the guidance it can offer us out of the morass of misinformation. To take the First Amendment's authority within our shared political project as unsettled would require that students consider alternatives and think creatively about what a better system might be. I contend that a more progressive and ambitious civic education should encourage students to engage with *Tinker* in this more critical and imaginative way.

Here, we begin to see a core tension in Driver's proposal. On the one hand, these cases offer common ground that a bipartisan group could use as the basis of a civic education curriculum. But, on the other hand, finding that common ground would likely lead us to take questions as closed that we would see as open if we were to educate students to critically reflect on the very foundations of our system of shared governance.

NAVIGATING PARTISAN DIVIDES

To further make my case, let me turn to *Brown v. Board of Education*. This is a seminal case in the "schoolhouse cases" that would comprise the material for Driver's civic education proposal. I am not a legal scholar, so you will have to excuse my cursory understanding of the depths of the *Brown* debate.[5] One way of looking at *Brown* is as a victory for racial equality. I expect many would be inclined to teach *Brown* in this way if they were motivated by the drive to seek consensus with the opposing side. We might imagine this playing very well in an affluent majority White suburban school. Moreover, we cannot deny that, as Driver writes, "*Brown*, properly understood, provided supporters of racial equality with a powerful rhetorical and moral weapon that helped to catalyze the nation toward the goal of racial equality."[6] Nevertheless, it is precisely the rhetorical power of *Brown* that might obscure questions that we should be asking in a civic education classroom.

Another analysis of *Brown*, put forward by critical legal theorists, considers it a symbolic and regressive decision. They hold that the decision was motivated by a desire to satisfy calls for racial equity without making meaningful changes to the education received by most Black and Brown Americans. Derrick Bell suggests that

> viewing *Brown* as a symbol of what might have been, however, only serves to mask the continuing manifestations of inequality that divide us along lines of color and class. These divisions are exploited to enable an uneasy social stability, but at a cost that is no less onerous because it is all too obvious to blacks, and all but oblivious to a great many whites.[7]

According to this alternative analysis, *Brown* allows those who benefit from racial discrimination to feel that this issue has been handled while it continues to damage the lives of those who suffer the effects of underfunded, segregated schools. This critical reading of *Brown* might resonate more with the many Black and Brown low-income students still attending segregated schools. However, this analysis also forces us to consider the limitations of a strategy for advancing racial equality through the courts.

Here we have two radically different ways of thinking about the same case—one that would see, in this case, the continuing power of the founding documents of the United States, and one that would focus on its inherent limitations. The first would take the courts as an effective path to pursuing an ever more perfect union. The second sees the courts as often playing the role of an obstacle to true equality. I suspect that citizens aligned with the two main political parties in the United States might also be split on which version of the case to teach in K-12 schools. It would seem, then, that we cannot get away from the bitter partisan divides we see in current debates regarding how to teach American history by turning to Supreme Court cases about students.

If we are to teach *Brown* as a civics lesson, can we do so without talking to students about how this is "a nation borne on the backs of two evils of history—the violent takeover of Indigenous territory and near decimation of Indigenous peoples as the nation's borders advanced, and what many refer to as the holocaust of African enslavement?"[8] Even in discussing which "facts" count, we see political polarization at play. For example, some Texas schools are encouraging teaching about the Holocaust to include countervailing perspectives on this mass atrocity.[9] Even the most settled historical facts are up for contention as "opinions" in our current political climate.

However, if we retreat from confronting these facts because they might be potentially polarizing, can we truly be said to be teaching students the critical thinking skills they need to be good citizens? Critical thinking requires that students be well versed in "uncovering how power operates" in their civic communities.[10] To fail to do so is to inculcate in students a conservativism at odds with forging a better future. The approach put forward by Driver has the materials from which we could "trojan horse" a more progressive, radical approach to civic education, but it is difficult to see how we might do so without challenging the foundation of what makes this approach potentially bipartisan.

Citing Robert Gordon, Derrick Bell writes that "things seem to change in history when people break out of their accustomed ways of responding to domination by acting as if the constraints on them are not real and they have the power to change things."[11] If civic education takes the framework of our political project to be set entirely by the Constitution and its interpreters on the court, it will foster an uncritical conservative habitus toward the terms of our shared political project. Civic education should, in my view, disrupt that impulse. However, a civic education that does is unlikely to thread the needle in the way Driver envisions.

Civic Education in Polarized and Segregated Classrooms

Where does this leave us? In *The Political Classroom*, Diana Hess and Paul McAvoy describe how two very ideologically like-minded schools, one liberal and one conservative, sought to discuss controversial issues in the classroom and equip future citizens with the skills to be engaged, thoughtful participants in the political arena. Their richly described cases show the potential and limitations of doing so within classrooms that lack diversity. If we envision Driver's schoolhouse cases being taught in those types of classrooms, we start to get a sense of what we might expect. In some school districts, teachers, parents, and administrators will be open to the more critical version of this course. There, students will be encouraged to challenge and reimagine the terms of our shared political enterprise. In others, the more conservative version will prevail. Students will be encouraged to hew their discussion more closely to established precedent. They would be expected to limit their challenges to those that fall within the parameters set by a particular understanding of the Constitution.

One might argue that the flexibility of the approach licensed by the implementation of Driver's educational program is a strength of the account; it has room for many interpretations. Still, others might argue that even if students learn, for example, that *Brown* was a great victory in the fight for racial equality, discussing it with their peers in the way that Driver envisions would function as a trojan horse to deeper and more complex debates about the role of the courts, America's history of racial domination, and the failures of the education system.

In considering Driver's proposal, we must also bear in mind that this civic education course would be happening against the background of socioeconomic, racial, and political segregation. Creating a more engaged and civically minded citizenry requires that we learn how to live together across differences and that people in different parts of the country come away with a shared understanding of our political project. However, in our divided America, students are much more likely to participate in this civic education course in classrooms with other students like themselves—politically, racially, and economically. A civic education curriculum that allows students to avoid engaging with different viewpoints, and to walk away with vastly different ways of understanding our joint political project, might not sufficiently narrow existing divides.

Scholars from a range of disciplines have been grappling with questions of how to approach civic education in this complex era. The National Academy of Education recently compiled a thorough report on Civic Reasoning and Discourse. The group, convened by Carol Lee, gathered scholars from across the academy—philosophers, historians, cognitive scientists, education researchers, and political scientists—to discuss how to implement a civic education program. In their chapter on the history of education, Nancy Beadie and Zoe Burkholder show how the umbrella of civic education has "often functioned as a program of forced assimilation and violence against Native, Black, and Latinx communities."[12] However, their report also details how civic education has been used to advance the cause of racial and gender equality. They argue that civic education is a big umbrella—in some historical contexts, it has reified existing inequalities, and in others, it has bucked against them. They write that to be effective, "we must understand *where we are in history, understand ourselves as historical agents,* and *believe that engagement matters*" (original emphasis).[13]

This lesson is essential as we consider avenues toward building consensus around civic education. It might very well be that we cannot do better at this historical moment in the United States than aiming for common ground around understanding one of the branches of government that still retains some, albeit quickly eroding, credibility. Building civic education by discussing the Schoolhouse cases with students brings us back to basics. It would lead students to graduate with a better understanding than they currently have of their rights as enshrined in the Constitution, how the courts work, and the relationship between the judiciary and other branches of government. These are essential lessons. Insofar as Driver's proposal offers a pedagogically incisive way to teach them to students, we should applaud it. It lays the foundation for civic understanding that is necessary, though not sufficient, for the solidarity and civic friendship required to embark on more ambitious progressive projects.[14] However, as I have noted, there is a risk—one that we can see most plainly in the legacy of *Brown*, especially when we consider data on how segregated and unequal our schools and communities remain. Sometimes taking smaller steps toward a progressive vision prevents us from agitating for a more radical refashioning of the political project. The problem with our political situation is that there is so little political shared knowledge and good will that perhaps some progress, no matter how small, might be the best we can do for now. But we should not take this to reflect the limits of our civic project, but of how far we have come from that ideal.

NOTES

1 Carol D. Lee, Gregory White, and Dian Dong, "Educating for Civic Reasoning and Discourse," National Academy of Education, 2021.

2 Diana E. Hess and Paula McAvoy, *The Political Classroom: Evidence and Ethics in Democratic Education* (New York: Routledge, 2014).

3 Of course, some students have done this and more. However, those are not the students that we worry about when thinking about the lack of civic education in schools.

4 Hess and McAvoy, *The Political Classroom.*

5 Though we should note that most teachers, administrators, and others who would be involved in making these decisions will also have a superficial understanding of these issues.

6 Justin Driver, *The Schoolhouse Gate: Public Education, the Supreme Court, and the Battle for the American Mind* (New York: Vintage Books, 2019), 312.

7 Derrick A. Bell Jr., "The Unintended Lessons in Brown v. Board of Education," *NYLS Law Review* 49, no. 4 (2005): 1065.

8 Lee et al., "Educating for Civic Reasoning and Discourse."

9 Francine Prose, "Texas Schools Are Being Told to Teach 'Opposing Views' of the Holocaust. Why?" *The Guardian*, October 19, 2021. www.theguardian.com. Accessed August 25, 2022.

10 Lee et al., "Educating for Civic Reasoning and Discourse," 33.

11 Bell Jr., "The Unintended Lessons in Brown v. Board of Education," 1066.

12 Lee et al., "Educating for Civic Reasoning and Discourse," 143.

13 Lee et al., "Educating for Civic Reasoning and Discourse," 143.

14 Danielle S. Allen, *Talking to Strangers. Anxieties of Citizenship since Brown v. Board of Education* (Chicago: University of Chicago Press, 2004).

6

RACE, EQUITY, AND CIVIC EDUCATION

LISA GARCÍA BEDOLLA

In "Civic Education, Students' Rights, and the Supreme Court," Justin Driver raises the critical question of the state of civic education in the United States and how the lack of robust civic education practices in schools has helped to exacerbate political tensions and conflict. He also emphasizes the important role that an analysis of US Supreme Court cases and a focus on the legal debates around constitutional rights could play in fostering an engaging and impactful civic education experience for K-12 students. I agree wholeheartedly with his call to action and for the need to consider how best to educate US youth for democratic citizenship. However, I would suggest that there are some key considerations that need to be added to his analysis and his ideas for developing a civic education program focused on student rights. First, there is need for a clarification regarding his view of the goal of "civic education." Second, there should be a consideration of the robust literature on the best pedagogical and organizing practices for fostering youth civic engagement. Finally, there is need for some deeper reflection on school context, including the profound racial, gender, and socioeconomic inequalities, among others, that exist in US schools and society, and how this context needs to be taken into consideration when attempting to teach students about the US polity and make them feel efficacy and engagement within it. I will discuss each of these issues in turn.

DEFINING CIVIC EDUCATION AND ITS PURPOSE

In Driver's chapter, "civic education" seems to be doing very different kinds of political work. At the most basic level, it would be

143

helpful if Driver defined what he means by civic education. For example, Rogers et al. define civic learning as

> a process through which young people develop the knowledge, skills, and commitments to interact effectively with fellow community members to address shared problems. It includes preparation for both civic engagement (or practices seeking to promote the public good through non-governmental organizations and informal community work) and political engagement (or activities aiming to influence state action through formal avenues such as voting, lobbying, petitioning, or protesting).[1]

This type of definition assumes that civic education is about more than just fostering civic knowledge. Instead, civic knowledge is only valuable insofar as it serves the purpose of helping students become actively engaged in civic life. I would argue, similarly, that successful civic education must include the development of culturally competent democratic understanding *and* engagement, rather than simply the ability to know one's congressperson, or name all three branches of government, or understand the function of the Supreme Court and the importance of its landmark decisions. Driver, however, seems to waver between holding a narrower view and a broader view of the goals of civic learning. In his initial discussion, Driver seems to be using a narrow civic knowledge framing as the purpose of civic education, talking about how few students know the causes behind the Declaration of Independence or could name all three branches of government. Yet, at the end of the chapter, when discussing the outcome of a mock court session and a student's stated desire to become a judge, Driver seems to be arguing that the purpose of a student-centered civic education is to foster students' "civically minded ambitions." More clarity on the goals of his civic education program is needed.

Returning to the political work Driver is asking civic education to do, by my reading he is arguing that a student-centered civic education would decrease political polarization by helping students develop empathy for those with opposing viewpoints, would help students see themselves as agents in the political process, and would lead to more civic-minded outcomes. Those goals are quite distinct and require different pedagogical approaches in order for them to be achieved. I will discuss the pedagogical piece below. Here, I want to focus on students' development of empathy for opposing viewpoints and seeing themselves as political actors. The ability of the student-centered civic education model to serve these two laudable purposes is limited by the fact that the framework seems to have been developed with a student who is imagined as a "universal subject." In other words, the assumption is that all students, regardless of social position, need the same sort of civic education and will respond to that education in the same sort of way. As an example, Driver mentions students' inability to report the causes leading to the Declaration of Independence as a sign of poor civic education in the United States. But, as Rogers Smith and other scholars have pointed out, there were multiple factors leading to the development of a US national identity distinct from that of Great Britain. These included not merely an economic concern about "taxation without representation" but also racial and gendered framings of US interests and needs that were in conflict with those of the British Empire.[2] That is, the factors leading to the Declaration of Independence are not simple and, most likely, this complex understanding is not being taught in most schools. Moreover, an array of scholarship shows that one of our standard national myths is, in fact, a contested one, the understanding of which can depend on a particular student's social position and point of view.

Another example of the assumed universal student subject in Driver's contribution is that he argues that his student-centered civic education "foregrounds the major Supreme Court decisions that have shaped the everyday lives of students across the nation." Have they? Or have most of those decisions only shaped the lives of the most privileged students of our nation? We know from decades of research in education that high-poverty schools infringe on students' civil rights and liberties most often, with metal detectors, random searches of students' belongings, significant control over student behavior, bodies, and free speech, etc. Driver provides the example of student clothing being policed by schools. This and other more egregious limitations on students' rights happen every day in schools across the United States. Driver seems to assume either that these rights are self-enforcing, or that parents and students have the resources to hire lawyers to protect those rights. I would argue that it is only students with very particular types of privilege, or those rare students who can gain assistance from sympathetic public interest lawyers, who are able to use the courts to advance their rights. As such, a Supreme Court–based civic education curriculum could have a demobilizing effect—making it clear to students how often their rights are violated while not providing them with the means to do anything about it. At a minimum, if the goal of civic education is to prepare students for democratic citizenship, we must appreciate that students' social position will affect how they interpret and understand the material provided to them. We cannot assume a universal response, given the diversity of US youth, across all dimensions.

INCORPORATING EFFECTIVE CIVIC PEDAGOGIES

I appreciate that Justin Driver is a legal scholar, and therefore I have no expectation that he should be an expert in pedagogical practice. However, as a legal scholar making a recommendation about what should happen in classrooms, it would be helpful if he could develop a proposal rooted in the robust literature on teaching, learning, and civic education that currently exists.[3] I cannot do justice to that literature here. But, at a minimum, that research teaches us some considerations that seem crucial to take into account when devising or implementing a civic education program in today's school contexts, which I describe next.

The Need for Problem-Based Learning Approaches

Research shows that problem-based approaches to civic education are most effective. By problem-based I mean that students are asked to identify a problem in their community and then, working in groups with a mentor to guide them, asked to study who is in charge of that problem in order to arrive at an approach for addressing it. Having students learn about the role of federalism, jurisdictional overlap, and the role of governmental and nongovernmental actors in this way gives them a much more grounded understanding of government, its forms, its powers, and, most important, the avenues into government that are available to them to foster change regarding the things they care most about.[4] How might Driver draw on these lessons to make his plan for teaching "student-centered" education more robust? Does having students participate in mock trials or moot courts provide an adequate method for helping students understand what they might do if they believed a right was being violated? This research suggests it would, if the approach incorporated what we know about the effectiveness of problem-based learning and an intentional focus on how power and inequality might have played a role in the outcomes of these cases.

Structuring Contentious Topics and Conversations

There is also research showing the importance of political discussion, including "contentious conversations" about topics such as politics, constitutional rights, and so on, for civic learning.[5] However, teachers struggle, sometimes for political reasons, to hold contentious conversations in their classrooms. They worry about parents' responses and, in general, are not trained in how to foster and manage such discussions. That reality has only become more challenging in our current political moment.[6] Moreover, while we know that students benefit greatly from having contentious conversations, it is important to think about how to help teachers structure and facilitate those conversations: Research shows that these conversations will be most effective and most conducive for civic learning when the structure of the classroom is more democratic, meaning that student voice and opinion are valued and not overridden by the teacher.[7] Unfortunately, students of color and economically precarious students are much less likely than more wealthy, white students to be given the opportunity to participate in contentious conversations that are structured democratically, so there is a particular need for civic education approaches that can help address this gap.[8] Thus, I believe Driver should take this set of challenges into consideration if he wants his approach to civic learning to provide robust options for discussing rights controversies and other issues that may arise during these lessons.

The Challenges Arising from Current School Contexts

These studies and others suggest challenges inherent in our current school contexts, and how the politics and ideology that underlie the positionality of each person in the classroom—teacher and students—affects schools' capacities to provide effective civic education. First, teachers are often reluctant to raise topics that are seen as "political" in their classrooms, for fear of parents' or administrators' responses. This was true even before recent events and that has only intensified recently.[9] Studies have shown that teachers' beliefs matter and affect what they see as important for students to learn in reference to civics.[10] DiGiacomoa et al., in a recent study of civics teachers in a racially diverse school district, found that teachers lacked a shared understanding of what civic education was for, what the appropriate methods were for teaching civics, and that teachers lacked professional development in this area. These challenges made many of the teachers in their study shy away from addressing political issues within their classrooms.[11] At a minimum, these findings urge us to consider the politics inherent in teacher preparation and teachers' relationships with their administrators, both of which affect the ability of schools to effectively prepare their students for democratic citizenship.

Furthermore, in today's hypercompetitive high school classrooms, most students are there to do well and to receive a high grade. They are indoctrinated early not to contradict their teachers and to give teachers what they want to see when exam time comes. That training does not disappear in the civics classroom, limiting students' ability to be their authentic selves in those spaces and engage in contentious debate in the ways they need to in order to maximize the impact of those educational opportunities. Any approach to civic education that is meant to foster student agency would have to be intentionally designed to alleviate these contextual factors. The classroom is not a neutral setting; it reflects the profoundly unequal society within which it sits. If the goal is to nurture students' sense of power and place within the polity, then classroom structure and expectations also would need to change in significant and intentional ways.

TAKING SCHOOL AND STUDENT CONTEXT SERIOUSLY

These last points bring us to my final concern about the framing of Driver's chapter: his discussion of the causes and consequences of polarization. Appreciating that a look at vote choice in the 2020

presidential election is a superficial proxy measure of polarization, I would note that, according to CNN's exit poll, 87 percent
of Blacks, 65 percent of Latinos, and 61 percent of Asian Americans voted for Joe Biden for president. That is a relatively high
level of agreement within each group. Whites were the group that
was most split, with 58 percent voting for Donald Trump and 41
percent for Biden.[12] Looking at public opinion, whites were evenly
split (50/50) when asked whether or not they agreed with the statement, "Today discrimination against whites has become as big a
problem as discrimination against blacks and other minorities." In
contrast, 75 percent of Black respondents and 71 percent of Latinx
respondents said they disagreed with that statement.[13] Whites are
also the most segregated of any racial group in the United States,
and our K-12 public schools are highly segregated along the lines
of race and socioeconomic status.[14]

Thus, these types of indicators suggest that polarization is not
evenly distributed across the polity, and that whites may be the most
ideologically polarized racial group in the United States. In addition, as a recent Government Accountability Office report revealed,
white youth are likely to attend school mainly with other whites: 45
percent of white students attend schools that are at least 75 percent
white.[15] Given how ideology maps onto geography in the United
States, it is likely that progressive whites will mostly attend school
with other progressive whites, while conservative whites will mostly
attend school with other conservative whites. Those factors must
be taken into consideration when thinking about civic education
strategies, particularly if one of the goals of the exercise is to foster empathy for differing viewpoints. If students are only asked to
interact with (and debate) students like them, it is highly unlikely
that exercise will result in any significant changes in their worldview, given they rarely interact with anyone of another opinion or
of another race.

We can also think about how particular aspects of a student's
school and neighborhood context may limit Driver's program of
civic education. For students of color who attend high-poverty
schools, learning about students in the past who had the privilege
or good fortune to find a lawyer to take their case and then wait
years working through the courts to finally gain resolution, seems
unlikely to lead them to feelings of political efficacy given their

school contexts and lived experiences. In my own research, I have found that what is most important for fostering civic engagement is an individual being shown the degree to which people "like them," similarly situated to their personal circumstances, were able to effect change.[16] But this type of successful student-activist role model is not what students would see when reading most Supreme Court cases, or from a reading of the rare instances of student activism that resulted in support of student rights within schools. In California, "willful defiance," defined as "disrupting school activities or otherwise willfully defying the valid authority of school staff,"[17] was, until very recently, the most common justification for school suspension, even among elementary school children.[18] This policy was recently outlawed in California because its subjective nature made it possible for school personnel to suspend a student any time that student said or did anything the staff person did not like.

One can imagine that a student attending a school where these kinds of suspensions occur regularly would not necessarily be able to see themselves or their school context reflected in court cases upholding students' free speech rights. If those students learned those rights ideals in class and then attempted to exercise speech disliked by their schools, their most likely outcome would be suspension or some other harsh form of discipline.[19] As I mention above, schools' gendered and racialized enforcement of school dress codes is another example of how students' lived experiences can vary dramatically from what is theoretically protected or allowed from a legal standpoint.[20] For Driver's vision to be made real, those realities would need to change.

In closing, I want to argue that in developing his vision of civic education, Driver needs to grapple with these challenges, especially the challenges faced by public schools in our current era. I also want to urge that any conversation about the future of civic education needs to be informed by consideration of the complexities and mixed legacies of US history and the growth of public education. The early development of "common schools" (which would later become our public schools) in the United States stemmed from mixed motives, including both a belief in the importance of common learning and a desire to increase social conformity and control over culturally diverse immigrant groups and newly enfranchised working-class men.[21] The growth of common schools coincided with the removal of property restrictions on suffrage and the implementation of racial and gender restrictions on voting.[22] At the time, there were concerns among US political elites about how these unpropertied white men might vote. This contributed to beliefs that the state needed to educate them in order to ensure their ability to effectively (and appropriately) exercise the franchise. One initial purpose of our public schools, then, was to teach students a version of civic education with a common narrative about US politics and the role of the citizen within them.

The mixed legacy of that history is evident in civics and government classrooms today. Those narratives about US history and politics have been adjusted periodically in response to protest movements, but there has never been a national conversation about what civic education has to look like in order to support a truly inclusive multiracial democracy. Thus, while I agree with Driver that we need a national civic education conversation, I would humbly suggest that it must take account of both that exclusionary history and the profoundly unequal reality of our nation's public schools. Only by facing all our truths—the good and the bad—will we be able to teach our young people that this democracy truly is theirs and that they have both the power and the obligation to nurture and sustain it.

NOTES

1 John Rogers, Erica Hodgin, Joseph Kahne, Rebecca Cooper Geller, Alexander Kwako, Samia Alkam, and Cicely Bingener, *Reclaiming the Democratic Purpose of California's Public Schools* (Los Angeles, CA: Leveraging Equity & Access in Democratic Education Initiative at UCLA & UC Riverside, 2020), 2.

2 Rogers Smith, *Civic Ideals: Conflicting Views of Citizenship in U.S. History* (New Haven, CT: Yale University Press, 1997).

3 Carnegie Corporation of New York, CIRCLE. *The Civic Mission of Schools* (Carnegie Corporation of New York and CIRCLE, 2003). See also Jonathan Gould, Kathleen Hall Jamieson, Peter Levine, Ted McConnell, and David B. Smith, eds., *Guardian of Democracy: The Civic Mission of Schools* (Philadelphia: Leonore Annenberg Institute for Civics of the Annenberg Public Policy Center at the University of Pennsylvania, 2011).

4 Joseph Kahne and Ellen Middaugh, "High Quality Civic Education: What It Is and Who Gets It," *Social Education* 72, no. 1 (2008): 34–39.

5 Diana E. Hess and Paula McAvoy, *The Political Classroom: Evidence and Ethics in Democratic Education* (New York: Routledge, 2015).

6 Daniela Kruel DiGiacomo, Erica Hodgin, Joseph Kahne, and Sara Trapp, "Civic Education in a Politically Polarized Era," *Peabody Journal of Education* 96, no. 3 (2021): 261–274.

7 Cathy Cohen, Joseph Kahne, Ellen Middaugh, and Jon Rogowski, *Participatory Politics: New Media and Youth Political Action* (Oakland, CA: Youth and Participatory Politics Research Network, 2012).

8 Cohen et al., *Participatory Politics*.

9 DiGiacomo et al., "Civic Education."

10 See Ryan T. Knowles and Antonio J. Castro, "The Implications of Ideology on Teachers' Beliefs Regarding Civic Education," *Teaching and Teacher Education* 77 (2019): 226–239, and Steve Farkas and Ann M. Duffett, *High Schools, Civics, and Citizenship: What Social Studies Teachers Think and Do* (Washington, DC: American Enterprise Institute, 2010).

11 DiGiacomo et al., "Civic Education," 272.

12 CNN exit poll results from the November 2020 election. "National Results 2020 President Exit Polls," *CNN*, www.cnn.com, accessed September 1, 2022.

13 Results from the PRRI 2015. "American Values Survey 2015 Supplement," PRRI, www.prri.org, accessed September 1, 2022.

14 For residential segregation, see Sean F. Reardon, Lindsay Fox, and Joseph Townsend, "Neighborhood Income Composition by Household Race and Income, 1990–2009," *ANNALS of the American Academy of Political and Social Science* 660, no. 1 (2015): 78–97. For school segregation, see Will McGrew, *U.S. School Segregation in the 21st Century: Causes, Consequences, and Solutions* (Washington, DC: Washington Center for Equitable Growth, 2019).

15 GAO, *K-12 Education: Student Population Has Significantly Diversified, But Many Schools Remain Divided Along Racial, Ethnic, and Economic Lines* (Washington, DC: Government Accountability Office, June 2022), www.gao.gov, accessed September 1, 2022.

16 Lisa García Bedolla and Melissa Michelson, *Mobilizing Inclusion: Transforming the Electorate through Get-Out-the-Vote Campaigns* (New Haven, CT: Yale University Press, 2012).

17 Description of what the bill, AB420, changed in terms of school discipline policy in California, see www.fixschooldiscipline.org, accessed September 1, 2022.

18 Chloe Triplett, "Time to End 'Willful Defiance' Expulsions, Suspensions in K-12 Education," ACLU, www.aclusandiego.org, accessed September 1, 2022.

19 Pedro Noguera, "Schools, Prisons, and the Social Implications of Punishment: Rethinking Disciplinary Practices," *Theory into Practice* 42 (2003): 341–350.

20 See Jennifer L. Martin and Jennifer M. Brooks, "Loc'd and Faded, Yoga Pants, and Spaghetti Straps: Discrimination in Dress Codes and School Pushout," *International Journal of Education Policy & Leadership* 16 (2021), and Edward W. Morris, "'Tuck in that Shirt!' Race, Class, Gender, and Discipline in an Urban School," *Sociological Perspectives* 48 (2005): 25–48.

21 David Tyack, *Seeking Common Ground: Public Schools in a Diverse Society* (Cambridge, MA: Harvard University Press, 2003).

22 This resulted in the loss of voting rights for those few free blacks and women who, until then, had had the right to vote in some states, like New Jersey. See "For a Few Decades in the 18th Century, Women and African-Americans Could Vote in New Jersey," *Smithsonian Magazine*, www.smithsonianmag.com, accessed September 1, 2022.

7

MOVING BEYOND THE "POITIER EFFECT"

EXAMINING THE POTENTIAL TO ADVANCE CIVIC RESPECT THROUGH CROSS-COMMUNITY TEACHING

ILANA PAUL-BINYAMIN, WURUD JAYUSI, AND YAEL (YULI) TAMIR

One of the most iconic school-themed movies, *To Sir with Love*, features Sidney Poitier as a teacher in an inner-city London school who generates a transformative marvel of the kind Hollywood loves to admire. The movie reflects many people's beliefs about the capacities of the ideal teacher who, by the mere power of their charisma, overcomes all difficulties, unveils their students' hidden skills, and eases their way into maturity. But there is a twist in the plot. The teacher is Black, while most of the students are not. When the movie came out in the late 1960s, the idea of a transformative Black teacher wasn't at all to be taken for granted.

The movie elevated Poitier into an icon; the admirable young Black man who defied all expectations and captured the hearts and minds of his students and all other viewers. The film score, sung by Lulu, also became a hit, replayed in endless graduation ceremonies. As the girl in the song leaves school, she sends a message of gratitude to the teacher who shaped her life: "I know that I am leaving my best friend / A friend who taught me right from wrong /and weak from strong. That's a lot to learn / What! What can I give you in return?" When awarding Poitier the Presidential Medal of Freedom in 2009, President Obama defined him not as a movie star or filmmaker but as an instigator of artistic excellence and American progress. Poitier and his films were seen as milestones for promoting cross-community racial respect and integration in American life. This chapter reconsiders the mythical "Poitier effect" and the difficulties of promoting intergroup empathy and connection in the midst of polarization. Drawing on ideas of contact theory and studies of cross-cultural interactions in educational contexts, we argue that cross-community teaching and learning can have powerful effects for reducing prejudice and humanizing the other.

Going Beyond the Mythical "Poitier Effect"

In the late 1960s, Poitier was seen by many as an embodiment of all consensual values—this was his ticket into the mainstream. *To Sir with Love* is, then, a movie characteristic of an age that promoted what we can think of as "thin diversity" in which each person, including "the other," plays by the rules of the majority. In a polarized age characterized by a lack of common rules, where there is no agreement on how to distinguish "right from wrong and weak from strong," can teachers in general, and teachers from minority groups in particular, pave their students' way into civic maturity and connection, preparing them to become virtuous, active, interconnected citizens of a pluralist society?

The film version of the Poitier effect can be criticized as a misleading portrayal of racial reconciliation.[1] However, decades of real-world studies of contact theory show crucial potential for interactions between groups to reduce prejudice.

Gordon Allport's influential contact hypothesis claims that extensive integration between members of an in-group and an out-group is the best means for achieving social stability and harmony.[2] The theory holds that people who engage in intergroup contact are likely to be less prejudiced toward out-group members than are those who do not have such experiences.[3]

Based on research on contact theory in Israel, the United States, Germany, England, and Australia,[4] we argue that learning from an admirable teacher who belongs to "the other" has the potential to be transformative: to teach children how to respect diversity, and ameliorate social and political polarization. We believe this potential is especially important for helping societies navigate the real complexities of diversity and increasing polarization.

One high-profile example of this type of cross-community civic learning and connection occurred in 2020, when the Israeli prize for the "Teacher of the Year" was awarded to Alya Wadi Kadach, a Muslim woman, who covers her head with a hijab and wears traditional garments. When she enters a mall or a coffee shop in Israel, she is treated as a security suspect. In her school, however, she is a hero. She is an outstanding math teacher who works in Eilat, a city that votes mostly for right-wing parties and is not known for progressiveness. And yet parents and students alike recommended Alya for the teaching prize. Children testified that they love studying with her because she is not only a good teacher but also attentive and generous. Parents love Alya because her students passed their exams with distinction. Everyone agreed that Alya is one of the best assets of their school. For the lucky students, teachers, and parents who know Alya, the stereotype of traditional Arab women was shaken. Through their relationship with her they were able to humanize "the other" and appreciate the benefits that can come from diversity and connection across differences. When Alya's students meet Arab women wearing traditional garments, rather than being afraid, they are curious and say: "They look like Alya; let's ask if they know her."

THE CHALLENGE OF THICK DIVERSITY AND INCREASING POLARIZATION

One challenge facing schools and societies stems from increasing polarization and more complex and conflictual forms of thick diversity that are more difficult to navigate than the thinner forms of diversity circulating in the latter twentieth century. The type of diversity portrayed in Sydney Poitier's film role as a teacher can be seen as a version of "thin diversity." Thin diversity is grounded in one of two social conditions:

(1) The Broad Consensus Condition: Members of the diverse groups that constitute a society broadly share an agreed upon set of basic norms and principles.

(2) The Majority Rule with Minority Conformity Condition: The dominant or majority group in a society dictates the norms and principles while members of other groups conform to these rules.[5]

As a result, the society shares core values that are indisputable. These values define a neutral ideological space where teachers are sheltered from public pressures. Under these conditions, it is easier for civic education to nurture respect for consensual norms and rules and foster a productive social dialog. In these circumstances, civic education may focus on teaching children the importance of a democratic theory of education that "in the face of our social disagreements, helps us judge (a) who should have authority to make decisions about education, and (b) what the moral boundaries of that authority are."[6]

However, while many assume that in modern democracies thin diversity is a stable state of affairs, thick diversity is brewing below the surface. Thick diversity is a social condition in which there is no agreement on basic social values, social norms are contested, and no group has the power to enforce its set of values on all others. Hence, social disagreements go all the way down from the political sphere to the classroom. Lacking a common set of propositions to relay on social dialog often leads to greater hostility and a sense of despair, which in turn draws the different social groups apart.

Polarization is the next step of social disintegration. It is characterized by an unwillingness of the different parties to engage in a cross-communal dialog, and quite often with a desire to delegitimize the "other" in order to justify the process of disengagement.

Polarization is not the same as disagreement about how to solve public policy problems, which is healthy and natural in a democracy. Polarization is more than just having a different opinion from your neighbor about certain issues. Polarization occurs when we refuse to live next to a neighbor who doesn't share our politics, or when we won't send our children to a racially integrated school. The force that empowers polarization is tribalism: clustering ourselves into groups that compete against each other in a zero-sum game, where negotiation and compromise are perceived as betrayal, whether those groups are political, racial, economic, religious, gender, or generational. [7]

Gidron, Adams, and Horne define this kind of polarization as *affective polarization* marked by a breakdown of epistemological and moral norms that leads to growing social isolationism, geographical segregation, partisan sources of information, and territorial voting patterns.[8]

In polarized societies, attempts to draft an agreed upon civic curriculum lead to the realization that *all* views are contested. No opinion can be sheltered under the protection of "neutrality." Disagreement is everywhere. Each group tries to gain more ground.

One recent example of an attempt to pre-structure teachers' speech took place in the United States. On September 15, 2021, a bill was passed in the Wisconsin Assembly declaring that all schools must follow a statewide civics curriculum, and all students must take at least half a credit in civic education in order to graduate. The required civics curriculum would have to include teaching the history and context of the Declaration of Independence, US Constitution, and the Bill of Rights as well as "a sense of civic pride and desire to participate regularly with government at all levels," and yet it also prohibited discussion of a long list of terms and concepts. It was passed in the Assembly in a 60–38 party-line vote, stirring a nationwide controversy.[9]

Opponents argued that the bill intends to prevent teachers from teaching Critical Race Theory as well as the historical and contemporary implications of racism. The Bill's supporters argued that Critical Race Theory is, itself, racist as it assumes that all white people, due to their race affiliation and regardless of their own actions, are to be blamed for past injustices toward Blacks. It forces children to feel shameful and blameworthy for something they did not do.

In testimony before a joint meeting of the Assembly and Senate education committees in August, Rep. Chuck Wichgers, one of the co-authors of the Bill, outlined a list of terms and concepts that the authors believe violate the Equal Protection Clause of the US Constitution and should be prohibited from discussion in classrooms. The very long list makes one wonder what moral and political issues could be discussed in schools if the following one hundred concepts are banned:

Critical Race Theory (CRT); Action Civics; Social Emotional Learning (SEL); Diversity, Equity, and Inclusion (DEI); Culturally responsive teaching; Abolitionist teaching; Affinity groups; Anti-racism; Anti-bias training; Anti-blackness; Anti-meritocracy; Obtuse meritocracy; Centering or de-centering; Collective guilt; Colorism; Conscious and unconscious bias; Critical ethnic studies; Critical pedagogy; Critical self-awareness; Critical self-reflection; Cultural appropriation/misappropriation; Cultural awareness; Cultural competence; Cultural proficiency; Cultural relevance; Cultural responsiveness; Culturally responsive practices; De-centering whiteness; Deconstruct knowledges; Diversity focused; Diversity training; Dominant discourses; Educational justice; Equitable; Equity; Examine "systems"; Free radical therapy; Free radical self/collective care; Hegemony; Identity deconstruction; Implicit/Explicit bias; Inclusivity education; Institutional bias; Institutional oppression; Internalized racial superiority; Internalized racism; Internalized white supremacy; Interrupting racism; Intersection; Intersectionality; Intersectional identities; Intersectional studies; Land acknowledgment; Marginalized identities; Marginalized/Minoritized/Underrepresented communities; Microaggressions; Multiculturalism; Neo-segregation; Normativity; Oppressor vs. oppressed; Patriarchy; Protect vulnerable identities; Race essentialism; Racial healing; Racialized identity; Racial justice; Racial prejudice; Racial sensitivity training; Racial supremacy; Reflective exercises; Representation and inclusion; Restorative justice; Restorative practices; Social justice; Spirit murdering; Structural bias; Structural inequity; Structural racism; Systemic bias; Systemic oppression; Systemic racism; Systems of power and oppression; Unconscious bias; White fragility; White privilege; White social capital; White supremacy; Whiteness; Woke.[10]

A desire to influence curricular content or rephrase language to shape moral discourse is not unique to Wisconsin, since bills to ban certain topics or concepts have also been introduced or passed in many other US states. Moreover, efforts to control curricular content and language can occur across the right-left political spectrum. For instance, recently the liberal-leaning Brandeis University published a "suggested language list" including concepts that should not be used in the classroom as they may be considered violent. The list is described as a compilation of alternatives to words and phrases with "roots, histories, and/or current usage that can serve to reinforce systems of oppression," and it flags words like "victim" and "survivor." A Brandeis spokesperson stated that while Brandeis is firmly committed to principles of free expression, the list is an accessible resource for anyone who wants to consider their own language "in an effort to be respectful of others who may have different reactions to certain norms and behaviors."

Under these types of circumstances of extreme disagreement, civic education, and many other fields of knowledge, can become volatile, with each discussion likely to trigger insoluble conflicts that schools are eager to avoid.[11] Schools thus adhere to teaching the minimums of social agreement, mostly structural and procedural issues. The moral heart of civics as a field of study is uprooted from the curricular body, which can make civic learning lifeless. It is no wonder fewer teachers want to teach civics and fewer students are eager to study it.

When discourse is avoided or silenced, one needs to seek a set of actions that will allow for a safe meeting space, taking actions that have the potential to reduce hostility, humanize others, and promote attentiveness to their needs. Research shows that one way of humanizing the other is through personal contact. We thus turn to Contact Theory, examining its effects on mitigating conflictual, polarized realities and nurturing civic virtues.[12]

Rather than attempting to overcome differences and reduce hostility by rational deliberations, Contact Theory posits humanizing others by getting to know them, spending time together doing things all participants enjoy and care about. Are such meetings effective in creating a common ground for shared citizenship, and could these be especially important in situations of thick diversity and polarization?

The Challenge of Separate Schools and Groups: Israel's Efforts for Intergroup Contact and Cross-Cultural Teaching as a Case Study

We turn to the complex circumstances of education in Israel to consider the possibilities for intergroup contact to help promote more cross-community awareness, appreciation, and connection. Because the Israeli education system preceded the state of Israel, pre-state separatism replicated itself in the formal state system and led to the formation of four separate public school systems:

General or largely secular Jewish, Religious Jewish, Ultra-Orthodox Jewish, and Arab, each serving its own community. In the absence of a joint or integrated school system, children and teachers from the different communities rarely meet and engage with each other. To confront these problematic social divisions, in recent decades proponents of a shared society in Israel have drawn on the insights and approaches of Contact Theory to attempt to structure opportunities for teachers and students to engage in cross-cultural, cross-religious contacts. The most common approach has been to have meetings designed to break the separatist reality by bringing children together to a limited number of joint activities. These episodic meetings offer direct, unmediated interaction between members of estranged and hostile groups. The hope is that such meetings will ignite a sense of community, of mutual responsibilities, and common goals.

Because of the explosive power of direct dialog, meetings are usually set up not to discuss any social and political conflicts but simply to involve children in playing or studying together. The theory is that meeting "the other" in a friendly environment allows participants to open up and see each other in a different light. When playing together, children may find that the other individual is a good sport, or a generous teammate, or that they share a sense of humor or a love of music. They may want others to be on their team or teach them something they don't know.

In recent decades, thousands of such encounters between members of conflicted groups were initiated in Israel with an attempt to fight prejudice and racism, or advance active and egalitarian citizenship. The research on such efforts has been mixed, showing some benefits but also some problematic outcomes. Scholar Yifat Maoz followed and analyzed Jewish-Arab encounters over a period of twenty years, investigating their effects.[13] In her meta-analysis, she argues that contacts attempting to promote coexistence or stimulate joint projects by "putting aside" controversial issues tend to preserve and perpetuate the dominance and control of the Jewish majority group, encouraging Arab submission and passivity. In contrast, contacts that invited a discussion on more controversial issues positively influence trust and empathy and increase understanding of the intricacies of the conflict. However, for some participants these engagements with controversy also stimulated verbal hostility and led to the escalation of the conflict. The research indicates that for some participants, discussing controversial issues deepens hostility.

Other research also indicates that finding effective approaches to cross-group interactions is a difficult task, and that not every type of interaction will generate benefits. Paul-Binyamin and Haj-Yehia (who examined the structure of encounters between Israeli Jews and Palestinians), found that folkloristic encounters that were based on sharing experiences, customs, music, and food, frustrated the participants, while conflictual meetings kept them apart.[14] In other work, Paul-Binyamin and Haj-Yehia, Jayusi, and Rosen and Perkins have argued that sporadic approaches to cross-communal encounters are too limited, because although they may contribute to a short-term change in standpoints of young adults, they are likely to have negligible long-term effects.[15] Participants feel that the encounters are an external "project" that invades their daily routine and will soon fade away.

Thus, the goal of reducing hostility and prejudice between conflicting groups seems to require a more long-term investment and ongoing interactions. One crucial method for this is cross-cultural or cross-community teaching. Cross-cultural teaching that places Israeli Palestinian teachers in Jewish schools and Jewish teachers in Arab schools is an attempt to create continuous engagements that become an integral part of school life. When teachers enter a school of "the other," a relationship between equal-status partners is created and the existing social and political hierarchy turns upside down. The encounter enables students to experience the other not only as a human being, but also as a knowledgeable agent, an authority, and often as a beloved educational figure.

Minority Teachers in Majority Schools

It is a widely held assumption that placement of minority teachers in majority schools helps overcome cultural and linguistic barriers.[16] There is also some important research on the contributions and influences of minority teachers. In the United States, for instance, the issue of integrating teachers of color in majority schools has been researched since the 1970s.[17] Researchers unanimously agree that teachers from diverse cultural and ethnic backgrounds contribute extensively to creating a more open and egalitarian school system.[18] Similarly, Cherng and Halpin claim that students who were exposed to minority teachers had a more favorable perception of Black and Latino teachers than of non-minority teachers.[19] McNamara and Basit examined the experiences of British teachers of Asian and African / Caribbean origin teaching outside their communities, concluding that the majority of the teachers found their schools supportive and their instruction process valuable.[20] Moreover, they felt that they play an important social role in building bridges between antagonistic communities and countering prejudice and racism both within schools and in the wider society.

Research in other countries also shows important benefits of teachers from minority backgrounds. In Germany, for instance, studies found that hiring more minority teachers is considered a promising means of dealing with existing difficulties in diverse schools.[21] Looking to Australia, an investigation of the experiences of indigenous teachers and ethnic minority teachers in Australian schools suggested that the teachers' "knowledge of self" regarding ethnicity and social class enabled them to empathize with diverse groups of students from perspectives not available to teachers from the dominant cultural majority.[22] As a further example, a study in Hong Kong examining twelve minority teachers (American, Canadian, Indian, Nepalese, and Pakistani), indicated that ethnic minority teachers were able to create a culturally responsive environment.[23]

Thus, Israel is among a number of countries interested in the possibilities of cross-cultural teaching. In 2013, the Israeli Ministry of Education decided to expand cross-cultural teaching, aiming to incorporate five hundred Israeli Palestinian teachers into Jewish schools. Merchavim, an Israeli nongovernmental organization, was recruited to support Arab teachers in Jewish schools and study the progress they made. In the first year, 465 Arab teachers were recruited, and approximately one hundred more have been recruited each year since, reaching almost 1,400 teachers by 2021 (out of Israel's 200,000 teachers) These teachers teach not only Arabic, but a variety of other subjects such as English, science, special education, and other subjects.[24]

The Merchavim program's cross-cultural teaching is a relatively small sample, but following its impact is important when aiming to scale up. Research shows that crossing the cultural and communal lines affects both teachers and students. Fragman investigated the integration of Israeli Palestinian teachers who taught spoken Arabic in elementary schools and found that they are satisfied with their position and feel empowered by their self-definition as "ambassadors of good will."[25] And yet, as the term "ambassador" indicates, they perceive themselves as external to the community, teaching their language to "others." Unfortunately, for the most part, they did not feel well-supported, and also often felt lonely, isolated, and vulnerable.

Some other recent research sheds further light on some of the complex dimensions of these cross-community teaching and learning efforts. Gindi and Erlich Ron examined the way 163 Israeli Palestinian teachers placed in Jewish schools handled power relationships within their workplace and found that they were forced to navigate between their national and professional identities.[26] And yet other studies of these efforts by Jayusi and Bekerman indicate that these teachers can have some important benefits despite these difficulties.[27] They conclude that Israeli Palestinian teachers in Jewish schools experience a strong sense of self-efficacy, they believe their work helps reduce prejudice and increases mutual understanding among the groups in conflict. As one of these teachers reports:

> I had many experiences that changed and shaped my professional identity as a teacher and changed and shaped the attitude of students, parents and colleges towards the society from which I came. My presence in a Jewish school makes a difference. My students were curious to learn more about the "other," not to judge, [but rather] accept differences. My message is clear, the fact that we are different doesn't make any of us less worthy of care and respect.[28]

Although there are some promising results from these studies, thus far the presence of Israeli Palestinian teachers in Jewish schools is too limited to provide more than anecdotal evidence. Nevertheless, some preliminary inferences can be drawn from what we have learned so far: Ongoing encounters between teachers and students can reduce hostility and diminish alienation when three supportive conditions are in place:

1. when highly qualified teachers who teach a variety of subjects (not just Arabic) enter Jewish schools;
2. when the schools are coached on how to accommodate and support these teachers;
3. when the teachers themselves are well prepared to teach cross-culturally and receive ongoing support.

There could be no better example of Derrick Bell's interest convergence theory than this case. Bell argues that the rights of Black people only advance when they converge with the interests of white people. Twenty-five years after the US Supreme Court's ruling in *Brown v. Board of Education*, Bell argued that the aftermath of the decision "cannot be understood without some consideration of the decision's value to whites, not simply those concerned about the immorality of racial inequality, but also those whites in policymaking positions able to see the economic and political advances at home and abroad that would follow abandonment of segregation."[29]

It is unclear whether interest convergence could be seen as a necessary and sufficient condition for the success of cross-cultural teaching. Many external circumstances can alter the results of such an exchange. So, is it a necessary condition? Can cross-community teaching succeed in cases where there is no interest conversion?: for example, when teachers of one community think that teachers from the other community take their jobs, or parents suspect that cross-teaching is a way of introducing their children to a set of beliefs they are alienated from, or, as we have seen in some cases in Israel, that the minority leadership question the "real" role of the teachers, wondering whether they are agents of the state. In all such cases, the effectiveness of cross-group teaching is affected. In other words, the more supportive the environment is to the process of cross-teaching and the more it judges teachers by their performance irrespective of their origin, the more successful the exchange will be.

In is worth mentioning that Bell's idea of "interest convergence" helps us uncover two difficulties inherent in placing excellent minority teachers in majority schools. It forces teachers to excel in their performance as failure will reflect on the whole group and break up the convergence. Consequently, minority schools may be losing their best workforce. Neither of these issues should be ignored.

Majority Teachers in Minority Schools

Very few studies examine the influence of teachers from majority groups teaching in minority schools. Some evaluate the influence of white teachers on the achievements, attitudes, and academic performance of Black students.[30] A cross-sectional study examined the attitudes of 174 minority pre-adolescents (aged 9–13) toward the Dutch majority, indicating that Turkish and Moroccan students who studied with a teacher from the majority group had more positive attitudes toward the Dutch out-group. In such cross-communal teachings the positive aspect of the relationship ("closeness") was more important than the negative aspect ("conflict").[31]

In recent years, a limited number of Jewish teachers were placed in Arab schools to help Arab students learn to speak fluent Hebrew. Gara investigated this process and found that most teachers reported they had a good and interesting experience.[32] They saw their work as an opportunity to win the hearts of Arab students, reducing prejudice and misconceptions. Thus, while more research is needed, there are some indications that benefits can accrue from cross-community teaching and learning when teachers are from the majority or dominant group and students are from minority groups.

In addition to such findings, our research suggests that there can be important positive effects on the broader community of teachers at schools that include a teacher from a different group. We consider these effects now.

Potential Benefits of Cross-Cultural Teaching for Communities of Teachers: Some Stages and Developments Reported by Teachers

In our study of cases of cross-cultural teaching in Israel, we found that teachers often went through an eight-stage process of experiences and development. We have defined these stages below. While not every teacher or every school will reach the latter stages of this developmental process, all of them pass through the initial stages, and the few who will not transcend the initial stages usually withdraw from cross-teaching.

Stage 1: Mutual Cultural Alienation

In the first stage, estrangement is prevalent as stereotypes and the differences embedded in the way of life, religious beliefs, norms and values, and habitual behavior distance the participants and emphasize their otherness. In the Israeli case, national ceremonies are the most stressful occasions: "It is especially difficult for me to sing the anthem at school events; days like Independence Day, Memorial Day or Holocaust Day emphasize my otherness," says an Israeli Palestinian teacher. "On Memorial Day," says a Jewish teacher, "it feels awkward to see an Arab teacher standing next to the memorial site commemorating fallen students from our community."

Stage 2: Creating a Preliminary Community

"Warming up" happens in the second stage. It allows communication among members of the various groups, blurring the boundaries between "us" and "them" to create a joint community, such as "the Teachers' Room," where all members have equal rights. The Teachers' Room is a new community that embodies the principles of tolerance, respect, and trust. "The atmosphere in the staffroom is positive," reported an Israeli Palestinian teacher. "I think I succeeded in reducing prejudices among a lot of teachers. The most moving moment was when a teacher who had lost her son in war and conveyed explicit hostility at the beginning of the year saying she hates all Arabs, befriended me later on."

Stage 3: Cross-Cultural Dialogs

In the third stage, there can be opportunities to move toward more exchange and interaction. Willingness to learn about each other, and comparing differences and similarities, opens the door for more honest, personal conversations based on respectful dialog motivated by a desire to work together in the newly created community of the Teachers' Room.

Stage 4: Undermining Stereotypes

In this stage, we can begin to see the reduction of prejudice and hostility by breaking down problematic stereotypes. The creation of community and beginning of dialog can generate more open-mindedness, which allows teachers to de-emphasize the role of stereotypes and external indicators that were operating during the first stages. Teachers now see each other as individuals with an independent identity and personality rather than anonymous members of the group of "the other."

Stage 5: Communication and Problem-Solving

The transformation of previously stereotyped or culturally identified individuals into distinct human "persons" allows teachers to continue to the next stage, focusing on professional issues and seeking solutions to common problems while getting to know each other. Teachers can work together on pedagogical issues, discuss ways to cope with their students' difficulties, and complain about school life. Many teachers are also mothers, and they may exchange experiences about child rearing, married life, communal celebrations—they bring food to the teachers' room, eat together, and exchange recipes. Thus, in these stages the communication transcends the professional sphere and becomes much more personalized.

Stage 6: Accepting the Other as a Member of the Profession

Professional communication, openness, the desire to hear the "other" and perhaps even learn from them, gives teachers an opportunity to view their fellow teachers as colleagues. In the research material we have examined, we saw that both sides attested to feelings of professional respect and recognition: "She is just like any other colleague of mine; regardless of being Jewish or Arab." Teachers who have reached this stage see themselves as having a joint professional identity and affiliation, emphasizing similarities rather than differences, seeking possible collaborations in an attempt to solve mutual problems. For them, the Teachers' Room represents a unified professional space: "It's our school," both Jewish and Arab teachers say. "We have a common mission to succeed."

Stage 7: Increasing Collegiality and Openness

In a few cases, professional communications led to high levels of collegiality and some personal closeness: "Being honest, having open conversations, expressing empathy"; "When you know each other the relationship deepens, and you find more and more resemblances."

Stage 8: Accepting the Other as a Personal Friend

For school sites with the greatest success, the process can progress to the stage that teachers belonging to different cultural groups, who started from a point of mutual alienation, establish friendships and share thoughts and hopes for a better future. The fact that they coalesce into a community reflects also on their students and the way they perceive the role of "the other" in their educational community.

We believe the opportunities and possibilities we observed from these teachers are extremely important for creating more positive interaction and connection. A functional and inclusive school community teaches by example. Coexistence is created before entering direct and lengthy discussions of heated controversies that could exacerbate tensions. Through living and working together, teachers and students practice self- and mutual respect across religious, national, and gender communities, embodying civic virtues even if they do not explicitly define these actions as a means to a civic end.

To be sure, cross-cultural teaching is not guaranteed to bring benefits, but requires careful planning and preparation. Much of the success of processes of integration depends on the role played by the school principal, a support system, and pre-contact preparation, which make a considerable difference in both the scope and the depth of the mutual acceptance process. One thing of utmost importance is the role of a school principal in publicly and consistently supporting a minoritized teacher by establishing norms and rejecting discrimination against demographic groups, including groups to which teachers belong. School principals play a key role in creating a school climate through public statements, explaining why they appreciate diversity in the teaching force in general and emphasizing that, in particular, they are keen to have an Arab teacher as part of their cohort.

In divided societies, civic virtue demands that we will learn to live with "others," hence diversity among the teaching cohort is a double blessing. Not only does it help recruit qualified teachers, it also transforms the atmosphere in the school to make it "diversity accommodating"—something that has inherent educational value, reducing the prejudice and hostility that often persist in diverse communities.

When teachers from the non-dominant group support students' academic achievement, this can also open the door for additional civic learning and connection. Along the way, teachers from the non-dominant group develop individual relationships with students that can result in those students humanizing the minoritized teachers. This allows for interest convergence as the dominant group has an interest in having their children receive an excellent education, and the non-dominant group has an interest in having more opportunities for positions and professional advancement. This is particularly true in the Israeli context, where there is a shortage of teachers in the Jewish sector and an abundance of teachers in the Palestinian one.

CONCLUSION

There is certainly room for more research on cross-cultural exchanges. Yet, based on existing findings, we offer the following conclusions: Some common approaches to teaching civics in a polarized society often increase rather than decrease social and political tensions. Educational segregation leads groups to converse only with their own group in ways that can intensify polarization. Internal and external intervention can pressure teachers to shy away from dealing with core issues that could trigger violence and accentuate social cleavages. The result is that the most volatile and important civic questions are left out of the curriculum and schools focus on technical issues, procedures, and institutions.[33]

We urge that the creation of a community of common concern and respect is best pursued by creating ongoing cross-group classroom interaction and learning on noncontroversial topics rather than by focusing on staging direct discussions of the most polarizing issues. Drawing inspiration from Contact Theory, we reviewed the effect of numerous cross-cultural, cross-religious encounters, which have been found to have some valuable short-term effects, but also some limitations. We then examined the option of cross-cultural / religious / ethnic teaching and discovered that this approach may have deeper, more lasting effects, including positive effects on the broad community of teachers at a school.

To learn more, we intend to follow teachers from Beit-Berl College who were trained to work in cross-communal settings. We recognize that cross-cultural, religious, ethnic teaching alone is not enough to help bring a society together, and other means must be implemented to revive a spirit of civic coexistence. Yet cross-teaching has an exceptional potential to contribute to the development of an inclusive society and the nurturing of civic virtues needed to create more empathetic and just societies. Most of all, we believe cross-community teaching is an effective means of humanizing the other and reducing harmful prejudice. As Seneca wrote at the end of his treatise on the destructive effects of anger and hatred, "Soon we shall breathe our last. Meanwhile, while we live, while we are among human beings, let us cultivate our humanity."[34]

Postscript: *Even after the horrific events of the 7th of October and the war in Gaza that left us all wounded, pained and angry, we continue to believe in coexistence and to seek a way to live together respectfully. We will keep striving to develop cross communal activities and hope for better days to come.*

Notes

1 We are well aware that the idea of "the Poitier effect" has some problematic dimensions and may operate as a double-edged sword for minorities. Sharon Willis points out that, "as Hollywood's first Black leading man, Poitier came to signify to the white status quo a form of racial reconciliation." His role as a teacher overcoming the prejudice of students in *To Sir with Love* could be seen as carrying a silent but false message that race no longer matters. See Sharon Willis, *The Poitier Effect: Racial Melodrama and Fantasies of Reconciliation* (Minneapolis: University of Minnesota Press, 2015). As this chapter unfolds, we hope it will be clear that we are encouraging a different type of intergroup contact effect that dignifies the identity of all of the participants, including those from minority or outsider groups. Moreover, it wishes to make diversity, and the complexity it carries, present in the life of children and the general community.

2 Gordon W. Allport, *The Nature of Prejudice* (Reading, MA: Addison-Wesley, 1954).

3 Rupert Brown and Miles Hewstone, "An Integrative Theory of Intergroup Contact," *Advances in Experimental Social Psychology* 37 (2005): 255–343.

4 Donald Easton-Brooks, Chance Lewis, and Yubo Yang, "Ethnic-Matching: The Influence of African American Teachers on the Reading Scores of African American Students," *National Journal of Urban Education & Practice* 3, no. 1 (2010): 230–243; Jacqueline Jordan Irvine, "Beyond Role Models: An Examination of Cultural Influences on the Pedagogical Perspectives of Black Teachers," *Peabody Journal of Education* 66, no. 4 (1989): 51–63, https://doi.org/10.1080/01619568909538662; Jacqueline Jordan Irvine and Leslie T. Fenwick, "Teachers and Teaching for the New Millennium: The Role of HBCUs," *Journal of Negro Education* 80, no. 3 (2011): 197–208; Dririt Lengyel and Lisa Rosen, "Minority Teachers in Different Educational Contexts: Introduction," *Tertium Comparationis* 21, no. 2 (2015): 153–160; Olwen McNamara and Tehmina N. Basit, "Equal Opportunities or Affirmative Action? The Induction of Minority Ethnic Teachers," *Journal of Education for Teaching* 30, no. 2 (2004): 97–115; Ninetta Santoro, "'Outsiders' and 'Others': 'Different' Teachers Teaching in Culturally Diverse Classrooms," *Teachers and Teaching* 13, no. 1 (2007): 81–97; Josef Strasser and Wiebke Waburg, "Students' Perspectives on Minority Teachers in Germany," *Tertium Comparationis* 2, no. 2 (2015): 251–274.

5 This is a similar distinction to the concepts of thin and thick multiculturalism that Yael (Yuli) Tamir offers in "Two Concepts of Multiculturalism," *Journal of Philosophy of Education* 29, no. 2 (1995): 161–173.

6 Amy Gutmann, *Democratic Education* (Princeton, NJ: Princeton University Press, 1987), 11.

7 Zaid Jilani and Jeremy Adam Smith, "What Is the True Cost of Polarization in America?," *The Greater Good Magazine*, March 4, 2019.

8 Noam Gidron, James Adams, and Will Horne, *American Affective Polarization in Comparative Perspective. Elements in American Politics* (Cambridge: Cambridge University Press, 2020).

9 Associated Press, "Wisconsin Assembly Approves Bill Requiring Civics Education," September 28, 2021.

10 Riley Vetterkind, "Wisconsin Assembly Passes Ban on Teaching Critical Race Theory," *Wisconsin State Journal*, September 29, 2021.

11 Diana E. Hess, *Controversy in the Classroom: The Democratic Power of Discussion* (New York and London: Routledge, 2009); Diana E. Hess, "Teaching Controversial Issues: An Introduction," *Social Education* 82, no. 6 (2018): 306; Ilana Paul-Binyamin and Tali Hayosh, "'Safe Space' for Jewish and Arab Teachers Dealing with Controversial Issues," *Leadership and Policy in Schools* (2021), 1–16.

12 Gordon W. Allport, *The Nature of Prejudice* (Reading, MA: Addison-Wesley, 1954); Thomas F. Pettigrew, Linda R. Tropp, Ulrich Wagner, and Oliver Christ, "Recent Advances in Intergroup Contact Theory," *International Journal of Intercultural Relations* 35, no. 3 (2011): 271–280.

13 Ifat Maoz, "Does Contact Work in Protracted Asymmetrical Conflict? Appraising 20 Years of Reconciliation-Aimed Encounters between Israeli Jews and Palestinians," *Journal of Peace Research* 48, no. 1 (2011): 115–125.

14 Ilana Paul-Binyamin and Kussai Haj-Yehia, "Multicultural Education in Teacher Education: Shared Experience and Awareness of Power Relations as a Prerequisite for Conflictual Identities Dialogue in Israel," *Teaching and Teacher Education* 85 (2019): 249–259.

15 Paul-Binyamin and Haj-Yehia, "Multicultural Education in Teacher Education"; Wurud Jayusi, "Restoring the Attitudes of Palestinian and Jewish Students Who Participated in Peace Education Programs Through Peer-Tutoring," *Al-Hasad* 1 (2011): 101–133 [in Arabic]; and Yigal Rosen and David Perkins, "Shallow Roots Require Constant Watering: The Challenge of Sustained Impact in Educational Programs," *International Journal of Higher Education* 2, no. 4 (2013): 91–100.

16 J. J. Irvine, "Beyond Role Models: An Examination of Cultural Influences on the Pedagogical Perspectives of Black Teachers," *Peabody Journal of Education* 66, no. 4 (1989): 51–63; https://doi.org/10.1080/01619568909538662; Strasser and Waburg, "Students' Perspectives on Minority Teachers in Germany."

17 Sabrina Hope King, "The Limited Presence of African-American Teachers," *Review of Educational Research* 63, no. 2 (1993): 115–149. https://doi.org/10.3102/00346543063002115.

18 D. Easton-Brooks, C. Lewis, and Y. Yang, "Ethnic-Matching: The Influence of African American Teachers on the Reading Scores of African American Students," *National Journal of Urban Education & Practice* 3, no. 1 (2010): 230–243; J. J. Irvine and L. T. Fenwick, "Teachers and Teaching for the New Millennium: The Role of HBCUs," *Journal of Negro Education* 80, no. 3 (2011): 197–208.

19 Hua-Yu Sebastian Cherng and Peter F. Halpin, "The Importance of Minority Teachers: Student Perceptions of Minority Versus White Teachers," *Educational Researcher* 45, no. 7 (2016): 407–420.

20 O. McNamara and T. N. Basit, "Equal Opportunities or Affirmative Action? The Induction of Minority Ethnic Teachers," *Journal of Education for Teaching* 30, no. 2 (2004): 97–115.

21 Strasser and Waburg, "Students' Perspectives on Minority Teachers in Germany."

22 N. Santoro, "'Outsiders' and 'Others': 'Different' Teachers Teaching in Culturally Diverse Classrooms," *Teachers and Teaching* 13, no. 1 2007): 81–97.

23 Ming Tak Hue and Kerry John Kennedy, "The Challenge of Promoting Ethnic Minority Education and Cultural Diversity in Hong Kong Schools: From Policy to Practice," *Revista española de educación comparada* 23 (2014): 117–134.

24 Merchavim, The Institute for the Advancement of Shared Citizenship in Israel. Retrieved from http://www.machon-merchavim.org.il. 2021. Accessed October 15, 2021.

25 Alon Fragman, "The Integration of Arab Native Teachers as Teachers of Arabic in Hebrew-Speaking Schools: Intended Policy or Arbitrary Strategy," *Annual of Language & Politics and Politics of Identity* 2 (2008): 55–80.

26 Shahar Gindi and Rakefet Erlich-Ron, "Bargaining with the System: A Mixed-Methods Study of Arab Teachers in Israel," *International Journal of Intercultural Relations* 69 (2019): 44–53.

27 Wurud Jayusi and Zvi Bekerman, "Yes, We Can!—Palestinian-Israeli Teachers in Jewish-Israeli Schools," *Journal of Teacher Education* 71, no. 3 (2019): 1–13. https://doi.org/10.1177/00224871198498.

28 Jayusi and Bekerman, "Yes, We Can!."

29 Derrick A. Bell, "Brown v. Board of Education and the Interest Convergence Dilemma," *Harvard Law Review* 93, no. 3 (1980): 518–533.

30 Bruce Douglas, Chance Lewis, Adrian Douglas, Malcolm Earl Scott, and Dorothy Garrison-Wade, "The Impact of White Teachers on the Academic Achievement of Black Students: An Exploratory Qualitative Analysis," *Educational Foundations* 22, no. 1/2 (2008): 47–62; Carla Bidwell and David W. Stinson, "Crossing 'The Problem of the Color Line': White Mathematics Teachers and Black Students." In *Proceedings of the 38th Annual Meeting of the North American Chapter of the International Group for the Psychology of Mathematics. Education,* ed. M. B. Wood, E. E. Tuner, M. Civil, and J. A. Eli, 2016.

31 Jochem Thijs and Maykel Verkuyten, "Ethnic Attitudes of Minority Students and Their Contact with Majority Group Teachers," *Journal of Applied Developmental Psychology* 33, no. 5 (2012): 260–268.

32 A. Gara, Proposal for a research thesis submitted as partial fulfillment of the requirements towards a master's degree in education / teaching program. MA dissertation. Beit berl, 2021. [in Hebrew].

33 Yael (Yuli) Tamir, "Teachers in the Social Trenches: Teaching Civics in a Divided Society," *Theory and Research in Education* 13, no. 1 (2015): 121–136.

34 M. Nussbaum, *Cultivating Humanity: A Classical Defense of Reform in Liberal Education* (Cambridge, MA: Harvard University Press, 1997).

8

THE CHALLENGES OF THICK DIVERSITY, POLARIZATION, DEBIASING, AND TOKENIZATION FOR CROSS-GROUP TEACHING

RIMA BASU

Teachers play an important role in our development. It is a running joke on Twitter that if you were ever your English or art teacher's favorite, you're probably gay now. I was often the favorite of both, so I guess that explains some things. More to the point, it's likely that most people can recall a teacher who made a significant positive impact on their lives. That is, a teacher who was a stabilizing source, a teacher who inspired, a teacher who believed in them when others didn't. A teacher who pushed them to become better than they were.

The powerful role that teachers can play in our development is the focus of Paul-Binyamin, Jayusi, and Tamir's chapter in this volume. They argue that teachers, in particular teachers who don't share the same background as their students, can help counter the increasing polarization that characterizes our current era.[1] This so-called Poitier effect, named after actor Sidney Poitier and his role as an inspirational teacher breaking down racial divides in the movie *To Sir with Love*, is the type of transformative debiasing phenomenon that the authors seek to reproduce. That is, can cross-group teaching reduce racial and cultural biases and divides and create greater mutual respect?

However, in asking whether the Poitier effect can be adapted for today's classrooms, Paul-Binyamin, Jayusi, and Tamir note that there

175

is a challenge for their project—a challenge that they identify as emerging from how different our current era is from the era in which *To Sir with Love* was released. According to the authors, the film and its reception occurred in a culture of *thin diversity*. The challenge for adapting the strategy for current classrooms is that our current era is, the authors claim, marked by a culture of *thick diversity*. Although we aren't given a full characterization of these two accounts of diversity, we are told that the distinction between thin and thick diversity should be regarded as similar to the distinction between thin and thick multiculturalism, as discussed in Tamir.[2]

To judge the proposal put forward by Paul-Binyamin, Jayusi, and Tamir, we must first bring to the surface three underlying assumptions and consider some important issues that might otherwise be obscured. These issues, I will argue, raise serious questions about whether cross-group teaching could help reduce polarization as well as whether this model of teaching could be implemented in a way that does not create additional burdens or harms for minority teachers or students.

First, we must question whether our current era is rightly characterized as one of *thick diversity* as opposed to *thin diversity*. Further, we must also judge whether it is thick diversity that gives rise to polarization. To address these questions, I first attempt to give a fuller account of thick diversity by drawing on Tamir's account of thick multiculturalism.[3] Although I grant that our current society might be characterized as one of thick diversity as opposed to thin diversity, I note that much more argument is needed to make the case for the claim that thick diversity is responsible for the polarization we see today. There are many mechanisms by which polarization can occur, but I will outline just a few of them, focusing on some purely rational mechanisms by which polarization can occur. That is, polarization doesn't only occur between people stubbornly refusing to engage with the other side and dogmatically holding onto their beliefs. Polarization can occur among reasonable people following epistemically sound practices. That is, there's reason to think polarization can occur in communities characterized by thin diversity as well. As a result, polarization is not a problem unique to thick diversity or thick multiculturalism.

Second, with a better understanding of the processes of polarization, we then must judge whether attempts to recreate the Poitier effect can be a counterforce or bulwark against increasing polarization. That is, whether, as the authors claim, "meeting an admirable teacher who belongs to 'the other' has the potential to be transformative, teach children how to respect diversity, and ameliorate social and political polarization."[4] Central to this claim is the psychological theory put forth in Gordon Allport's contact hypothesis.[5] However, as I'll demonstrate, there are a number of reasons to doubt that contact with "the other" can have this transformative effect on prejudice. Research in social psychology since the publication of Allport's *The Nature of Prejudice* has shown that increased contact can lead to a number of backlash effects and unintended consequences that increase rather than decrease prejudice.

Third, and following from the first and second points, as is clear by now, I am not as optimistic as Paul-Binyamin, Jayusi, and Tamir about the power of teachers to reverse the polarization that plagues society today. But as I hope to make clear here, my lack of optimism doesn't stem merely from my general disposition toward pessimism, nor from any lack of faith in the ability of talented teachers to connect with and inspire their students. Rather, the source of my pessimism stems primarily from serious concerns about the costs that minority teachers and minority students would have to bear under this proposal. So, I then turn to worries about problems of tokenization, instrumental rationales for diversity, and the combination of the "politics of deference" and "being-in-the-room privilege" that could occur with this type of teaching model.[6]

THICK DIVERSITY AND POLARIZATION

Thin vs. Thick Diversity and Thin vs. Thick Multiculturalism

As I noted in the previous section, although a central claim of Paul-Binyamin, Jayusi, and Tamir's chapter is that our current era is one marked by thick diversity as opposed to thin diversity, the reader isn't given a full characterization of these key concepts. Rather, the authors state that the distinction between thin and thick diversity should be regarded as similar to the distinction between thin and thick multiculturalism, as discussed in Tamir's "Two Concepts of Multiculturalism."[7] To judge whether thick diversity gives rise to polarization, however, we must first understand precisely what is meant by thick diversity. Let us turn to that now by first explicating this distinction between thin and thick multiculturalism so we may then understand the distinction between thin and thick diversity.

According to Tamir, thin multiculturalism involves different liberal cultures, whereas thick multiculturalism involves both liberal and illiberal cultures. For thin multiculturalism, Tamir's example is the debate between English- and French-speaking communities in Canada wherein "the two communities share a set of liberal-democratic beliefs, [as a result] the debate is an intra-liberal one."[8] In short, the two communities have a shared set of beliefs and, as a result, "disagreements over basic principles do not arise."[9] For thick multiculturalism, Tamir's example is the French ban on face coverings, which "French officials see as imposing neutrality [whereas] Muslims see as a campaign against Islam."[10] This is a deeper disparity than the first example because there is a deep disagreement about whether religion can or should remain strictly private.

Our current era, Paul-Binyamin, Jayusi, and Tamir claim, is one marked by a lack of common ground, one in which there's no agreement on common rules, one in which we are increasingly polarized and segregated. That is, just as thick multiculturalism is marked by deep disagreement about fundamental matters, thick diversity is similarly marked by deep, intractable disagreement.

At first glance this might seem like an odd claim to make about our current time period in contrast to the 1960s. However, a report published on the sixty-fifth anniversary of *Brown v. Board of Education* observes "a disconcerting increase of black segregation in all parts of the country."[11] And as reported in Vox, "black students in the South are less likely to attend a school that is majority white than about 50 years ago."[12] Growing polarization exists hand in hand with growing segregation. For example, a 2014 report from the Pew Research Center notes that "Republicans and Democrats are more divided along ideological lines—and partisan antipathy is deeper and more extensive—than at any point in the last two decades."[13] These are not the conditions under which civic education can thrive.

So, what are the conditions under which civic education can pave a path toward virtuous active citizenry? Paul-Binyamin, Jayusi, and Tamir identify two conditions that I reproduce below.

(a) Members of the diverse groups that constitute a society share an agreed upon set of basic norms and principles; or

(b) The dominant group dictates the norms and principles while members of other groups abide by these rules.[14]

They note that this characterization resembles the characterization of thin diversity outlined earlier. Although the argument isn't explicitly given this form, their remarks may seem to suggest that combating polarization requires returning to thin diversity. That is, one might think that the liberal culture of thin diversity or thin multiculturalism is either more rational or at the very least less likely to lead to polarization than thick diversity because of the shared set of basic beliefs. Such a view, however, would be mistaken, as polarization can result from a number of mechanisms, including rational ones. I turn next to spelling out how.

The Processes of Polarization

Although it might seem intuitive, at first blush, to assume that belief polarization is the result of epistemically irrational processes, there has been pushback against this view in recent years. For example, as Tom Kelly has argued, paying more attention to evidence for views we disagree with—a practice you might think would help counteract polarization—can actually increase polarization.[15] Kevin Dorst argues, more forcefully, that many of the reasoning "biases" discussed in the psychological literature, e.g., searching for confirming arguments, interpreting conflicting evidence as confirmatory, and becoming more extreme in reaction to discussion, are in fact *rational* processes.[16]

On the one hand, demonstrating that polarization is a rational process can help bolster Paul-Binyamin et al.'s point that in a polarized society we cannot overcome differences and reduce hostility through rational deliberations. On the other hand, in demonstrating how polarization happens, it's also clear that polarization is not a problem *that arises uniquely because of* thick diversity. That is, polarization can also occur in cultures of thin diversity.

To demonstrate rational polarization, I want to consider some results from a computer simulation run by Singer et al.[17] Let's assume two groups, A and B. Each group has a set of beliefs that are epistemically rational for them to hold. And now each group shares the reasons for their beliefs with one another. For the simulation, it does not seem to matter whether the groups' beliefs are distinct from one another or whether there are beliefs shared in common. Singer et al. found that in their simulation, "agents with unlimited memories in pure deliberation (with no outside input) [. . .] eventually end up with the same set of reasons, giving them the same view with the same strength."[18] However, we're not agents with unlimited memories.[19] A more rational strategy for us is that of what Singer et al. call a *coherence-minded agent*, that is, one who, given their limited memory, prioritizes remembering the reasons for the view that is best supported by all their reasons. What Singer et al. find in their simulations is that such agents *always polarize*. Importantly, these coherence-minded agents do not commit the epistemic sins that most of the literature on polarization focus on. Coherence-minded agents in Singer et al.'s simulations aren't overtly biased, they do not "misjudge the content or strength of their evidence, nor do they misprocess evidence they receive. Our agents incorporate new reasons before deciding what to forget, and as such they aren't irrationally stubborn like biased assimilators."[20]

So, what can we learn from this? Critically, polarization is a structural problem. That is, it is not a problem that is necessarily tied to individual biases (implicit or explicit) or individual prejudices. For example, as Eduardo Bonilla-Silva has argued, racism can persist without racists.[21] Returning to polarization, polarization can occur in societies characterized by both thin and thick diversity. Whatever explains the greater polarization of our current society is not merely a matter of greater disagreement or divergence among racial or ethnic groups. Proposing a solution to growing polarization requires identifying the mechanisms for our growing polarization.

Furthermore, in assessing whether teachers can be a bulwark against polarization in our current political climate, Paul-Binyamin et al.'s own discussion of the panic over critical race theory suggests that teachers might in fact be poorly situated or limited in their capacity to turn back the tides of polarization. There are reasons to doubt whether the presence of minority teachers in classrooms can be effective in reducing bias in a highly polarized society. For example, consider more closely the US context and the moral panic over critical race theory. Although teachers are in a position to change students' minds because of the authority their positions represent, that is precisely why they are seen as a threat and are being targeted in the current debates about critical race theory in schools.[22] A process that we see being employed is what Endre Begby calls *evidential preemption*, and this process is central to the creation of *echo chambers*.[23] Understanding these processes can help us understand impediments to cultivating a form of the Poitier effect.

Expanding on these concepts, evidential preemption is most easily recognizable as the following sort of claim: "My opponents will tell you that *q*, but I say *p*."[24] As Begby notes, this type of argument is characteristic of many right-wing pundits, such as Bill O'Reilly and Newt Gingrich. Evidential preemption turns disagreement into a way to reinforce the views of the group. For example, if you've been primed that others will try to undermine your belief in some conspiracy theory by drawing your attention to x, y, or z, then when in conversation someone brings up x, y, or z, that's evidence that your conspiracy theory is right. Further, as C. Thi Nguyen notes, "by making undermining predictions about contrary testimony, inside authorities not only discredit that contrary testimony, but increase their trustworthiness for future predictions."[25]

To see this in action, consider how students may be warned that universities are full of the illiberal left who are intolerant of conservative viewpoints. That is, students may be given a preemptory warning that their teachers will try to undermine their faith or turn them into atheists.[26] When someone is evidentially preempted in such a way, any pushback that they experience in response to their views will then be seen as precisely the kind of threat they were warned against and as evidence of a left-wing conspiracy against conservatives.[27] This helps to create an echo chamber, which Nguyen defines as follows:

> I use "echo chamber" to mean an epistemic community which creates a significant disparity in trust between members and non-members. This disparity is created by excluding non-members through epistemic discrediting, while simultaneously amplifying members' epistemic credentials. Finally, echo chambers are such

that general agreement with some core set of beliefs is a prerequisite for membership, where those core beliefs include beliefs that support that disparity in trust.[28]

In support of Paul-Binyamin, Jayusi, and Tamir's distinction between thin and thick diversity, it is worth noting how this definition of an echo chamber closely resembles the kind of illiberal communities that were Tamir's concern with regard to thick multiculturalism. In her earlier paper, Tamir notes:

> liberals expose their children to illiberal forms of life while defenders of illiberal cultures make a special effort to shelter their children from any form of cultural diversity. Taking into account that complete closure is impossible, members of illiberal cultures also make sure to disparage other cultures, religions and traditions as sources of knowledge and self-reflection. In fact they often ridicule the idea of self-reflection, contrasting it with the idea of absolute truth proclaimed through revelation or the handing down of wisdom from one generation of sages to another. By claiming that the only valid source of knowledge is internal to the group they attempt to lessen the importance of multicultural exchanges and to render them less harmful.[29]

However, given these mechanisms of evidential preemption and the creation and maintenance of echo chambers in highly polarized societies, one must wonder whether learning from minority teachers will be enough to create a common ground for reducing bias and generating shared citizenship. This brings me to my second concern.

THE CONTACT HYPOTHESIS: UNINTENDED CONSEQUENCES AND BACKLASH EFFECTS

In the face of such extreme polarization, the promise of civic education for promoting civic bonds seems unachievable. However, by exploring the use of some methods of cross-cultural interaction and teaching as practiced in the Israeli education system, Paul-Binyamin, Jayusi, and Tamir suggest that there may be some hope for overcoming the forms of polarization we see today. Notably, their methods build on the insights and operation of contact theory, which was initially developed by Gordon Allport as a method to humanize the other through ongoing personal contact. That is, according to the contact hypothesis, prejudice between two groups can be reduced through ongoing contact (provided certain conditions are met).

I will begin with some reason for hope for contact theory before I turn to my critical comments. In Nguyen's discussion of how to escape from an echo chamber, he highlights the story of Derek Black. Derek Black is not only the son of the creator of the white nationalist site Stormfront but also the godson of David Duke, a white supremacist, far-right politician, and former Grand Wizard of the KKK. Thus, Derek Black was heralded as the heir to the white nationalist movement. As reported in the *Washington Post*, he was pulled from his "public school in West Palm Beach at the end of third grade, when [his parents] heard his black teacher say the word 'ain't.'"[30] At New College, however, where Derek enrolled to study medieval European history, things changed. As Nguyen writes:

> Black went to college and was shunned by almost everyone in his college community. But then Matthew Stevenson, a Jewish fellow undergraduate, began to invite Black to his Shabbat dinners. Stevenson was unfailingly kind, open, and generous, and he slowly earned Black's trust. This eventually lead to a massive upheaval for Black—a slow dawning realization of the depths to which he had been systematically misled. Black went through a profound transformation and is now an anti-Nazi spokesperson.[31]

Notice, however, that this involved a friendship among peers, and the trust that one can earn in extending a promise of friendship to another. Although peer-to-peer friendship is not a relationship teachers can have with their students, the model of peer-to-peer friendship is an important part not only of making depolarizing efforts possible, but it's also a key part of integration. So, I turn now to discussing the specifics of the teacher-student model for depolarization.[32]

Is it the case that increasing the number of minority teachers in the classroom will help to reduce racial hostilities, thereby creating

more virtuous and active citizens who respect diversity? It is easy to
see why the contact hypothesis would be important to this thesis.
After all, according to the contact hypothesis, increased contact
between individuals from different backgrounds can reduce prejudice. However, it is worth noting that since being introduced in
1954, the claim that contact reduces prejudice is not a matter of
consensus among social psychologists. Given how much the success
of developing a new Poitier effect depends on the contact hypothesis, one cannot gloss over the ways in which contact can have
both unintended consequences and backlash effects that worsen
prejudice. These complications and points of contention aren't discussed by Paul-Binyamin, Jayusi, and Tamir, so I will discuss them
here. For these points I draw on Alex Madva's work on structural
interventions to reduce bias.[33]

First, let us question whether the presence of counter-
stereotypical exemplars—in the form of minority teachers—will
be sufficient for reducing prejudice and bias to create more virtuous students. This type of contact can have the unintended consequence of preserving an unjust status quo, as Paul-Binyamin et al.
acknowledge. For example, Madva notes:

> In particular, it leads members of low-status groups (including blacks
> in South Africa, Arabs in Israel, Muslims in India, and black college
> students in the US) to perceive the status quo to be fair, to be less
> supportive of structural reform, and to (often mistakenly) expect
> fair treatment from members of high-status groups. "When the dis-
> advantaged come to like the advantaged, when they assume they are
> trustworthy and good human beings, when their personal experi-
> ences suggest that the collective discrimination might not be so bad
> after all, then they become more likely to abandon the project of
> collective action to change inequitable societies" (Dixon et al. 2012:
> 11). In short, social contact leads them to like the advantaged group
> more, but also saps their motivation to fight for social change.[34]

In addition to the morally bad consequences of preserving an unjust
status quo and sapping the motivation of students to fight for social
change—surely we want active and engaged students who want to
make the world better!—there is also reason to doubt the ability of
counter-stereotypical exemplars, in the form of minority teachers,

to debias their students. Madva notes that although undergraduate women are more likely to pursue STEM majors if they have women math and science professors:

> research increasingly suggests that having women professors has no effect whatsoever on undergraduate men's implicit or explicit stereotypes about math ability and gender. This particular debiasing effect applies only to ingroup members (women) rather than outgroup members (men). Moreover, even this ingroup effect depends on several contingent psychological factors, such as the extent to which individuals perceive themselves to be similar to the counterstereotypical exemplar. For example, the effect increases when participants believe that the exemplar graduated from their own university. But if women believe that the exemplar is an exceptional "superstar" genius, then the effect reverses: they report fewer career aspirations, think of themselves as less assertive, and lose interest in math and science.[35]

What these unintended consequences and backlash effects call into question is the efficacy of minority teachers to accomplish Step 4 in Paul-Binyamin, Jayusi, and Tamir's proposed eight-stage process: the blurring of stereotypes. I've lost count of the number of times I've been told that I'm not like those other immigrants, or that I should disregard disparaging remarks about Indians because they weren't talking about me, etc. My presence as a counter-stereotype to stereotypes about people who look like me can be easily assimilated by treating me as an exception, thus leaving the stereotype untouched. So let me now turn to this worry about being treated as a token, which preserves the underlying social hierarchy and leaves stereotypes untouched. That is, I turn next to some concerns about typecasting, tokenization, the politics of deference, being-in-the-room privilege, and more generally, the kind of compulsory representation of "the other" that minority teachers will be required to perform.

TOKENIZATION AND THE UNJUST DISTRIBUTION OF BURDENS IN COMBATING INJUSTICE

As Paul-Binyamin and colleagues note, their hope in trying to adapt the Poitier effect is that minority teachers can enable encounters where others, notably students, "experience the other not only as a human being, but also as a knowledgeable agent, an authority, and often as a beloved educational figure."[36] However, they also note that the first stage of the eight-stage process for creating a transformative cross-group teaching effect is cultural alienation. Here I want to focus on these feelings of alienation and estrangement from a community that you've been placed in and explore in greater detail just how harmful that can be.[37] I've often experienced this feeling of being a token, especially in philosophy where it's not uncommon to be the only brown person in the room.[38] As Emmalon Davis has documented more thoroughly, there are many harms that stem from the practice of tokenization.[39] As Davis notes:

> The harms stemming from this practice are abundant. First, tagging marginalized individuals as spokespersons perpetuates the myth that the members of nondominant social groups share one monolithic experience. Second, targets are placed under tremendous pressure to deliver on behalf of their entire constituency. Indeed, targets may experience anxiety, embarrassment, or even anger at having their social identity made into a public spectacle. Alternatively, the target may fear public shaming or ridicule if she does not possess (and transfer) the knowledge prejudicially attributed.[40]

Now, I want to be clear that I'm not saying that the process discussed by Paul-Binyamin et al. necessarily involves tokenization, but the risk is there and efforts must be made to ensure that the negative effects don't eventuate for the minority teachers. Minority teachers should not be used as objects for the betterment of their students.

What I am reminded of here is how discussions regarding the benefit of diversity are often presented as primarily a good for white students rather than as a good for Black students. A study by Starck, Sinclair, and Shelton notes that the instrumental rationale that universities offer, i.e., that diversity promotes learning, or that diversity prepares students for a diverse workplace, is preferred by white students, whereas Black students prefer moral rationales for diversity, i.e., that it's the right thing to do, that increasing diversity is a matter of justice.[41] For example, Starck et al. note that "the purported educational benefits described in instrumental diversity rationales largely serve to provide educational value to White individuals."[42] And furthermore, that "as conceptualized, these objectives were to be achieved by introducing novel points of view to campus, implying that the educational beneficiaries of these efforts were those for whom minority perspectives were novel (i.e., majority group members)."[43] Whereas moral rationales for diversity, i.e., the rationales preferred by Black students, heighten white students' "concern with being labeled prejudiced due to their race."[44]

Thus, we find ourselves facing the following dilemma: using instrumental rationales in order to preserve white students' sense of belonging at the cost of moral rationales that boost Black students' sense of belonging.[45] Ordinarily in a dilemma, both horns are equally bad and undesirable. However, in this dilemma we can recognize that, given historical injustice, choosing one horn over the other is likely to detrimentally affect some students more than others, and especially students from groups that have been historically oppressed, disadvantaged, or negatively stereotyped. The opting for instrumental rationales for diversity naturally raises the following question: Whose interests are being sidelined for whose? Further, is that just?[46]

Furthermore, there are additional worries that go beyond tokenization and instrumental rationales for diversity as opposed to moral rationales that must also be raised here. First, the act of offering the disadvantaged a seat in the room, even if it's in the front of the room, can itself be a problematic exercise of what Olúfémi O Táíwò calls *the politics of deference*.[47] As Táíwò warns, adding a minority voice to the room can often end up being at most a symbolic act and at worst "a performance that sanitizes, apologizes for, or simply distracts from the fact that the deferrer has enough 'in the room' privilege for their 'lifting up' of a perspective to be of consequence—to reflect well on *them*."[48] Although the politics of deference is right to pay attention to lived experience, and the sharing of lived experience by being a counter-stereotypical exemplar in the room can be a powerful tool, it puts too much weight on the ability of mere stories and contact to change the unjust structures underlying why you were originally left out of the room.[49] As Táíwò notes, if we focus on merely elevating "the voices and perspectives *in* the room, the harder it becomes to change the world *outside* of the room."[50] That is, we can be concerned that, in its current, preliminary formulation, Paul-Binyamin et al.'s proposal seems to ask little of the rooms the teachers are in, little of the larger social structure, and it allows the material differences to stay the same.

CONCLUSION

Although my comments have been critical, I offer them in a friendly spirit to aid further work on these topics. Anyone interested in cultivating some beneficial version of the Poitier effect as a bulwark against polarization must do so with a fuller understanding of the processes of polarization and of the controversy surrounding the contact hypothesis. Perhaps most important, they ought also to be mindful of how the burdens of correcting the injustices of racial and ethnic oppression and prejudice will be distributed. This is not to say that Paul-Binyamin et al. have not been mindful of these concerns, but rather that there is *a lot* to consider and these critical comments scratch just the surface of complicated issues of addressing injustice in an unjust world.

As a final note, just as Paul-Binyamin, Jayusi, and Tamir end on a quote, I follow suit with a quote from Táíwò that captures the spirit of their proposal: Let us "be accountable and responsive to people who aren't yet in the room, and [let us] build the kinds of rooms in which we can sit together, rather than merely seek to navigate more gracefully the rooms history has built for us."[51]

NOTES

1 See Paul-Binyamin, Jayusi, and Tamir's chapter in this volume.
2 Yael Tamir, "Two Concepts of Multiculturalism," *Journal of Philosophy of Education* 29, no. 2 (1995): 161–172.
3 Tamir, "Two Concepts of Multiculturalism."
4 Paul-Binyamin et al., in this volume.
5 Gordon W. Allport, *The Nature of Prejudice* (Reading, MA: Addison-Wesley, 1954).
6 I want to note that I am in general quite optimistic about the power of teachers and other attachment figures to shape who we become; see Rima Basu, "The Ethics of Expectations," in *Oxford Studies in Normative Ethics*, volume 13, ed. Mark Timmons (New York: Oxford University Press, 2023), 149–169, but teachers can only do so much when they operate against greater sociohistorical injustices that give rise to

racism and prejudice. I should also note that although Paul-Binyamin, Jayusi, and Tamir's focus is on replicating the Poitier effect in schools in Israel, in my critical comments I focus on issues of polarization and segregation and sociohistorical injustice in the United States as it is the context I am more familiar with.

7 Tamir, "Two Concepts of Multiculturalism."

8 Tamir, "Two Concepts of Multiculturalism," 161.

9 Tamir, "Two Concepts of Multiculturalism," 162.

10 Tamir, "Two Concepts of Multiculturalism," 167.

11 Erika Frankenberg, Jongyeon Ee, Jennifer B. Ayscue, and Gary Orfield, "Harming Our Common Future: America's Segregated Schools 65 Years After *Brown*," www.civilrightsproject.ucla.edu, May 10, 2019 (research). Retrieved from https://escholarship.org, 8.

12 Alvin Chang, "The Data Proves That School Segregation Is Getting Worse," *Vox* (Vox, March 5, 2018), www.vox.com. However, it is important to note that these statistics are also due to a declining number of white students in public schools and the changing demographics of the United States as discussed by Frankenberg et al., "Harming Our Common Future."

13 "Political Polarization in the American Public," Pew Research Center—US Politics & Policy (Pew Research Center, April 9, 2021), www.pewresearch.org.

14 Paul-Binyamin, Jayusi, and Tamir, chapter in this volume.

15 Thomas Kelly, "Disagreement, Dogmatism, and Belief Polarization," *Journal of Philosophy* 105, no. 10 (2008): 611–622.

16 Kevin Dorst, "Why Rational People Polarize," *The Phenomenal World*, January 24, 2019, www.phenomenalworld.org. For the more general point that biases can be rational and part of epistemically sound reasoning processes, see also Louise M. Antony, "Bias: Friend or Foe? Reflections on Saulish Skepticism," in *Implicit Bias and Philosophy, Volume 1: Metaphysics and Epistemology*, ed. Michael Brownstein and Jennifer Saul (Oxford: Oxford University Press, 2016), and Gabbrielle M. Johnson, "The Structure of Bias," *Mind* 129, no. 516 (2020): 1193–1236.

17 Daniel J. Singer, Aaron Bramson, Patrick Grim, Bennett Holman, Jiin Jung, Karen Kovaka, Anika Ranginani, and William J. Berger, "Rational Social and Political Polarization," *Philosophical Studies* 176, no. 9 (2019): 2243–2267.

18 Singer et al., "Rational Social and Political Polarization," 7.

19 It is not necessarily a bad thing that we're not agents with unlimited memories, as I discuss in Rima Basu, "The Importance of Forgetting," *Episteme* 19, no. 4 (2022): 471–490.

20 Singer et al."Rational Social and Political Polarization," 17.

21 Eduardo Bonilla-Silva, *Racism without Racists: Color-Blind Racism and the Persistence of Racial Inequality in America*, 3rd ed. (Lanham: Rowman & Littlefield, 2009). Similarly, I've argued that one can have racist beliefs without harboring any explicit or implicit racist attitudes or ill-will, rather you might have racist beliefs simply from responding in seemingly rational ways to the evidence. See Rima Basu, "The Wrongs of Racist Beliefs," *Philosophical Studies* 176, no. 9 (2019): 2497–2515.

22 Unfortunately, since the original presentation of both Paul-Binyamin et al.'s paper and my comments, the situation with respect to education in the United States has gotten worse. In addition to the panic over critical race theory, teachers, in particular LGBTQIA+ teachers, are now being accused of "grooming" children. For example, the popular TikTok account "Libs of TikTok" reposts content by "activist" and "groomer" teachers to more than a million followers, resulting in events involving drag queens being attacked by far-right extremist groups and death threats against school officials.

23 Endre Begby, "Evidential Preemption," *Philosophy and Phenomenological Research* 102, no. 3(2021): 515–530. For discussion of echo chambers, see C. Thi Nguyen, "Echo Chambers and Epistemic Bubbles," *Episteme* 17, no. 2 (2020): 141–161. For another account of the processes by which individuals can be groomed for this kind of evidential preemption, see Lauren Leydon-Hardy, "Predatory Grooming and Epistemic Infringement," in *Applied Epistemology*, ed. Jennifer Lackey (Oxford: Oxford University Press, 2021), 119–150.

24 Begby, "Evidential Preemption," 2.

25 Nguyen, "Echo Chambers," 147.

26 In contrast to *To Sir with Love* consider the movie *God's Not Dead*, where Kevin Sorbo plays a left-wing atheist philosophy professor who insists his students declare that God is dead.

27 This is not to be considered only a right-wing phenomenon. As Nguyen notes, "echo chambers surely exist elsewhere on the political spectrum, though, to my mind, [however] the left-wing echo chambers have been unable to exert a similar level of political force" ("Echo Chambers," 150).

28 Nguyen, "Echo Chambers," 146.

29 Tamir, "Two Concepts of Multiculturalism," 169–170.

30 Eli Saslow, "The White Flight of Derek Black," *Washington Post*, October 15, 2016, www.washingtonpost.com.

31 Nguyen, "Echo Chambers," 158.

32 For more on this point see Elizabeth Anderson, *The Imperative of Integration* (Princeton, NJ: Princeton University Press, 2010).

33 Alex Madva, "A Plea for Anti-Anti-Individualism: How Oversimple Psychology Misleads Social Policy," *Ergo, an Open Access Journal of Philosophy* 3, no. 27 (2016): 701–728.

34 Madva, "A Plea for Anti-Anti-Individualism," 707–708. This result seems to be corroborated by the meta-analysis Paul-Binyaminet al. discuss in their chapter, where a study cited discovered that "contacts attempting to promote coexistence or stimulate joint projects tend to preserve and perpetuate the dominance and control of the Jewish majority group, encouraging Arab submission and passivity."

35 Madva, "A Plea for Anti-Anti-Individualism," 713.

36 Paul-Binyamin et al., chapter in this volume.

37 See Tommie Shelby, *Dark Ghettos: Injustice, Dissent, and Reform* (Cambridge, MA: Harvard University Press, 2018), for criticisms of Anderson along these lines.

38 See Eric Schwitzgebel, Liam Kofi Bright, Carolyn Dicey Jennings, Morgan Thompson, and Eric Winsberg, "The Diversity of Philosophy Students and Faculty," *Philosopher's Magazine* 93, no. 1 (2021): 71–90.

39 Emmalon Davis, "Typecasts, Tokens, and Spokespersons: A Case for Credibility Excess as Testimonial Injustice," *Hypatia* 31, no. 3 (2016): 485–501.

40 Davis, "Typecasts, Tokens," 492.

41 Jordan G. Starck, Stacey Sinclair, and J. Nicole Shelton, "How University Diversity Rationales Inform Student Preferences and Outcomes," *Proceedings of the National Academy of Sciences* 118, no. 16 (2021): 1–7.

42 Starck et al., "How University Diversity Rationales Inform Student Preferences," 2.

43 Starck et al., "How University Diversity Rationales Inform Student Preferences," 2.

44 Starck et al., "How University Diversity Rationales Inform Student Preferences," 2.

45 However, it should be noted that a reason these instrumental rationales dominate is because they have been important for schools' attempts to justify and protect forms of affirmative action. For more on this point, see in particular Kristine Bowman's contribution to this volume and Bowman's discussion of Derrick Bell's interest convergence dilemma (Derrick A. Bell Jr., "*Brown v. Board of Education* and the Interest-Convergence Dilemma," *Harvard Law Review* 93, no. 3 (1980): 518–533). Thanks to Elizabeth Beaumont for pressing me to say more on this point. Also, for an accounting of these different rationales for diversity, see Natasha Warikoo, *The Diversity Bargain and Other Dilemmas of Race, Admission, and Meritocracy at Elite Universities* (Chicago: University of Chicago Press, 2016).

46 For more on unjust burdens befalling those already disadvantaged in the system, see also Sally Haslanger, "Studying While Black: Trust, Opportunity, and Disrespect," *Du Bois Review: Social Science Research on Race* 11, no. 1 (2014): 109–136.

47 Olúfémi O Táíwò, *Elite Capture: How the Powerful Took Over Identity Politics (And Everything Else)* (Chicago: Pluto Press, 2022).

48 Táíwò, *Elite Capture*, 74.

49 See also Darien Pollock's "Political Action, Epistemic Detachment, and the Problem of White-Mindedness," *Philosophical Issues* 31 (2021): 299, where Pollock notes "how it's possible for institutional actors to fail to properly represent the interests of a politically disenfranchised group, even if these institutions include certain members of the disenfranchised group as a part of their organizing efforts."

50 Táíwò, *Elite Capture*, 83.

51 Táíwò, *Elite Capture*, 84. This approach he calls "the constructive approach to standpoint epistemology." For more on standpoint epistemology, see Briana Toole's "From Standpoint Epistemology to Epistemic Oppression," *Hypatia* 34, no. 4 (2019): 598–618, for an overview.

9

EXPLORING AN EPISTEMIC CONFLICT OVER FREE SPEECH ON AMERICAN COLLEGE CAMPUSES, AND THE PROMISE OF THE NEW DEMOCRATIC MODEL

KRISTINE L. BOWMAN

Given the growing political polarization around the world, it is not surprising that scholars across disciplines are turning their attention once again to educational institutions, thinking deeply about how schools, colleges, and universities can help sustain and strengthen democracy. The idea that educational institutions shape democratic citizens is not new: The US Supreme Court and many scholars often have described a central purpose of public elementary and secondary schools as creating the next generation of citizens.[1] An array of scholars also have described educating citizens as one of many aims of colleges and universities.[2]

In this volume, the chapter "Moving Beyond the 'Poitier Effect': Examining the Potential to Advance Civic Respect through Cross-Community Teaching," by Ilana Paul-Binyamin, Wurud Jayusi, and Yael Tamir expands this legal and scholarly tradition by considering how bringing students into contact with different "others" can help combat polarization. Paul-Binyamin et al. do not mince words about what is at stake in the current moment: "The move from diverse to polarized societies," they say, "marks the erosion of the foundations of social agreement."[3] Responding to this threat, they leverage insights from

193

contact theory, which explains how and why sustained personal contact with "the other" can create individual relationships that reduce stereotypes and thus help break down the borders of tribalism.[4] Although contact theory has focused mostly on peer relationships, Paul-Binyamin et al. use it as a lens to explore the positive social changes that can occur when "the other" is in a position of authority. Because teachers are one of the most significant authority figures in children's lives, the authors contend that significant, long-term social changes can take place when these educators teach students who are demographically unlike them and majority students thus see "the other" as a leader with authority and expertise, as well as a mentor and even friend.[5]

In this chapter, I aim to complement Paul-Binyamin et al.'s work by exploring two different views of higher education and free speech and how they may relate to polarization; this is an important consideration as higher education institutions are increasingly diverse, and for many students the most diverse environment they have yet experienced.[6] I argue that we need to develop a deep understanding of the epistemic disconnect between the two dominant conceptions of the purpose of the university and the differing role of free speech on campus that results from each purpose. Specifically, I ask: What view of the purpose(s) of the university does the current literature about free speech in colleges and universities use as its foundation? How does a particular view of the purpose of the university influence conceptions of free speech in campus contexts? And ultimately, how may different understandings of free speech relate to combating polarization?

I begin this work by exploring what I term the "knowledge-production model" of the university, well-known in the higher education literature as the "American University model."[7] This model came to dominate higher education globally in the first half of the twentieth century; it is embodied by a large, comprehensive, research university serving graduate and undergraduate students alike. The understanding of free speech that flows from this model is a near-absolutist understanding that took shape around the same time that the model developed. I then turn to what I call the "new democratic model" of the university, the model that began to emerge in the mid-twentieth century in the United States as multiple barriers were reduced and the rapidly growing American community college system led the worldwide massification of higher education. The new democratic model has been defined in large part by struggles for, and with, equality, and more recently by the desire to create inclusive spaces of learning and knowledge creation. It leads to a different understanding of free speech, one that includes a redistributive component that can consider the impact of harmful speech on future access to speech communities, rather than framing free speech as only an individual negative right, as the near-absolutist approach does. In the knowledge-creation model, a university's role in free speech is relatively hands-off; under the new democratic model, the institutional role in free speech is greater and may be somewhat redistributive.[8] Although a near-absolutist perspective dominates First Amendment law and American culture, a redistributive lens is present in the regulation of free speech at state and local levels in the United States, in non-legal American scholarship, and in courts and scholarly work outside the United States regarding free speech.[9]

Ultimately, I conclude that the traditional, near-absolutist understanding of free speech is not very well-positioned to combat polarization. Rather, a democratic and redistributive understanding of free speech, which emphasizes inclusion and seeks to balance individual liberty with consideration of potential harm or benefit to others, is somewhat better positioned to combat polarization. That said, the near-absolutist understanding is so entrenched in the Supreme Court's jurisprudence and our social fabric that I find it highly unlikely this understanding will be replaced anytime soon. However, I do expect that support for an understanding of free speech that includes a redistributive element will continue to grow and to compete with the near-absolutist understanding outside of courts. Thus, I encourage readers to develop a more nuanced understanding of the strengths and limitations of each conception of the purpose of the university and the understanding of free speech that flows from it, as these ideas seem highly likely to continue to co-exist on many campuses and thus the epistemic disconnect between the ideas will be an ongoing source of tension.

The Knowledge-Production Model of the University: Knowledge-Production, Negative Free Speech Rights, and Institutional Neutrality

The most common model of the university explicitly invoked in the recent literature about free speech on campus, particularly in the legal literature, is the "knowledge-production model." This model assumes a large, comprehensive university in which graduate study and the creation of new knowledge—all grounded in deep scholarly expertise—take place alongside teaching and undergraduate education. In this model, universities also seek to create benefit for the public, including lowering barriers to admission based on socioeconomic status, sex, race, and ethnicity.

The most extensive explication of this model in the relevant literature on free speech comes from political scientist Keith Whittington, who describes the knowledge-production model as beginning to gather steam in the late 1800s, ultimately replacing the dominance of the German Research University model. Reflecting the balance between research and graduate study on one hand, and teaching and undergraduate education on the other, Whittington describes the American University as being driven by a "twin mission" of "generating and disseminating knowledge," which can take different forms for different institutions.[10] He also hints at the "marketplace of ideas" concept in which better ideas are assumed to win out over worse ones, stating that in the university, "ideas are held up to critical scrutiny and our best understanding of the truth is identified and professed."[11] Whittington argues that the purpose of the university as he articulates it is the dominant model embraced by scholars today.[12] This understanding is indeed popular: It is the same model that anchors the widely adopted Chicago Principles, which foreground the pursuit of truth and creation of knowledge.[13] Legal scholars also regularly invoke this model, which embraces the "marketplace of ideas" approach, albeit usually through only a sentence or two.[14]

A common variation of the perspective taken by Whittington is to embrace the ideas of critical thinking, knowledge creation (research), and public purpose and also to briefly acknowledge the university's interest in supporting diversity, equity, and inclusion. Erwin Chemerinsky, Howard Gilman, and Michael Roth, all scholars and American university leaders with decades of administrative experience, adopt this approach.[15] Like Whittington, Chemerinsky and Gilman emphasize the knowledge-creation mission of the university. In their view, faculty must be allowed to push the boundaries of knowledge, which often means advancing unpopular ideas. Specifically, Chemerinsky and Gilman state that some of these approaches "may be considered crazy, distasteful, or offensive to the community."[16] Applying the knowledge-generation concept to students means nurturing critical thinkers who are willing and able to explore new ideas, challenge settled assumptions, and continually push forward in the pursuit of truth.[17] Similar to some other scholars,[18] Chemerinsky and Gilman go beyond the knowledge-creating purpose of a university to note the importance of inclusion, which they describe as "protect[ing] the learning experiences of all students," but they do not discuss the concept of inclusion or its execution in much detail.[19]

The approach taken by Whittington, Chemerinsky, Gilman, and Roth maintains the centrality of the knowledge-generation model and allows DEI goals to be advanced to the extent they are consistent with the knowledge-generation model. However, doing so is fundamentally different from embracing diversity, equity, and inclusion as central to the mission of the university alongside free speech as core, coequal values, and grappling with how to reconcile and integrate these two concepts.

Free Speech as a Negative Right and the Marketplace of Ideas

Each model of the university leads to a specific normative view about free speech on campus. The literature that embraces the knowledge-production model centers a negative rights approach to free speech, including the "marketplace of ideas" metaphor that dominates American law and culture today. A negative rights approach is highly individualistic and has been referred to as "absolutist" although in practice it is near-absolutist because time, place, and manner and the possibility of serious physical danger resulting from speech, among other factors, do constitutionally restrict what a speaker may say, so even a near-absolutist approach is not without exception. That said, aside from a handful of relatively limited exceptions, impact on others is usually not part of the equation for determining the permissibility of speech.

The marketplace metaphor emerged out of Justices Holmes's 1919 dissent in *Abrams v. United States*, a case where the US Supreme Court majority held that anti-war leaflets distributed to workers in munitions factories were not protected by the First Amendment. Disagreeing with that holding, Holmes (joined by Brandeis) famously wrote in dissent:

> [W]hen men have realized that time has upset many fighting faiths, they may come to believe, even more than they believe the very foundations of their own conduct, that the ultimate good desired is better reached by free trade in ideas—that the best test of truth is the power of the thought to get itself accepted in the competition of the market. That at any rate is the theory of our Constitution.[20]

Through this metaphor, Holmes invoked an economic model and implied that both the marketplace for goods and marketplace for ideas function best when individuals are allowed to make choices without government interference.[21] Over the past century, Holmes's metaphor has come to anchor nearly all of the many subfields of the Court's First Amendment jurisprudence, although scholars debate its utility.[22]

Using the marketplace of ideas concept to ground an argument about free speech on campus has at least four significant conceptual ramifications, all of which act to maintain or increase polarization.

First, Holmes suggested that the marketplace of ideas will reveal and prioritize truth, a result especially important in the context of the university in which the pursuit of truth and creation of knowledge are at the heart of the enterprise. However, upon further examination, the assumption that if all possible ideas are in play, then the more true ideas will win out over the less true ones, is problematic. Foundationally, aggregating individuals' choices in a market reveals the prevailing good or idea selected by those who can most readily participate in the market. As history has shown us, the most popular idea at a given time may or may not constitute truth.[23] For example, despite the widespread practice and legal permissibility of slavery from the initial colonial settlement of the

United States through the Civil War, slavery is now understood to be a deep moral wrong.[24]

The marketplace metaphor is thus arguably a better fit for determining political consensus about policy than to ascertain empirical or theoretical truth. This is consistent with the emphasis in the Supreme Court's First Amendment jurisprudence on protecting public discourse as part of the work of sustaining democracy.[25] However, it is also important to acknowledge that political consensus is shaped by preexisting social power and privilege. For example, a dominant group's primary incentive to compromise often is pragmatic—it must compromise if it cannot do what it wants to do on its own. Furthermore, pragmatic political compromise is a far cry from the empathy required to humanize the other.

The disconnect between the public square and the specific institutional context of higher education leads constitutional law scholar Robert Post to contend that although academic freedom protection is essential in higher education (a view with which I wholeheartedly agree), the First Amendment should not be interpreted as protecting all speech in colleges and universities, which must make content-based distinctions in both research and teaching.[26] This view is consistent with what others, including legal scholar James Weinstein, have expressed: American free speech doctrine is anchored by a commitment to participatory democracy which is most important in the public sphere.[27] In articulating the First Amendment's inapplicability to colleges and universities, Post is an outlier; the vast majority of scholars writing in this area begin with the premise that the First Amendment does apply to public colleges or universities, as state actors, and then seek to shape the conception of free speech to advance the aims of higher education.

Second, the marketplace of ideas metaphor dovetails with the conventional understanding that American free speech rights are negative rights.[28] In contrast to positive rights—affirmative rights to ensure a capacity or receive a particular benefit or type of treatment—negative rights are rights to be free from government interference.[29] When free speech rights are understood as negative rights, the starting point of analysis is that the government cannot limit individual expression of ideas, although this presumption is rebuttable in the event a strong, specific reason exists.[30] The limits on government action as Holmes characterized them—"Congress certainly cannot forbid all effort to change the mind of the country"[31]—are framed in negative terms, with the focus on Congress controlling individuals' speech rather than Congress ensuring that all have meaningful access to the speech marketplace.[32]

A practical consequence of this negative rights, anti-censorship framing is evident on college and university campuses, and in other venues, today. Exclusionary views are equally entitled to be present as inclusionary views. Restricting such exclusionary speech—and sometimes, even engaging in counterspeech to oppose the exclusionary speech—is framed as an infringement on the liberty of the exclusionary speaker which impermissibly prioritizes inclusion "over" free speech.[33] The negative rights approach which grounds the marketplace of ideas metaphor thus limits the potential relationship between diversity, equity, and inclusion (DEI) values and free speech to an either/or dynamic, rather than an approach that can conceive of the relationship as a both/and dynamic. Viewing free speech rights as a competition, and more specifically a zero-sum game, is anchored in a defensive approach in which speakers (or those with an interest in the speech space) strategize to maintain or expand their turf in competition with those they perceive to have conflicting interests. This approach is highly unlikely to produce the sort of openness and vulnerability that can help reduce polarization, and in fact may be more likely to increase polarization.[34]

Third, and relatedly, Holmes's conceptualization of the idealized, neoclassical market disregards varying levels of power and privilege among speakers and also fails to account for common human characteristics that distort any market, ranging from habit, to bigotry, to altruism.[35] A significant consequence of this approach is that Holmes's metaphor assumes that all ideas not only can be but in fact will be in play because there is no cost to participating in the marketplace and therefore no barrier to doing so; economists rejected this understanding of markets decades ago.[36] To be clear: This approach assumes that dynamics of power and privilege that shape potential speakers' lived realities are not relevant in the operation of the marketplace or do not determine which ideas "sell" or "win." It also illustrates a libertarian view of the relationship between free speech and inclusion, which contends that government should not put its proverbial thumb on the scale even in pursuit of greater social equality because such action would be improperly coercive and inevitably misguided at some point.[37] This belief in the marketplace as a fair and neutral arbiter exacerbates the zero-sum view of free speech rights which, as discussed above, may be more likely to increase polarization than to help reduce it.

Concretely, imagine a campus that has buildings named for known Ku Klux Klan members and monuments to them. Under a negative rights approach, Black students who may perceive from these endorsements of white supremacy that they are fully or partially excluded from the environment of learning and knowledge creation would not be able to frame the buildings' names as a free speech issue because Black students have the same formal right to speak and learn on campus as non-Black students, regardless of which names are on buildings and which monuments exist on campus. However, as this example shows, failing to acknowledge informal barriers to participation, as the marketplace metaphor does, leads to a situation in which the lived realities of historically marginalized and minoritized members of the community are only partially accounted for. By failing to consider a role for government in maintaining a marketplace with more equitable opportunities for involvement, the libertarian approach similarly perpetuates existing systemic discrimination and exclusion. These negative approaches to free speech, which dominate First Amendment doctrine, are therefore anti-redistributive in nature.[38]

Fourth, the marketplace of ideas concept is central to the unique First Amendment culture in which speakers' free speech rights in the United States are less restricted than in any other country in the world.[39] This culture, which spotlights individual liberty, is both the source and result of continual iteration by courts through judicial decisions as well as by official and everyday social practices.[40] In this context, free speech claims have a disproportionate salience, and "free speech" is used interchangeably with "First Amendment."[41] The rhetoric prominent legal scholars use to describe this culture helps illustrate its significance: Robert Tsai describes the First Amendment's "promise" as "the redemptive power of freedom of expression."[42] Frederick Schauer writes about the First Amendment's "cultural magnetism" to describe how cases about everything from sexual harassment to panhandling to securities regulation have become First Amendment battles.[43] And, Genevieve Lakier writes about the "mythological" First Amendment.[44]

Whether inside a public university or in the public square, in First Amendment culture, perceived threats to freedom of expression are defined broadly and potential limitations on speech are perceived as exceptionally dangerous. I do not suggest we consider these issues narrowly or take them lightly, but broadening a discussion about free speech to include law and culture in other democracies, such as the United Kingdom, Canada, and Australia, would challenge us to think about how other countries take a more redistributive approach without seeming to compromise the core of their democracy.[45] Put differently and more generally, the robustly libertarian American understanding of free speech, embodied in the marketplace of ideas metaphor, is not the only possible (much less acceptable) approach in a modern democracy, and yet dominant First Amendment culture assumes that it is.[46]

Individually and collectively, these four implications of the marketplace of ideas metaphor demonstrate why the near-absolutist view of free speech is severely limited in its ability to reduce polarization, and in fact may lead to more polarization rather than less. Quoting Zaid Jilani and Jeremy Adam Smith, Paul-Binyamin et al. point to the source of polarization as "tribalism: clustering ourselves into groups that compete against each other in a zero-sum game, where negotiation and compromise are perceived as a betrayal, whether those groups are political, racial, economic, religious, gender, or generational." The way forward, they contend, is by "taking actions that have the potential to reduce hostility, humanize others, and promote attentiveness to their needs." In other words, the way forward is to empathize with the other and to focus on the larger community rather than oneself.

As discussed throughout this section, the marketplace metaphor leads to the reinforcement of tribalism rather than its reduction. The libertarian assumptions that run through the near-absolutist view of free speech focus strongly on the individual speaker and their rights, without space to consider, much less take seriously, the perspective of the other. Relatedly, popularity and politics are fundamentally about seeking dominance, not about building empathy for the other. A search for the most popular idea is built on competition, not cooperation, and competing over free speech rights means viewing such rights as a zero-sum game and viewing the other as an opponent. Such a search also unwittingly interpolates and reinforces structural and institutional racism, sexism, and other inequalities that are woven into the fabric of our society, because power and privilege impact the popularity of ideas and yet the marketplace is framed as searching not for the most popular ideas but for the most true ones. The negative rights approach and marketplace of ideas metaphor may dominate American law and society, but they do not lead to creating empathy.

Institutional Neutrality and Polarization

A key premise in free speech absolutism is the idea that the government should not discriminate among individuals' viewpoints. Where this becomes thorny is when we ask about the government's *own* viewpoint, because what is policymaking if not choosing one viewpoint over another? As I have written elsewhere, these two ideas—government agnosticism regarding individual viewpoints on one hand, and government monopolization of a speech environment on the other hand—appear in First Amendment jurisprudence in the forum analysis doctrine and government speech doctrine, respectively.[47] Interestingly, judicial opinions talk about these doctrines as though they never overlap and as though situations present either forum analysis questions or government speech questions, but never both. However, this either-or approach limits government to either the role of neutral, and presumably viewpoint-silent, moderator, or a speaker who can exclude all other speakers and viewpoints. Thus, continuing to theorize this doctrine, I have elsewhere proposed a way in which we can understand, consistent with First Amendment doctrine and liberal political theory, the government as a speaker within a forum it also neutrally moderates.[48] This is particularly important for the context of public colleges and universities today because many call for university leaders to express their support for those who are the targets of harmful speech and to affirm the importance of marginalized and minoritized members of the campus community. If a university leader is either relegated to being a viewpoint-silent moderator or one who can dominate the entire forum, this leaves little room for engagement.

Related to all of this is a necessary, deeper engagement with
the meaning of "neutrality." As I have noted above, much of the
doctrine assumes that the government (including public universities) is silent regarding its own viewpoint when it moderates. Yet, as
Katharine Gelber and I have demonstrated via the use of speech act
theory, which explains what speech does in the world, institutional
silence in the face of harmful speech is not neutrality—rather,
institutional silence allows the discriminatory norms in the harmful speech to shape the norms of the community, changing what
becomes acceptable going forward.[49] As we note, often neglected
in conversations about speech neutrality is a deep understanding
of the harmful consequences of some speech. By putting the burden for creating and maintaining a robust free speech community on individual speakers and limiting the institutional role to a
regulatory one of moderating, the law fails to grapple sufficiently
with the lived experience of those who are the target of harmful
speech. Thus, a near-absolutist approach to free speech, which
assumes that government is a neutral—usually viewpoint-silent—
moderator, reinforces existing power dynamics and thus strength-
ens polarization.

Yet, it seems that active moderators who also speak in further-
ance of equality can be more helpful to those who seek to move
through polarization than those who do not do so. If we are currently limited in our ability to engage across difference, then our
discourse needs facilitation. It is not readily apparent how such
facilitation is compatible with a near-absolutist approach to free
speech, which centers the speaker and their rights and almost never
looks outward. Thus, a near-absolutist approach to free speech is
inherently limited in its ability to be at the center of a path that
moves through polarization.

Centering Inclusion in Free Speech

The New Democratic Model of the University

The new democratic model of the university does not dominate the
literature, but it is increasingly prominent. Two scholars' separate,
extended engagements with this model are particularly illuminat-
ing. Political philosopher and education scholar Sigal Ben-Porath

invokes the new democratic model by articulating what she calls a "revised social mission of the university." This revised social mission prioritizes the pursuit of truth in teaching and research alongside effectively serving a diverse student population.[50] Similarly, comparative literature scholar Ulrich Baer describes the purpose of the university as advancing knowledge, and he notes that such advancement must involve both a desire to pursue and identify truth, and the inclusion or exclusion of views based not on the identity of the speaker, but rather on the merit of the view.[51]

Equal participation in the university community is key to both Ben-Porath's and Baer's models of the university. Both scholars operationalize this by identifying inclusion as part of the truth-seeking mission of the university. Thus, rather than inclusion and truth-seeking being mutually exclusive, they are intertwined and mutually reinforcing. Ben-Porath weaves these two concepts together by discussing the importance of access to truth-seeking and knowledge-creation spaces, emphasizing that having access to these spaces means not only having the formal ability to enter the space (a negative rights approach), but also the substantive ability to engage in the space on the same terms as others, despite different experiences of privilege or marginalization (a positive rights approach). Importantly, an environment of free and open exchange exists when all members of the community can substantively access and engage in spaces where knowledge is created.[52] Thus, Ben-Porath contends that respecting all members and hearing all voices is the very definition of a campus where free and open expression exists.[53]

Education scholars Benjamin Bindewald and Joshua Hawkins similarly highlight the importance of valuing the dignity of all individuals in a campus community, particularly when considering free speech issues.[54] They further note that this baseline assumption is especially important in public colleges and universities, which have a duty to create a public good.

True equal participation is important not only because of its impact on knowledge creation and learning in the university, but also because of its connection to civic development. Ben-Porath notes that the largest constituency in colleges and universities is undergraduate students, whom she describes as "newly minted as full citizens . . . often not fully prepared for their civic roles."[55] She argues that fostering free and open exchange on campus assists these same students in developing skills to participate in demo-cratic spaces, and that supporting the development of these skills is part of the new democratic purpose of the university.[56] Further-more, she argues that this approach has the potential to help reduce social polarization by first reducing polarization around the very issue of free speech on campus, which reflects and is fed by larger culture wars.[57] Legal scholar Stephen Feldman writes more directly about subordinating speech that further under-mines marginalized groups' political standing to a shared interest in pluralist democracy.[58] In sharp contrast, the scholars who adopt a knowledge-production view of the university and negative view of speech rights come out on the other side of this type of conflict, prioritizing individual speech over the interests of the marginalized rather than reconciling the two.

The New Democratic Model of Free Speech as a Negative Right with Positive and Redistributive Dimensions

Beginning with the new democratic model shifts our understand-ing about free speech on campus substantially as compared to understandings about free speech on campus that grow from the earlier knowledge-production model. Perhaps most significantly, the new democratic model tends to treat free speech and inclu-sion as a mutually reinforcing double helix. This conceptualiza-tion departs significantly from the negative understanding of free speech that dominates the legal literature and public discourse, in which stronger support for inclusion means weaker support for free speech and vice versa.[59] Rather, under the new democratic model, it is possible to assume that free speech and inclusion can work in harmony—not just in parallel—much of the time. For this to occur, free speech rights must be framed as negative rights with a positive dimension so that free speech is understood to be robust if those who have been historically excluded and marginalized can exercise their speech on the same terms as the historically privi-leged and powerful, and thus fully engage in spaces of learning and knowledge creation. This approach casts free speech rights as somewhat redistributive in nature by making capacities for speech more equitable, and thus opens a different role for the state (here, the public university) to assist with the redistribution.[60]

Conceptualizing free speech in this way involves understanding free speech as a compound right in which considerations of individual autonomy and social utility both shape the scope of the right.[61] Specifically, the idea of speech as a negative right—an individual right that can be restricted only under limited circumstances—prioritizes the ability of individuals to speak freely with few restrictions. This is the traditional approach, and part of the knowledge-production model of the university. Understanding speech as a right with positive dimensions means taking seriously the ways in which individual speech interacts with other social values, such as equality, and employing a redistributive approach normatively anchored in utility-based values. Bringing both of these ideas together to form a compound right means seeking to maximize both the autonomy of the negative right and the utility value embraced by the positive dimension; the new democratic model employs this compound rights approach.

To illustrate the difference between free speech under the knowledge-production model and the new democratic model more concretely, consider a situation in which an outside speaker, such as white supremacist Richard Spencer, is invited to campus. Students then petition for the event to be canceled because the speaker previously engaged in speech that is harmful to marginalized members of the campus community, challenging their very right to be present in that space of learning and knowledge creation. Under the knowledge-production model and the negative, marketplace free speech understandings that follow from it, the main concern is to avoid violating the speaker's rights by "deplatforming" them or canceling their event.[62] Using that approach, which centers the harmful speaker and focuses almost exclusively on their speech rights, free speech and inclusion compete in a zero-sum game.

However, an alternative framing under the new democratic model, which centers both speech and inclusion by understanding free speech as a compound right, is that a robust free speech environment exists when all voices are included, not just formally but also substantively. Thus, in the situation discussed above, a public university that embraces the alternative approach could permit the event to go forward (as required by law unless an exception applied, such as serious safety concerns) while focusing on expressions and activities that reinforce the university's commitment to inclusion. This could include engaging in substantial counter-speech supporting the targeted students; scheduling counter-events to promote messages of inclusion; funding proactive, systemic supports for minoritized and marginalized members of the campus community; and working to create a more inclusive campus community in which speech harms are part of the conversation about free speech, alongside speech rights. Thus, instead of centering the harmful speaker and focusing almost exclusively on that individual's speech rights, the university would center the marginalized and minoritized members of its own community, using its voice and its funds to elevate voices and views that promote inclusion and thus ultimately enable the fulsome access to all speech environments, especially spaces of knowledge creation and learning.

Although the compound right approach I described above is permitted by the First Amendment, it does not flow from the knowledge-production model of the university and the near-absolutist understanding of free speech, including the "marketplace of ideas" concept. That said, as legal scholar Genevieve Lakier argues, the American "free speech tradition"—in which she includes First Amendment law and culture as well as local, state, and other federal laws—is much more pluralist in its approach than we have realized.[63] Looking to the past, Lakier contends that federal and state legislative history, statutes, and policy implementation from the late eighteenth century through the present moment reveal a tradition parallel to the broadly accepted libertarian story of free speech rights.[64] Specifically, in the history Lakier unearths, free speech has a positive dimension through which the government can act to regulate speech conditions when necessary to protect a democratic good, including political equality or the occurrence of robust debate.[65] This redistributive approach prioritizes equalizing access to speech opportunities and is commonplace in non–First Amendment free speech law.[66]

A more redistributive approach also is present in free speech scholarship, including that by political scientists and philosophers Katharine Gelber, Rae Langton, Mary Kate McGowan, Lynne Tirrell, and Jeremy Waldron; all foreground dignity and equality in their normative discussions of free speech.[67] Langton, McGowan, and Tirrell each deeply engage speech harms experienced by women and the systemic discrimination that results. Gelber,

Langton, McGowan, Tirrell, and Waldron all theorize speech harms, and potential responses to speech harms, more generally. Collectively, these scholars advance a fundamentally different view of free speech than the approach grounded in the marketplace of ideas because they frame questions around harmful speech as not merely about the downstream impact of and responses to individual speech, but also about the subsequent upstream constraints that exclusionary speech can impose on future speakers.

This framing of free speech complements Baer's and Ben Porath's work; all conceive of a non-negligible role for the state (or, in the case of those writing about higher education, the university) in ensuring meaningful access to free speech for all persons. In the specific context of this chapter, this means the university is not relegated to the sideline as a viewpoint-silent arbiter of a marketplace of ideas. Rather, the university can and arguably should work on behalf of the historically marginalized and minoritized to increase access to—and speech in—spaces of knowledge creation and learning, and thus support the open exchange of ideas by all, not just by the traditionally powerful and privileged. With this normative positioning, the university can take affirmative steps to root out upstream barriers that foreclose some members of its community from speech opportunities on campus. To revisit two examples discussed above, renaming buildings bearing the names of known Ku Klux Klan members can help to create a more inclusive environment for Black students and thus open speech opportunities for them that previously may have been chilled in a practical if not legal sense. Similarly, a university leader speaking in support of marginalized groups of students, faculty, and staff when those groups are targeted by harmful speech on campus or in the world can help to ensure that those members of the campus community feel empowered to engage fully in the learning and knowledge creation work of the university community.

The alternative framing of the new democratic model I have discussed here is gaining ground not just in the literature but also in society, and the cultural shift is part of what has led to the widespread and heightened tensions around free speech on campus since 2015. In particular, the current generation of college students understands speech harms differently than prior generations. Survey research reveals that current college students, who have grown up in elementary and secondary schools attentive to the harm that can result from bullying, take speech harms more seriously than prior generations, and overall, many in this generation seem to understand at a deep level that speech can both constitute and cause harm.[68] Accordingly, this generation is much more comfortable with restrictions on harmful and exclusionary speech than prior generations have been.[69] In the context of First Amendment culture discussed above, restrictions on individual speech and responses to it by powerful officials are both viewed with high levels of suspicion. Although proactive restriction and reactive counterspeech are often conflated, it is important to distinguish between them. I do not engage the former issue but instead contend, along with other scholars and consistently with the current government speech doctrine, that the government—including a public university—can use its own voice in support of equality.[70] As this chapter makes clear, I also contend normatively that it should do so.

Redistributive Free Speech and Implications for Combating Polarization

Democracies around the world take a more redistributive approach to free speech than does the United States, and still they are wracked by polarization. I do not claim that a redistributive understanding of free speech is a panacea; rather, I argue that it is more compatible with reducing polarization than a near-absolutist approach. If polarization and tribalism go hand in hand, and tribalism can be reduced through experiences that humanize the other, it seems that a certain openness to considering what one shares with the other is a necessary first step to reducing polarization.

A near-absolutist approach considers others, and different others, only through minimal standard time, place, and manner regulations necessary to preserve social order (e.g., noise ordinances, parade permit requirements, etc.), and only in very rare circumstances when severe physical harm is likely to result (e.g., communicating "serious threats of harm or bodily injury to others," and "inciting imminent lawless action"). Although a near-absolutist approach does not foreclose considering the impact of one's speech on others more broadly, it does not foreground the importance of such a consideration.

By contrast, when free speech is understood as a compound right, involving redistributive elements, speech rights at their core are about the individual speaker *and* the community. Under the compound right approach, even when speech is permitted largely unrestricted and unopposed (which is still often the case in the largely absolutist free speech tradition Lakier discusses), the existence of a community of hearers, the experience of those hearers, and thus the existence and experience of the other, are acknowledged from the beginning. Such acknowledgment is a necessary step in empathizing with the other, and an understanding of free speech that easily enables this acknowledgment and thus facilitates awareness and, potentially, engagement is thus better positioned to combat polarization.

Empathy by those who seek to exclude is necessary if polarization is to reduce. Paul-Binyamin and colleagues focus on contact theory as explaining one way in which empathy for the other can develop. While interpersonal contact can create a powerful impact for a member of the majority group, a substantial disadvantage of that approach is that members of the marginalized and minoritized group carry the burden of being the other and helping the majority group members become comfortable with them. Especially when members of a marginalized or minoritized group are being told they do not belong in an environment of learning and knowledge creation, universities that truly value inclusion should not ask these members of the community to further defend and justify their presence. Thus, the university's message of inclusion should help those in the more powerful position to develop empathy for the other. While this is more challenging in the midst of a particular campus free speech conflict, much groundwork can be laid through co-curricular activities beginning at student orientation that encourage perspective-taking as part of the college experience. This proactive work by the university can describe a robust campus speech environment in which the historically marginalized and minoritized can engage in environments of learning and knowledge creation on the same terms as those historically more powerful, and in which speakers have not only legal rights to speak but also moral responsibilities for the impact of their speech on individuals and on the campus community.

CONCLUSION

In this chapter, I have sought to deepen our understanding of the ways in which educational institutions can help to combat social polarization by further theorizing free speech in the context of US colleges and universities. To do this required first going back to the foundational purpose of the university, as any normative view about free speech on campus will flow from an understanding about the purpose of the institution. This revealed that two models of the purpose of the university vie for dominance in the recent literature about free speech on campus; not surprisingly, those two models lead to rather different understandings about what free speech means and what the role of the institution is in maintaining a robust speech environment. The traditional, knowledge-creation view is strongly absolutist, focuses on individual rights, and relegates the government (here, the university) to the role of neutral moderator. The emerging new democratic view understands free speech as a compound right in which autonomy, in the form of a negative right, weaves together utility in the form of a positive, redistributive approach. In contrast to the traditional view, the emerging, alternative view centers both the individual and the community and is much more compatible with the idea that the government (again, here, the university), can and should help ensure equitable access for all to a space of learning and knowledge creation.[71]

The question then becomes which of these two understandings of free speech better positions universities to combat polarization in society at large. I contend it is the alternative understanding of free speech as a compound right, contained in the emerging new democratic model, that does so. Although I do not expect First Amendment doctrine to shift in this direction any time soon, non–First Amendment free speech law already has, and the lived experience of free speech on college campuses increasingly reflects the understanding of free speech contained in the new democratic model. Thus, I am hopeful that the alternative, compound view of free speech is one of the many ways in which the new democratic model of the university may help combat the democratic recession and the polarization that is woven into it.

NOTES

1 Jonathan Gould, ed., *Guardian of Democracy: The Civic Mission of Schools* (Philadelphia: Leonore Annenberg Institute for Civics of the Annenberg Public Policy Center at the University of Pennsylvania, and the Campaign for the Civic Mission of Schools, 2011); National Task Force on Civic Learning and Democratic Engagement, *A Crucible Moment: College Learning and Democracy's Future* (Washington, DC: Association of American Colleges and Universities, 2012).

2 See Sigal Ben-Porath, *Free Speech on Campus* (Philadelphia: University of Pennsylvania Press, 2019); Ronald J. Daniels, *What Universities Owe Democracy* (Baltimore, MD: Johns Hopkins University Press, 2021); Amy Gutmann, *Democratic Education* (Princeton, NJ: Princeton University Press, 1999); Michael A. Rebell, *Flunking Democracy: Schools, Courts, and Civic Education* (Chicago: University of Chicago Press, 2018).

3 See "Moving Beyond the 'Poitier Effect'" by Ilana Paul-Binyamin, Wurud Jayusi, and Yael Tamir, in this volume.

4 See Paul-Binyamin et al., "Moving Beyond the 'Poitier Effect'," in this volume.

5 As a side note, if we were to apply Paul-Binyamin et al.'s policy proposal in US elementary and secondary schools (the authors write about Israeli policy), I would wonder about a couple of key questions. First, how would we take seriously the challenges for minoritized teachers of serving in the role of ambassador, as the authors do when they identify the isolation and vulnerability that initially impacts minoritized teachers significantly when they are assigned to teach in majority schools? Relatedly, how would we counteract the opportunities denied to minoritized students when they have even fewer teachers from the same racial group? The US teacher shortage, and in particular a shortage of Black teachers, who make up only about 7% of the teaching population? Growing the pipeline of teachers from underrepresented groups, and particularly Black teachers, would seem to be a critical component of such a policy proposal.

6 Ben-Porath, *Free Speech on Campus*, 32; Emily Bramhall, "Why Does Segregation Between School Districts Matter for Educational Equity?," Housing Matters (May 12, 2021), available at: https://housingmatters.urban.org; "$23 Billion," EdBuild (2019), available at: https://edbuild.org; Michael Lipka, "Many U.S. Congregations are Still Racially Segregated, But Things Are Changing," Pew Research Center (December 8, 2014), www.pewresearch.org; Kate Bahn and Carmen Sanchez Cummings, "Factsheet: U.S. Occupational Segregation by Race, Ethnicity, Gender," Washington Center for Equitable Growth (July 1, 2020), https://equitablegrowth.org; Pearson Education, "Diversity in Colleges: Statistics, History,

and Resources" (2022), available at: www.pearson.com; US Department of Education, "Advancing Diversity and Inclusion in Higher Education" (November 2016), available at: www2.ed.gov.

7 The higher education literature conceives of "the university" as having multiple, sequential dominant models. The recent free speech on campus literature often summarizes these models: (1) the medieval proto-university anchored in the church and focused on training individuals for professions, (2) the Oxbridge undergraduate tutorial model with the goal of developing undergraduates' critical thinking skills, (3) the German Research University, emerging in the late 1800s, distinguished by deep expertise via graduate education and research, (4) the American University, beginning early 1900s. Ben-Porath, *Free Speech on Campus*; Keith Whittington, *Speak Freely: Why Universities Must Defend Free Speech* (Princeton, NJ: Princeton University Press, 2019), 13, 16.

8 Genevieve Lakier, "The Non-First Amendment Law of Freedom of Speech," *Harvard Law Review* 134, no. 7 (2021): 2300–2381.

9 Ishani Maitra and Mary Kate McGowan, eds., *Speech and Harm: Controversies over Free Speech* (Oxford: Oxford University Press, 2012); Mary Kate McGowan, "Responding to Harmful Speech: The More Speech Response, Counter Speech, and the Complexity of Language Use," in *Voicing Dissent: The Ethics and Epistemology of Making Disagreement Public*, ed. Casey Rebecca Johnson (New York: Routledge, 2018), 182–199; Katharine Gelber, "Differentiating Hate Speech: A Systemic Discrimination Approach," *Critical Review of International Social and Political Philosophy* 24, no. 4 (2019): 1–22; Lynne Tirrell, "Toxic Misogyny and the Limits of Counterspeech," *Fordham Law Review* 87, no. 6 (2019): 2433–2452; Jeremy Waldron, "The Conditions of Legitimacy, A Response to James Weinstein," *Constitutional Commentary* 32, no. 3 (2017): 697–717; Jeremy Waldron, *The Harm in Hate Speech* (Cambridge, MA: Harvard University Press, 2012); and Jeremy Waldron, "How Law Protects Dignity," *Cambridge Law Journal* 71, no. 1 (2012): 200–222.

10 Whittington, *Speak Freely*, 13, 16.

11 Whittington, *Speak Freely*, 7.

12 Whittington, *Speak Freely*, 12, 25, 27.

13 Geoffrey Stone, "Report on the Committee on the Freedom of Expression," 2015. Available online at https://provost.uchicago.edu.

14 Christina Bohannon, "On the 50th Anniversary of *Tinker v. Des Moines*: Toward a Positive View of Free Speech on College Campuses," *Iowa Law Review* 105 (2020): 2233–2271; Mary Rose Papandrea, "The Free Speech Rights of Unviersity Students," *Minnesota Law Review* 101 (2017): 1801–208, 1803; Joseph Russomano, "Speech on Campus: How America's Crisis in Confidence Is Eroding Free Speech Values," *Hastings Constitutional Law Quarterly* 45, no. 2 (2018): 273–300; Keith E. Whittington, "Free

Speech and the Diverse University," *Fordham Law Review* 87, no. 6 (2019): 2453–2477; and Joseph W. Yockey, "Bias Response on Campus," *Journal of Law and Education* 48, no. 1 (2019): 1–50.

15 Erwin Chemerinsky and Howard Gillman, *Free Speech on Campus* (New Haven, CT: Yale University Press, 2017); Michael S. Roth, *Safe Enough Spaces: A Pragmatist's Approach to Inclusion, Free Speech, and Political Correctness on College Campuses* (New Haven, CT: Yale University Press, 2019).

16 Chemerinsky and Gillman, *Free Speech on Campus*, 63.

17 Chemerinsky and Gillman, *Free Speech on Campus*, 51.

Similarly, in work focused on academic freedom in Australia, Carolyn Evans and Adrienne Stone define academic freedom as "protect[ing] the pursuit and dissemination of knowledge through free inquiry" as distinct from free speech, which is a political freedom in democracies. They contend that academic freedom captures the mission of the university and manifests primarily through individual freedom in research and teaching. Evans and Stone's framing may be due in part to the somewhat different way freedom of speech is understood in Australia, as a political freedom that can fit more neatly into the non-classroom, non-research spaces Evans and Stone identify as its context, as opposed to the American context, in which free speech issues reach inside classroom and research spaces as well as on the campus quad. Although Evans and Stone (like Chemerinsky and Gilman, and Roth) do not situate diversity or inclusion as a core mission of today's university, Evans and Stone's analysis differs in that they do explore questions around harmful speech in a fulsome way. Notably, they explain why speech can harm and note that, in their view, universities may reasonably restrict severe hate speech. Carolyn Evans and Adrienne Stone, *Open Minds: Academic Freedom and Freedom of Speech in Australia* (Carlton, Vic.: La Trobe University Press, 2021), 73.

18 Anniina Leiviskä, "A Discourse Theoretical Model for Determining the Limits of Free Speech on Campus," *Educational Philosophy and Theory* 53, no. 11 (2021): 1171–1182; and Ryan Muldoon, "Free Speech and Learning from Difference," *Society* 54, no. 4 (2017): 331–336.

19 Chemerinsky and Gillman, *Free Speech on Campus*, 20–21.

Likely because Roth's own institution is an undergraduate liberal arts college, he focuses on the activities of teaching and research, a hallmark of the comprehensive university in the knowledge-generation model, as creating the greatest benefit to the society at large by driving innovation and solving pressing problems. Roth, *Safe Enough Spaces*, 6.

20 *Abrams v. United States*, 250 U.S. 616, 630 (Holmes, J., dissenting).

21 Steven P. Lee, "Hate Speech in the Marketplace of Ideas," in *Freedom of Expression in a Diverse World*, ed. Deirdre Golash (Dordrecht: Springer Netherlands, 2010), 13–25.

22 Joseph Blocher, "Institutions in the Marketplace of Ideas," *Duke Law Journal* 57, no. 4 (2008): 821–889, 829–838; and Rodney A. Smolla, "The Meaning of the 'Marketplace of Ideas' in First Amendment Law," *Communication Law and Policy* 24, no. 4 (2019): 437–475, 439–441.

23 Lee, "Hate Speech"; and Frederick Schauer, "Free Speech, the Search for Truth, and the Problem of Collective Knowledge," *Southern Methodist University Law Review* 70, no. 2 (2017): 231–251, 236.

24 Schauer cites more than a dozen sources (books, law review articles, economics articles) as "a sampling of the extensive literature supporting or challenging the underlying empirical assumptions of the claim that a free marketplace of ideas will have truth-identifying tendencies." Frederick Schauer, "Facts and the First Amendment," *UCLA Law Review* 57 (2010): 897–919, 899 n.16. See also Steve Mirsky, "Flat Earthers: What They Believe and Why," in *Behavior and Society*, produced by Scientific American, podcast, audio, 36:08, March 27, 2020, www.scientificamerican.com.

25 Robert Post, "The Classic First Amendment Tradition under Stress: Freedom of Speech and the University," in *The Free Speech Century*, ed. Lee C. Bollinger and Geoffrey R. Stone (New York: Oxford University Press, 2018); and Schauer, "Free Speech, the Search for Truth," 107–108.

26 Robert Post, "Academic Freedom and Legal Scholarship," *Journal of Legal Education* 64, no. 4 (2015): 530–541; and Post, "The Classic First Amendment Tradition."

27 James Weinstein, "Participatory Democracy as the Central Value of American Free Speech Doctrine," *Virginia Law Review* 97, no. 3 (2011): 633–679.

28 Schauer also samples the literature recounting the First Amendment's negative rights approach. Frederick Schauer, "The Boundaries of the First Amendment: A Preliminary Exploration of Constitutional Salience," *Harvard Law Review* 117, no. 6 (2004): 1765–1809, 1791.

29 Schauer, "The Boundaries of the First Amendment."

30 Weinstein, "Participatory Democracy," 638–639.

31 *Abrams* at 628 (Holmes, J., dissenting).

32 Robert Post, "Writing the Dissent in *Abrams*," *Seton Hall Law Review* 51, no. 1 (2020): 21–40, 36.

33 See, e.g., Richard Delgado, "Legal Realism and the Controversy over Campus Speech Codes," *Case Western Reserve Law Review* 69 (2018): 275–298.

34 As legal scholar Eric Heinze notes, even among those who oppose hate speech bans, few would support a right to engage in hate speech in face-to-face encounters that are otherwise understood as stalking, harassment, or criminal activity motivated by group-based animus. Eric Heinze,

"Hate Speech and the Normative Foundations of Regulation," *International Journal of Law in Context* 9, no. 4 (2013): 590–617.

35 Paul Brietzke, "How and Why the Marketplace of Ideas Fails," *Valparaiso University Law Review* 31 (1997): 951, 962–963.

36 Blocher, "Institutions in the Marketplace of Ideas," 825–833.

37 Corey Brettschneider, *When the State Speaks, What Should It Say?* (Princeton, NJ: Princeton University Press, 2011).

38 Lakier, "The Non-First Amendment Law," 2365.

39 Blocher, "Institutions in the Marketplace of Ideas"; Frederick Schauer, *The Exceptional First Amendment* (Cambridge, MA: Harvard University, 2005).

40 Robert L. Tsai, *Eloquence and Reason: Creating a First Amendment Culture* (New Haven, CT: Yale University Press, 2008), ix.

41 Schauer, "The Boundaries of the First Amendment," 2381.

42 Tsai, *Eloquence and Reason*, ix.

43 Schauer, "The Boundaries of the First Amendment," 1766–1767.

44 Lakier, "The Non-First Amendment Law," 2379.

45 Eric Barendt, "What Is the Harm of Hate Speech?," *Ethical Theory and Moral Practice* 22, no. 3 (2019): 539–553; Robert French, "Report of the Independent Review of Freedom of Speech in Australian Higher Education Providers," Australian Government Department of Education, March 19, 2019, www.dese.gov.au.

46 Tsai, *Eloquence and Reason*.

47 Kristine L. Bowman, "University Speech and the First Amendment," *Nebraska Law Review* 90 (2021): 896–936.

48 Bowman, "University Speech."

49 Kristine L. Bowman and Katharine Gelber, "Responding to Hate Speech: Counterspeech and the University," *Virginia Journal of Social Policy and the Law* 28 (2021): 249–274.

50 Ben-Porath, *Free Speech on Campus*.

51 Ulrich Baer, *What Snowflakes Get Right: Free Speech, Truth, and Equality on Campus* (New York: Oxford University Press, 2019), xi.

52 Ben-Porath, *Free Speech on Campus*, 37.

53 Ben-Porath, *Free Speech on Campus*, 37.

54 Benjamin Bindewald and Joshua Hawkins, "Speech and Inquiry in Public Institutions of Higher Education: Navigating Ethical and Epistemological Challenges," *Educational Philosophy and Theory* 53, no. 11 (2021): 1074–1085, 1073.

55 Ben-Porath, *Free Speech on Campus*, 31–32.

56 Ben-Porath, *Free Speech on Campus*, 45.

57 Ben-Porath, *Free Speech on Campus*, 31.

58 Stephen M. Feldman, "Broken Platforms, Broken Communities? Free Speech on Campus," *The William and Mary Bill of Rights Journal* 27, no. 4 (2019): 949–988.

59 Whittington discusses the pervasiveness of this framing, citing surveys by the Knight Foundation, Gallup, and the American Council on Education that employ this approach. Whittington, "Free Speech and the Diverse University." Pew Research has done the same, and inside the academy others repeat this framing as well. See, e.g., Bradley Campbell and Jason Manning, *The Rise of Victimhood Culture: Microaggressions, Safe Spaces, and the New Culture Wars* (Cham, Switzerland: Palgrave Macmillan, 2018); Pareena Lawrence, "When Core Values Collide: Diversity, Inclusion, and Free Speech," *Liberal Education* 104, no. 2 (2018): 14–19; and Monnica T. Williams, "Adverse Racial Climates in Academia: Conceptualization, Interventions, and Call to Action," *New Ideas in Psychology* 55 (2019): 58–67.

60 Lakier, "The Non-First Amendment Law," 2365.

61 Meir Dan-Cohen, *Rights, Persons, and Organizations: A Legal Theory for Bureaucratic Society*, 2nd ed. (New Orleans, LA: Quid Pro Quo Books, 2016), 77–92; Richard W. Miller, "Rights and Reality," *Philosophical Review* 40, no. 3 (1981): 383–407.

62 Acknowledging that exclusionary, hateful speech can cause serious harm does not, however, result in the conclusion that such speech should be restricted; here, I do not argue for extending restrictions on exclusionary, hateful speech from campuses or in other contexts beyond current legal restrictions.

63 Lakier, "The Non-First Amendment Law," 2300–2305.

64 Lakier, "The Non-First Amendment Law," 2309–2342. Lakier analyzes three sets of free speech statutes, also including the legislative history surrounding their enactment and their implementation: federal postal laws from the late eighteenth century, federal "common carrier" media and communications laws stretching from the early twentieth century to the present, and states' worker protection laws beginning in the 1830s.

65 Lakier, "The Non-First Amendment Law," 2347, 2353.

66 Lakier, "The Non-First Amendment Law," 2352 n.80, 2366–2368.

67 See, e.g., Maitra and McGowan, *Speech and Harm*; McGowan, "Responding to Harmful Speech"; Gelber, "Differentiating Hate Speech"; Tirrell, "Toxic Misogyny"; Waldron, "The Conditions of Legitimacy"; Waldron, *The Harm in Hate Speech*; and Waldron, "How Law Protects Dignity."

68 Chemerinsky and Gillman, *Free Speech on Campus*; and Catherine J. Ross, *Lessons in Censorship: How Schools and Courts Subvert Students' First Amendment Rights* (Cambridge, MA: Harvard University Press, 2015).

69 Knight Foundation, "Free Expression on Campus: What College Students Think About First Amendment Issues," March 12, 2018, https://knightfoundation.org.

70 Bowman, "University Speech"; Brettschneider, *When the State Speaks.*

71 In other work, I have argued that the university should do this by using its own voice in support of the marginalized and minoritized.

10

TEACHING COMPETITION AND COOPERATION IN CIVIC EDUCATION

SIGAL BEN-PORATH, AMY GUTMANN, AND DENNIS THOMPSON

Civic education in the nation's public schools has suffered neglect in recent years. In the 1960s, by no means a golden age, students usually took three civics courses in high school. Today many states do not require any civic education at all, and most of those that do, require no more than one course, often only a half course.[1] There are some signs of renewal, and we note some promising developments below. But whether or not the decline is persisting, it is fair to say that civic education today gets less attention than it should in a healthy democracy. Civic education is subject to not-so-benign neglect.

There are some conspicuous sources of this neglect. Civic education does not usually have a place on the standardized tests that, after No Child Left Behind, have come to dominate teaching. It often raises controversial issues that many teachers may prudently want to avoid. It is competing for attention in a crowded curriculum with new subjects such as computer science and personal finance. But there is another, less appreciated, source of the neglect: a divergence between the ostensible aim of most civics courses and the polarized state of American politics. The aim emphasizes cooperation while the politics manifests competition. Appreciating the implications of this divergence, we suggest, can guide efforts to strengthen civic education.

A typical civics course teaches students facts about democratic institutions and processes, which are a basic part of any kind of civic education.[2] But traditional civics courses and those promoted more recently impart basic knowledge as part of a broader goal of cultivating a nonpartisan sense of shared American citizenship.[3] This goal appears on its face to be more consistent with teaching cooperation than competition. Yet the aim of teaching cooperation rather than competition does not align with the realities of the polarized society that students are joining.[4] What these novice citizens find when they participate in political life is mostly competition, not cooperation. It is true that well-designed civic education can increase students' propensity to participate in community action and politics and raise the level of their political knowledge.[5] But it is also true that the politics in which they will participate is likely to remain hyperpolarized and competitive for the foreseeable future.

In civic education, the gap between what many educators seek to teach and how politics is practiced in democratic societies has long existed, but as hyperpartisanship has increased in recent decades, the gap has become all the more striking.[6] On almost every politically relevant issue, including where the dispute appears to rely on fundamental facts that are contested, Republicans and Democrats are so radically divided that finding a basis for cooperation appears to many as an idealist's errand, if not a fool's.[7]

Even the greatest health crisis of our lifetimes, the COVID-19 pandemic, when coupled with polarized politics, has sparked what could be called the Coronavirus culture wars over the wearing of masks, the efficacy of vaccines, and the use of certain medical treatments. In this context, it is hard to justify teaching students only how to cooperate for a common good, rather than also how to compete politically for what they have reason to believe will save lives.

Were pandemic politics an aberration, we could dismiss this case as an anomaly. But Americans are polarized in their perspectives on the facts and values surrounding many major civic issues including climate change, gender, racial, and religious discrimination, and economic and educational inequality. The pandemic is paradigmatic. Despite the consensus among public health and medical experts, and despite the life-and-death stakes that would put a premium on a politics that cooperatively searches for a common good, American politics at the national and state levels continues to be hypercompetitive and polarized beyond COVID-19 policy issues.

How should we deal with this gap between what civic educators are asked to teach and what political citizens practice? If one of the main goals of civic education is to develop effective democratic citizens, both competition and cooperation may be necessary (though not sufficient) means to achieving it. To help establish their joint necessity, we highlight the contribution of each separately.

Consider first an approach that emphasizes only competition. This approach would appear to be more useful in the hyperpolarized politics of our time. It would help teach students how to be more effective in fighting for their own causes. Students would be taught the skills of competition: strategies that are more appropriate for zero-sum politics, debates that are more specifically designed to sharpen and highlight differences, rhetoric that is more typical in campaigns and protest movements, and techniques that are more effective in mobilizing the like-minded. To prepare students to function effectively in a polarized and unequal society, we would aim to cultivate skills and attitudes more suitable for competing based on opposing interests rather than for cooperating in search of common ground or compromise across divides. Students who are not taught to compete politically for their own interests will be at an obvious disadvantage in advocating for what they deserve in policy debates such as those concerning the response to COVID-19. A competitive approach could also help civic education gain wider support as it is more easily recognized as practical: The skills it teaches are directly useful to the lives students are experiencing. Regardless of whether the neglect of the competitive approach impaired civic education in the past, its absence now is more damaging as politics has become more polarized and competitive.

However, it is also essential to recognize the incompleteness of an approach that emphasizes only competition. To adopt a competitive approach exclusively would ignore the potential for improvement in civic discourse, civic engagement, and alliances for the common good. A second approach—teaching to the ideals of cooperation—is critically important. Improvements in the direction of creating a more just society will redound to the greatest benefit of those who today are least advantaged and will do the most in the long term to close the civic empowerment gap.[8] Giving in to the realities of polarized politics and relentless competition risks widening the civic empowerment gap by giving up on civic education designed to create and sustain a more just society. Instead, by emphasizing cooperation, we would teach strategies for finding common ground, dialog that bridges differences, rhetoric that is mutually respectful, techniques that bring opponents together, and, generally, attitudes suitable for cooperating rather than competing. With regard to the need for broader public support, we should not abandon a cooperative approach just because it is not easy to sell. Gaining greater support for civic education is unavailing if it neglects what is needed to create a stronger, better democracy.

The contrast between these two approaches points to a fundamental dilemma of civic education in a polarized society: If we teach only cooperation, we do not prepare students for the democratic politics they will face. We fail to give students the skills, attitudes, and knowledge they need for actual citizenship. So we should educate for competition. If we teach only competition, we reproduce and reinforce the polarized politics that prevails. We fail to realize the potential of democratic citizenship for all. So we should educate for cooperation.[9]

This dilemma is distinct from the question of what knowledge should be taught. It concerns skills and attitudes rather than facts and other information about government, which are embraced by both approaches. Although we do not discuss disputes about facts and information, we note that if students are to have a role in resolving those disputes—as we believe they should—they will have to develop the skills and attitudes of both competition and cooperation that we do discuss. They can use these skills and attitudes to pursue the widest range of goals, including social justice and democratic rights.

A Broader Understanding of Civic Education

The dilemma that is illuminated by contrasting the competitive and cooperative approaches can be overcome by adopting a broader understanding of civic education that promotes teaching both competition and cooperation. Teaching the basic facts of civics, the Constitution, and history is of course necessary, but what we propose here is an understanding that goes beyond those pursuits and focuses on skills and attitudes in addition to important content. Including both competition and cooperation in civic education should have wider appeal to all sides in a polarized society. It offers something to both the competitive-minded and cooperative-minded. A more expansive understanding connects competition and cooperation just as they should be connected in a properly functioning democracy. This understanding does not lay claim to including all the attitudes and skills that civic education should promote. It is not in that respect comprehensive. But, importantly, it can provide an effective response to the civic empowerment gap. Learning to both compete and cooperate can help motivate students with different levels of training in civics to take steps to ensure that they are included in the civic sphere. For civic education to have the best chance of succeeding, it needs to engage disempowered students and others who deeply mistrust government and are profoundly skeptical of cooperating with privileged and ideological opponents. The approach we outline can do so in an effective and inclusive way across the political spectrum.

As in other domains of education, civic education needs to have one foot planted firmly in the reality of how democracy functions now, and another foot in an aspirational future in which democracy functions better. To that dual end, we grasp both horns of the dilemma of civic education. We defend a civic education that teaches both competition and cooperation.

Competition, as we understand it, is an activity in which participants, following agreed upon rules, try to establish relative advantage over others who are trying to do the same. Democratic politics is replete with competition, most conspicuously between rival parties, candidates for public offices, and policy alternatives. The competitive nature of party politics—as long as it does not devolve into hyperpartisanship—is often a positive reality of democratic politics, generating interest and engagement.[10] Voting is the quintessential competitive activity in a democracy, driving home to every citizen the importance of participating in (and doing what they can to ensure) a fair competition. In the classroom, fair competition can help students learn the skills they need to successfully engage in a polarized world.

Competition in civic education is a special case because the skill of competition itself can be a key learning goal. A competitive debate about how to address climate change not only exposes students to the subject but also teaches the skills of debating in general.[11] Debates, which are generally seen as promoting engagement in learning and society, can be more or less competitive. Debates are more competitive when the aim is to learn the skills of debating itself. The students are trying to learn the skills they need to win. They are less competitive when the primary aim is to learn content, such as the effects of and possible responses to climate change, or the provisions of the Constitution. Both sides are pursuing the same goal—greater knowledge of the content—and it matters less which side wins.

The primary aim of any particular competition is to win, but in civic education how one wins (and loses) is critical. The competition that students learn should be fair, governed by rules that do not favor either side. Students should learn to observe the spirit of the rules, which prohibit violence, fraud, and deceit. They should not demonize their opponents or take unreasonable advantage of them, and should accept the results of the competition even in defeat. All these are valuable preconditions for any minimally acceptable democratic process. Most students, drawing on their experience in competitive sports and other activities, probably have an intuitive sense of the difference between fair competition with its rule-governed contestation, and no-holds-barred competition with its dirty tricks and below-the-belt tactics. That basic difference—and its nuances—can be further explored through explicit discussion in the classroom both before and after the competitive exercise. The discussion could also be productively directed toward finding ways to counter hypercompetitive conflict that is prevalent in modern society.

In this way, competition, though reflective of the realities of democratic politics, has an ethical dimension. Unlike some of its more extreme manifestations in everyday politics, it could be considered an ideal in this respect. But it falls short of the full-blown ideal of cooperation that civic education also seeks to promote. While competitors try to win against their opponents, cooperators try to win over their opponents to pursue a common purpose. Cooperation is an activity in which participants work together toward the same end. The goal is a collective good shared by all, rather than only particular goods allocated individually. In a democracy where deep disagreements are to be expected, cooperation is necessary and desirable. It is necessary to enact any laws at all, and desirable to make the enacted laws legitimate.

While the debate is the typical competitive exercise, the collaborative project is the characteristic cooperative activity. Students learn to cooperate by engaging in activities that require them to not prioritize personal preferences that conflict with those of others and to seek either common ground or a classic compromise.[12] The classic compromise—where all sides gain something more for their own positions by ceding something they value to the others—is a cooperative activity that turns competition into cooperation. The results of cooperative activities, like those of classic compromise, are often different from what each would have preferred to start with and are therefore not simply the sum of the initial preferences. Both sides may have to sacrifice something each values. Provided the activity is carried out properly, both sides also can see that the result is better than anything each could have achieved alone.

Competition itself requires a minimal form of cooperation. Both are often found together, and neither appears in pure form in actual political life. If a contest takes place between teams, the members must be able to work together to develop their strategies, assign the roles each should play, and coordinate their interactions. Both teams need to agree on rules and mechanisms to resolve disagreements. But all this internal cooperation, valuable though it is, takes place in a context where the main aim is to defeat opponents, not to collaborate with them. Appreciating this distinction serves to underscore the fact that learning to cooperate with teammates is based on a different goal and different skill set than learning to cooperate with rivals. Similarly, the skills and attitudes of an activity that seeks to *include* those with whom you initially disagree are quite different from skills and attitudes that seek to *defeat* those with whom you disagree. Cooperating within a team, group, or party is not the same as cooperating with opponents or reaching across the aisle. In a way, the two are pulling in different directions: The better your cooperation with your own teammates, the stronger you might be positioned for defeating the opposing team, and thus the less likely you are to look for ways to cooperate with them. In this way, partisan cooperation can fuel polarization. To avoid that outcome, the lessons of competition have to be tempered with the lessons of cooperation.

In simple terms, educating for competition means teaching the skills and attitudes useful for winning in the face of disagreement; and educating for cooperation means teaching the skills and attitudes useful for collaborating in the face of disagreement. Both require the ability to spot the weaknesses in opponents' positions, but in competition students identify weaknesses so that they can exploit them, whereas in cooperation students identify the weaknesses so that they can compensate for them. Both require the ability to recognize differences, but in competition it is for the purpose of sharpening them, whereas in cooperation it is for the purpose of overcoming them. Both require a will to succeed, but in competition the will is applied to defeat opponents, whereas in cooperation it is applied to enlist opponents in a common cause. Both require a mutual regard that supports an ongoing peaceful engagement, but in competition the regard takes the form of an acknowledgment of a worthy opponent, whereas in cooperation it is a respect for those with whom one shares a common purpose.

THE PLACE OF DEMOCRATIC THEORY

The contrast between competition and cooperation has some affinities with the distinction between aggregative and deliberative theories of democracy.[13] Aggregative democracy emphasizes competition, and deliberative democracy stresses cooperation. But neither teaching for competition nor teaching for cooperation requires adopting a full-blown theory of democracy. It is important to formulate goals of civic education that can stand independently of any particular comprehensive theory of democracy because democratic citizens reasonably disagree about which theory is correct. An important aim of civic education is to prepare students to engage with manifestations of that disagreement.[14]

Students should be taught the skills and attitudes to help themselves advocate for the theoretical principles they find most compelling, and to adapt their favored principles in the face of the claims of other principles. While they may not be operating with complete theories, students are likely to be making some claims that favor one theory over another. They should be prepared to recognize and defend the broader implications of their claims. This means that civic education cannot settle in advance the question of which democratic theory is correct, but aspects of different democratic theories may inevitably and legitimately shape the ongoing discourse.

Nevertheless, the civic education we are proposing assumes a set of democratic values or principles that are integral to any acceptable theory of democracy. Specifically, on any defensible view of democracy in a polarized society, both competition and cooperation are necessary and desirable for many reasons, including those we have described. Competition and cooperation are themselves value-laden; the values they assume, such as fair play and mutual respect, are the basic norms that any acceptable democracy in a polarized society needs to endorse.

Teaching Competition and Cooperation Together

The most general reason to teach competition and cooperation together is that maintaining and improving democracy depends on everyone learning both how to defend their own interests and how to cooperate together. They are necessary not only for pursuing any legitimate policy goal but also for promoting democratic citizenship itself. One way to teach both is to engage students in the electoral process, either as voters or as activists encouraging others to vote. The core democratic activity of voting, which exemplifies democratic competition, also depends on alternation between competition (a majority or plurality vote wins) and cooperation (the outcome seeks democratic legitimacy and can be collectively reconsidered in anticipation of another election). Every person's vote is a competitive action (to gain advantage over the opposition) while the ongoing institutional practices (elections and governance) alternate competition with cooperation.

A more specific reason to teach competition and cooperation together is that learning to compete more effectively can motivate and empower all young people and especially marginalized students both to stand up for their interests and to collaborate with others to improve democracy. Engaging students in understanding the competitive and cooperative nature of voting in a democracy can help to advance the value of voting among our youngest citizens who vote at disturbingly low levels and whose interests are correspondingly neglected in American politics. When the least privileged students learn how they can successfully defend their own interests through competition—engaging in such practices as nonviolent protest, political campaigning, and turning out the vote—they are more likely to be willing to pursue common interests through cooperation. Although, as we indicated earlier, hyperpartisan competition tends to inhibit cooperation across divides, well-structured competition combined with cooperation can enhance both.

In the classroom, competition and cooperation can be taught together if they are introduced alternately. The key to achieving this aim is teaching students how to step in and out of the competitive and cooperative roles. To see what this means, consider this illustrative scenario. A class would first cooperatively decide on what controversial issue to consider. The teacher would then divide the class into teams to engage in a debate on the issue, designed to be a competitive exercise. After the debate, students would step out of their competitive roles and adopt a cooperative perspective to assess whether the debate was conducted fairly. Finally, they would try cooperatively to reach a collective decision on the issues that were the subjects of the debate. If, as would be likely, some students dissent from the collective decision, the class would discuss the value of dissent, how majority and minority might work together on related issues, and how majority and minority might change over time.

The point of introducing this scenario is not to suggest that it must be carried out in full in any actual classroom, but rather to show that effectively teaching competition and cooperation depends on students' moving back and forth between engaging in each. Students learn more about competition by cooperatively reflecting on its strengths and weaknesses, and more about cooperation by contrasting it with the experiences of competition.

By teaching competition, we bring out the difficulties of polarized politics, and by then teaching cooperation, we try to determine how they can be overcome. Neither alone is sufficient, as they are both connected in democratic politics and should be taught as such to help students engage in both. Competition without cooperation may engage students, but leaves the polarization in place. Cooperation without competition conceals the seriousness of the problem of polarization.

In effect, we begin by teaching students what they both want and need to know: How can they effectively compete for more than they have now? We continue by teaching them how to expand their circle of cooperation to win allies for causes that serve both them and a common good. Alternating the two is exemplified by teaching ways to compromise. Compromise is a bridge between the two that illustrates their shared centrality in democratic politics. As it is an activity and an end state, compromise contains elements of both competitive and cooperative activities.

While compromise requires cooperative skills and attitudes, it also relies on a competitive attitude in order to get the most for one's side.[15] Alternating competition and cooperation can help students engage with each other in their classrooms, which can lead to an increased sense of efficacy, and as a result, greater political participation.[16] The key feature of this scenario—the alternation of competition and cooperation—can be found in more and less nascent forms in several innovative curricula in the classroom as well as outside it.

COMPETITION AND COOPERATION IN THE CLASSROOM

A program that comes close to the approach we advocate is the Legislative Semester, an innovative curriculum that allows teachers to alternate competition and cooperation in the classroom.[17] We focus on the curriculum in a suburban school in the Midwest, which we call Oak Hills High.[18] The school uses a simulation of the legislative process that takes place over a semester. The students self-identify by party (Democratic, Republican, or Independent) and elect a Speaker, as well as Minority and Majority Leaders. Each class chooses a topic on which to legislate, and small teams of students draft bills on the topic. (This step is a reminder that in actual political discussion the goal comes first. The means to the goal—competition and cooperation—only then come into play.) Following parliamentary procedure, they formulate, amend, and vote on bills in a process that simulates a legislative committee. The leaders then choose which bills to bring to a debate and vote in the full assembly. Older students serve as lobbyists, offering or withholding "monetary" donations from legislators whose bills they wish to promote or defeat.

The program teaches both competition and cooperation. It encourages competition between parties as well as among teams and interest groups that advance specific bills. It also teaches cooperation, not only among members of teams that write bills together, but also principally in the committees, where students form alliances across party lines and propose amendments that might persuade Independents and members of the opposing party to support a bill. Some progressive students, for example, strongly advocated for a bill to enfranchise undocumented residents. Some of these students were themselves undocumented, which served to underscore the high stakes of their competitive advocacy. The bill received only modest support at first, but after an amendment that limited participation to local rather than national elections, the bill gained broader support and moved forward. The compromise illustrates cooperation in action, turning competition into cooperation. One teacher reported that when students engage on more contentious issues, as in the example of immigration, "there are often 5–10 kids who cross party lines and help write a more moderate bill. In the past we did not let kids cross party lines, and now they can move by policy preference, which made the class way more cooperative."[19] This example also shows the importance of a diverse classroom in carrying out not only the Legislative Semester but all forms of civic education.

Teachers report that the class is effective for learning about how government (or at least the legislative branch) operates; and for learning skills such as public speaking. Equally important, students learn the skills of both competition and cooperation. Because the topics are known in advance, students of all skill levels are more likely to participate. The Legislative Semester is popular at Oak Hills High, and nearly all students participate with enthusiasm. In this and other forms of civic education we are recommending, the demands on the teachers are considerable. Teachers therefore need to be given more time for preparation and more support for carrying out their plans than they usually receive.

Teachers who have engaged in these legislative simulations are also alert to guarding against some potential pitfalls. Even accepting the fact that partisanship is an endemic and valuable part of democracy, students may become hyperpartisan in ways that can reinforce polarization and inhibit cooperation. One teacher worries that the emphasis on competition comes at the expense of cooperation: "It's a competitive system and some win and some lose—it's winner takes all. Teaching the kids to live within the system that allows only some to win. It teaches kids that this is the main or only way to do democracy—combative, two sided. Being on the opposite side of your friends, the 'other tribe'."[20] To avoid this pitfall, a simulation can and should strike a balance between competition and cooperation, and support compromise to enact both.

Another way the Legislative Semester falls short is the relative lack of discussion of the process itself, especially after it has concluded. As some teachers note, the required amount of basic knowledge and the complexity of the process leave little time for reflection on the results of the simulation. This is the reason that these civically minded teachers—with their school's support (an essential ingredient for any successful civic education)—are now planning to move to a year-long simulation. For the purpose of teaching competition and cooperation, more explicit reflection on the process itself can enrich the lessons the students learn.

Part of that reflection may include discussion of how compromise enables both sides to reach an agreement that makes everyone better off, and how the majority might work with the minority in pursuing future projects. That reflection could also include considering whether there are structural problems in the process or even in the laws and constitution that govern the process.

The Legislative Semester and other forms of civic education are not likely to be successful unless students are exposed to civics in other classes earlier in their education. Middle schools can also productively offer a civic education that incorporates both competition and cooperation. An innovative example is the year-long, eighth grade civics curriculum that was developed by the Democratic Knowledge Project and has been implemented in more than a dozen Massachusetts districts.[21] The "10 Questions" undergirding the curriculum—starting with "who am I?" and moving toward understanding citizens' relationships to each other and to their government—teach students to identify areas in their community that require change, and empower them to act toward promoting such change.

After the initial foundation, some teachers have the students engage in a competitive debate to decide which topic they want to endorse as a class. The students in rotating teams then brain-storm some key issues that need change in their school, commu-nity, or town. In a process of deliberation, advocacy, and voting, which alternate competition for votes and cooperation around a set of shared interests, the students choose an issue that most students care about. One class chose to investigate the availability of social workers in local schools; another decided to try to make the public bus schedule more reliable, and yet others looked at issues of national concern such as bullying or vaping. One teacher reports being impressed by "hearing the conversations students were having. There was real discussion about whether they thought changing public opinion or changing laws was more important, about why they did or did not think they could play a role in social change."[22]

Students research their topic collaboratively in teams. Compe-tition returns when newly formed interest groups aim to effect change through competing with others in a public context, contact-ing public officials, and engaging in public advocacy—for example, meeting with the superintendent to advocate for more mental health professionals in their schools, or teaming up with a local legislator to ban the sale of flavored vapes to children. The partici-pating teachers report that their students were highly engaged in the process, that they developed a keen interest in the political and civic process, and that some of them expressed a greater interest in becoming active in politics or activism. The Democratic Knowl-edge Project leaves structured time for cooperative reflection by students as they step back from competing and assess their efforts and gains. Some students continue working on their topic even after the coursework is done.

COMPETITION AND COOPERATION IN
EXTRACURRICULAR ACTIVITIES

Another potential source for civic education of the kind we rec-ommend can be found in extracurricular activities. These learning opportunities are more limited in their reach to the extent that only some students take advantage of them. However, such oppor-tunities should be offered to as many students as possible: They can improve not only students' civic skills but also the schools' civic environments, which otherwise may turn into "civic deserts."[23] The more schools and teachers treat all effective civic learning activities outside the classroom as not just extra- but also co-curricular, the more likely they will see the need to provide more inclusive access to them.

The Ethics Bowl is an extracurricular activity that teaches competition and cooperation in a distinctive way. The National High School Ethics Bowl and the regional ethics bowls it supports are "competitive yet collaborative events in which students discuss real-life ethical issues."[24] The bowls focus on a wide variety of ethical issues, all involving social issues of significance for civic life and policymaking. Teams take turns presenting their analyses of challenging ethical dilemmas and then respond to questions from other teams and the judges, who are generally experts in ethics but are sometimes well-prepared students themselves. The Ethics Bowl is distinct from a debate in which students are assigned opposing views. Instead, students "defend whichever position they think is correct, provide each other with constructive criticism, and win by demonstrating that they have thought rigorously and systematically about the cases and engaged respectfully and supportively with all participants."[25]

Model UN, a more familiar extracurricular program, promotes similar aims as the Ethics Bowl through different means.[26] Model UN brings together teams of students to emulate both the international body's cooperative deliberations and its competitive processes of decision-making on controversial policies. Limited in its reach, Model UN and its international subsidiaries nonetheless represent an opportunity for a wide range of students from around the globe to take part in a process that combines teaching both competitive and cooperative skills and attitudes. Its civic educational value, like that of the Ethics Bowl, could be multiplied by making it more accessible to more students.

A long-standing tradition in many schools involves inviting students to organize a student government.[27] While student government has not always had significant influence, the structure and process provide an opportunity for students and their representatives to make their voices heard. If used not merely to arrange social events or to assist teachers in implementing administrators' decisions, but also to incorporate students' voices into significant decision making, student government can foster civic habits of both competition and cooperation. Competing to be elected, and then cooperating in this nascent form of governance, encourages students to appreciate the value of both competition and cooperation.

BEYOND THE SCHOOL

A form of civic education that moves beyond the school, still in the spirit of alternating competition and cooperation, goes by the name of "Action Civics."[28] In contrast to the more common knowledge-based civic education, Action Civics seeks to teach political engagement through taking action on local issues students care about. According to the National Action Civics Collaborative, Action Civics is designed to create "an engaged citizenry capable of effective participation in the political process, in their communities and in the larger society."[29] Most programs try to focus on noncontroversial topics by staying local and nonpartisan (although this has become harder to achieve in a polarized environment in which more and more issues become contentious). Students engage in a "cycle of research, action, and reflection," partially mirroring the alternation scenario described in this chapter.[30]

The focus of Action Civics is on issues that are of significant concern to the community. Students learn how to collaborate with one another in the process of competing for the attention of community leaders. They then stand back and reflect on their successes and failures. During the pandemic, some now-virtual classrooms pivoted to mounting social media campaigns on issues they care about, competing for the best hashtags and then cooperating to amplify messages about masks and related topics.

Action Civics makes room for both competition and cooperation and for opportunities to reflect on each. It might do so even more effectively if students were encouraged to tackle controversial political issues directly.[31] But Action Civics as it stands offers an important model in the way it encourages students to do background research, compete and collaborate together to present their positions to political leaders, and then reflect on what they have done. Reflection on the process itself, as we suggested earlier, can enrich the lessons the students learn. Similar efforts around the country train students to participate in conducting the Census, which can help them learn how to collaborate in a shared activity that benefits their community, while competing for resources and representation.[32]

A notably inventive approach to Action Civics, called "Lived Civics," has been tried in Chicago in recent years.[33] This approach "emphasizes theories and practices that are rooted in and responsive to the lived reality of young people, with a focus on race and ethnicity."[34] In this context, identity—and particularly ethnic and racial identity—is central to the introduction of competition and cooperation in civics classes. Students and teachers acknowledge their multiple and competing experiences and visions about identity and privilege, and their divergent experiences with governing institutions, such as interactions with police, or access to social services. They then work together to embrace their diverse identities and develop projects that can address their multiple interests.

Implications for Pedagogy

The dilemma of civic education—the tension between teaching to the political reality of competition and teaching to the civic ideal of cooperation—reappears in decisions about pedagogy.

How do educators decide what issues to discuss in the classroom? Teaching controversial topics in the classroom is one of the recognized features of successful civic education.[35] But how best to teach controversial subjects is itself a subject of controversy.[36] If students discuss only issues that are currently controversial in the competitive society in which they now live, then polarization may be reinforced, and opportunities for finding agreement limited. But if they discuss only issues that are settled and can be more easily approached with a cooperative attitude, then the curriculum seems removed from actual politics and the opportunity for vigorous argument is lost. Controversy and competition increase engagement both in learning and in politics.[37] A solution would be to begin with issues that are now settled in mainstream American society but were once contentious (such as slavery and women's suffrage), and after the skills of respectful argument are reasonably well developed, move on to issues that are controversial now (such as immigration reform and legalizing marijuana).

Should teachers express their own views about controversial issues in the classroom? If they do not, then students may falsely assume authority figures can and should be politically neutral. A model of neutrality does not reflect actual competitive politics and does not help students learn how to contend with authority figures who have opinions that differ from theirs. But if teachers do express their own opinions on controversial issues, students may be less likely to develop or share their own views since teachers are by their very position authority figures. Teachers' taking controversial political positions in the classroom can lead to disengagement or to further polarization, as the students who hold views different from the teacher's may be marginalized and driven into their ideological corner.

In choosing between disclosing and not disclosing, teachers should be guided by this principle: Choose the alternative that is most likely to help students develop and defend their own views. In general, not disclosing seems the approach most likely to achieve this objective. Teachers can still make clear that they have views of their own, but for the purpose of encouraging students to develop theirs, they are not revealing them. This nondisclosure approach is well-expressed by Ms. Heller of Adams High: "We, as teachers, really have a very strong opinion that to create a safe environment, we should not say what our opinions are on any issue. We don't want the kids to feel pressured to sort of brown-nose and take on our opinion . . . We will play devil's advocate every so often with questions. We will restate things just to stir the pot . . . But we will never, no, we never say what we think on any issue . . . I told the kids I will take out a full-page ad in the school newspaper the day I retire and let them all know."[38]

However, this approach may not suit all situations. What works best in particular circumstances to stimulate students to develop their own views is likely to vary with both the details of classroom demographics and the issue at hand. In some cases it would make more sense for teachers to express their views strongly, especially in discussing issues such as climate change, which, though controversial, have strong scientific consensus on one side. In such a case, to express the controversy in terms of "on the one hand, on the other hand" contradicts the educational mission. More generally, teachers should present and strongly affirm their own views about

the value of democracy and its ideals. That is, to recognize why civic
education is important in the first place. Even as they teach the
techniques of competition, teachers should not fall into the cynicism of polarized politics or the habit of thinking that just because
individuals are entitled to their own opinions they are entitled to
their own facts.

Should civic education be taught differently according to the
population that the school serves? If it is, then students lose the
experience of a common curriculum and its potential for cultivating the pursuit of a common good. But if it is not taught differently,
it may neglect the needs of marginalized or disadvantaged students
who have been ill-served by society, and who may therefore deeply
mistrust government and elites.[39] It could end up serving mostly
advantaged students. It should be possible to maintain a common
curriculum if steps are taken to ensure that students find their own
voices within it.[40] This can begin with exercises that teach students
to protest when they believe they are denied what is rightfully
theirs. This approach initially puts more emphasis on the skills of
competition but subsequently includes exercises in which students
learn to cooperate with each other in a common cause. This way
of gaining students' attention is especially valuable for those who
are disadvantaged and anticipate being effectively disenfranchised.
By engaging with an issue about which they already care—whether
it be school uniforms, cafeteria menus, or gun safety—students
become more receptive to the value of learning about a broad
spectrum of issues that affect all of society. This kind of student
engagement also can deliver a bonus in civic educational value by
inspiring adults to address neglected issues.[41]

CONCLUSION

We have explored the tension between teaching to the ideals of
civic education and teaching to the realities of political life. The
tension creates what we call the dilemma of civic education: Should
civic education teach the skills for cooperation (as the ideals pre-
scribe) or the skills for competition (as the realities dictate)? We
have argued that it can and should do both. Moreover, when
civic education is seen as instrumental to the successful pursuit of
students' own civic interests as well as to their contributions to a

common good, the practical case for strengthening civic education becomes more powerful. Combining competition and cooperation creates a civic education that stands a better chance of receiving a higher priority in the curriculum than it has had in the past. We have shown how our approach can be applied in the classroom and the community. It can also help to clarify a number of important pedagogical dilemmas. The ultimate goal of the approach is to provide guidance for a civic education that can be both relevant and inspiring.

NOTES

The views expressed in this article are the views of the authors and reflect the official position of neither the Department of State nor the US Government.

1 Courses tend to focus on facts about governance structures rather than on skills or attitudes: James Youniss and Peter Levine, *Engaging Young People in Civic Life* (Nashville, TN: Vanderbilt University Press, 2009). On the poor record of performance on the National Assessment of Educational Progress civics exam, see Sarah Shapiro and Catherine Brown, *The State of Civics Education.* Center for American Progress (February 21, 2018). For a more recent discussion of the neglect of civic education, see "Educating for American Democracy: Excellence in History and Civics for All Learners," iCivics, March 2, 2021. www.educatingforamericandemocracy.org, pp. 9–10; and an analysis of state requirements in civics and history across the grades, which identifies 10 states that have no such requirements along with other states with weak requirements, in Jeremy A. Stern et al., "State of State Standards for Civics and U.S. History in 2021," Washington DC: Thomas B. Fordham Institute (June 2021). https://fordhaminstitute.org.

2 Jonathan Gould, ed., *Guardian of Democracy: The Civic Mission of Schools* (Carnegie Corporation of New York and CIRCLE, 2011), 6. Educating for American Democracy [EAD] argues that civic education should go beyond facts and promote in-depth inquiry (p. 15). We agree, but here we emphasize attitudes and skills in addition to knowledge. Our emphasis is in keeping with the "pride of place" that EAD gives to developing "skills and virtues for civil, productive disagreement" (p. 8).

3 For the more recent efforts, see Michael Hansen, Elizabeth Mann Levesque, Jon Valant, and Dianan Quintero, "Brown Center Report on American Education: How Well Are American Students Learning?," Brown Center on Education Policy at Brookings, June 2018.

4 For other valuable ways of dealing with these realities, see Eamonn Callan, *Creating Citizens: Political Education and Liberal Democracy* (Oxford: Oxford University Press, 1997); Michael X. Delli Carpini and Scott Keeter, *What Americans Know About Politics and Why It Matters* (New Haven, CT: Yale University Press, 1996); and Stephen Macedo, *Diversity and Distrust: Civic Education in a Multicultural Society* (Cambridge, MA: Harvard University Press, 2000).

5 David E. Campbell, "What Social Scientists Have Learned About Civic Education: A Review of the Literature," *Peabody Journal of Education* 94, no. 1 (2019): 32–47.

6 Polarization is accompanied by changing attitudes toward democracy itself. Nearly a quarter of US youth ages 16 to 24 believe that democracy is a "bad" or "very bad" way of governing: Roberto S. Foa and Yascha Mouk, "The Danger of Deconsolidation: The Democratic Disconnect." *Journal of Democracy* 27, no. 3 (2016): 5–17.

7 Larry M. Bartels, "Partisanship in the Trump Era," *Journal of Politics* 80, no. 4 (October 2018): 1483–1494.

8 On the civic empowerment gap, see Meira Levinson, *No Citizen Left Behind* (Cambridge, MA: Harvard University Press, 2012), 23–59; on students' voices in schools serving marginalized students, see Sigal Ben-Porath, "Deferring Virtue: The New Management of Students and the Civic Role of Schools," *Theory and Research in Education* 11, no. 2 (July 2013): 111–128.

9 Hess and McAvoy pose a related problem that they call the "paradox" of civic education: the need both "to provide students with a nonpartisan political education" and "to prepare them to participate in the actual highly partisan political community," in Diana Hess and Paula McAvoy, *The Political Classroom: Evidence and Ethics in Democratic Education* (New York: Routledge, 2015), 4. The dilemma we pose is somewhat different: the apparent conflict between teaching skills and attitudes that prepare students to compete and those that prepare them to cooperate. We emphasize that civic education should prepare students not only to participate in the actual partisan politics, but also to improve the democratic quality of that politics.

10 Nancy Rosenblum, *On the Side of Angels: An Appreciation of Parties and Partisanship* (Princeton, NJ: Princeton University Press, 2010).

11 On the educational value of debates, see David W. Johnson and Roger Johnson, "Classroom Conflict: Controversy Versus Debate in Learning Groups," *American Educational Research Journal* 22, no. 2 (1985): 237–256; and Walter Parker, "Listening to Strangers: Classroom Discussion in Democratic Education," *Teachers College Record* 11, no. 11 (2010): 2815–2832.

12 On the classic compromise, see Amy Gutmann and Dennis Thompson, *The Spirit of Compromise* (Princeton, NJ: Princeton University Press, 2012), 12–16, 212–213.

13 Amy Gutmann and Dennis Thompson, *Why Deliberative Democracy?* (Princeton, NJ: Princeton University Press, 2004), 13–21.

14 More generally, "since conceptions of the greater good will differ, justice-oriented students must develop the ability to communicate with and learn from those who hold different perspectives" (Joel Westheimer and Joseph Kahne, "What Kind of Citizen? The Politics of Educating for Democracy," *American Educational Research Journal* 41, no. 2 (2004): 237–269). For the centrality to democratic education of cultivating the capacity for robust and civil disagreement, see Amy Gutmann, *Democratic Education* (Princeton, NJ: Princeton University Press, 1999).

15 The report on Educating for American Democracy (p. 17) emphasizes the importance of teaching "the value and the danger of compromise" but ignores teaching the value and danger of competition and how compromise can serve as a bridge between cooperation and competition.

16 On the connection between encouraging political engagement in the classroom and subsequent participation, see John B. Holbein and Sunshine Hillygus, *Making Young Voters: Converting Civic Attitudes into Civic Action* (Cambridge: Cambridge University Press, 2020), 142–154.

17 The program can be seen as an expanded "civics lab" of the type recommended by CivXNow (www.civxnow.org), a coalition advocating for civic learning.

18 This account is based on interviews with faculty at a large suburban high school in the Midwest (conducted remotely in summer 2020 by Sigal Ben-Porath), along with other related research. To protect confidentiality, we refer to the school with a pseudonym. For a pioneering study of a similar program, which has influenced our work, see Hess and McAvoy, *The Political Classroom.*

19 Interview with a Legislative Semester teacher at Oak Hills High, August 2020.

20 Interview with a Legislative Semester teacher at Oak Hills High, July 2020.

21 The Democratic Knowledge Project, spearheaded by Danielle Allen in 2018, co-created an innovative social studies curriculum in collaboration with a local school district in Massachusetts and trained teachers in implementing it; https://yppactionframe.fas.harvard.edu. The information about the project here is based on www.democraticknowledgeproject. org, accessed August 2023; interviews with educators, as well as a review of the curriculum, case studies, and teachers' reflections, provided in the Massachusetts Department of Elementary and Secondary Education Civ-

ics Project Guidebook, October 2019, www.doe.mass.edu, accessed August 2020.

22 MA Guidebook, p. 29.

23 For additional information, refer to https://tischcollege.tufts.edu.

24 National High School Ethics Bowl, Parr Center for Ethics, University of North Carolina, Chapel Hill, https://nhseb.unc.edu, accessed July 28, 2020.

25 National High School Ethics Bowl.

26 See an overview at www.un.org/en/mun, accessed September 4, 2020.

27 James Youniss, Jeffrey A. McLellan, and Miranda Yates, "What We Know About Engendering Civic Identity," *American Behavioral Scientist* 40, no. 5 (1997): 620–631.

28 Parissa J. Ballard, Allison K. Cohen, and Joshua Littenberg-Tobias, "Action Civics for Promoting Civic Development: Main Effects of Program Participation and Differences by Project Characteristics," *American Journal of Community Psychology* 58, nos. 3–4 (2016): 377–390.

29 National Action Civics Collaborative, "Action Civics: A Declaration for Rejuvenating Our Democratic Tradition," http://actioncivicscollaborative.org, accessed August 4, 2020.

30 Levinson, *No Citizen Left Behind*, 224.

31 Many of these programs tend to be apolitical, to their detriment: Cliff Zukin, Scott Keeter, Molly Andolina, Krista Jenkins, and Michael X. Delli Carpini, *A New Engagement? Political Participation, Civic Life, and the Changing American Citizen* (New York: Oxford University Press, 2006).

32 Evie Blad, "For Students in Coal Country, the Census Is a Hands-on Civics Lesson," *Education Week*, November 12, 2019, www.edweek.org, accessed May 14, 2020.

33 Cathy Cohen, Joseph Kahne, and Jessica Marshall, with Veronica Anderson, Margaret Brower, and David Knight, "Let's Go There: Race, Ethnicity, and a Lived Civics Approach to Civic Education," GenForward at the University of Chicago, Chicago, Illinois, 2018.

34 Cohen et al., "Let's Go There," 4.

35 On this and other accepted features of civic education, see Peter Levine and Kei Kawashima-Ginsberg, "The Republic Is (Still) at Risk—and Civics Is Part of the Solution" (Medford, MA: Jonathan M. Tisch College of Civic Life, Tufts University, 2017).

36 Diana E. Hess, *Controversy in the Classroom: The Democratic Power of Discussion* (New York: Routledge, 2009).

37 Jonathan Zimmerman and Emily Robertson, *The Case for Contention* (Chicago: University of Chicago Press, 2017).

38 Hess and McAvoy, *The Political Classroom*, 92.

39 Civic outcomes for Latinx students varied from those of their non-Latinx peers in classrooms using the same civics curriculum and pedagogy, depending on students' sense of ethnic identity: Judith Torney-Purta, Carolyn Barber, and Britt Wilkenfeld, "Latino Adolescents' Civic Development in the United States: Research Results from the IEA Civic Education Study," *Journal of Youth and Adolescence* 36, no. 2 (2007): 111–125. Also see David Campbell and Richard Niemi, "Testing Civics: State-Level Civic Education Requirements and Political Knowledge," *American Political Science Review* 110, no. 3 (2016): 495–511; and Kenneth P. Langton and M. Kent Jennings, "Political Socialization and the High School Civics Curriculum in the United States," *American Political Science Review* 62, no. 3 (1968): 852–867.

40 David E. Campbell, "Voice in the Classroom: How an Open Classroom Climate Fosters Political Engagement Among Adolescents," *Political Behavior* 30 (2008): 437–454.

41 For an important example of Black youth informing adults about carceral violence, see Cathy Cohen and Matthew D. Luttig, "Reconceptualizing Political Knowledge: Race, Ethnicity, and Carceral Violence," *Perspectives on Politics* 18, no. 3 (2020): 805–818.

INDEX